Timothy A. Sexton

A Little Gleam of Time

Archway Publishing books may be ordered through booksellers or by contacting:

Archway Publishing
1663 Liberty Drive
Bloomington, IN 47403
www.archwaypublishing.com
1 (888) 242-5904

Because of the dynamic nature of the Internet, any web addresses or links contained in this book may have changed since publication and may no longer be valid. The views expressed in this work are solely those of the author and do not necessarily reflect the views of the publisher, and the publisher hereby disclaims any responsibility for them.

Any people depicted in stock imagery provided by Thinkstock are models, and such images are being used for illustrative purposes only.
Certain stock imagery © Thinkstock.

ISBN: 978-1-4808-4412-4 (sc)
ISBN: 978-1-4808-4411-7 (hc)
ISBN: 978-1-4808-4413-1 (e)

Library of Congress Control Number: 2017905679

Print information available on the last page.

Archway Publishing rev. date: 05/03/2017

This book is dedicated to Joe and Mary Elaine

Acknowledgements

I want to thank Dr. Roger Little, the man who had the inspiration for this book. Across a table in a noisy room, Roger planted the seed for this story. It would take months before that seed would take root and grow into this work; though the effort was mine, the idea was his.

Two other individuals deserve notice: my brother, Dan, and my sister Mary. Dan was instrumental in my search for pictures. As a depository of thousands of family photos, his collection proved invaluable.

Mary was a great depository of family facts. With possibly one of the most accurate memories of my siblings, she helped me keep the details of this story as precise as attainable.

Contents

Part Three

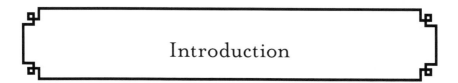

Introduction

One life—a little gleam of time between two eternities.

Thomas Carlyle

Hanging above the rows of books in my library is a black and white picture, roughly ten inches by ten inches. There is one central figure striding like a giant on the pictured landscape, filling the frame from top to bottom. The only other figure who appears in the photo is my brother Dan looking abnormally small. He is roughly seven or eight years old with a butch hair cut which accentuates his protruding ears. The central figure is my father, Joe Sexton, but he isn't posing for the camera. His gaze is momentarily transfixed upon the small white golf ball in the lower part of the frame. His body is tense, his muscles are taut, and you can read determination in his face. For those who knew him, the photo captures him precisely. But this photo also has a story to tell. He is hitting his final tee shot of a golf tournament, the Meadowbrook Invitational. It was tournament he probably played in for more than twenty –five years. On the day of this particular picture, he was one shot behind his friend and chronic opponent Art Cooper from Dubuque, Iowa. Just seconds after this picture, Joe's tee shot soared over the crest of the 18th hole (#9), a hole of 254 yards terminating in a domed round green immediately to the left of the remnant of an old sand green. The ball would come to rest ten to fifteen feet from the hole. He would go on to make the putt. Cheered by a small gallery of locals, he scored an eagle, two under par, which would secure a win by one stroke over Art. Both the story and the picture speak volumes about my father.

The same intensity portrayed in the picture invaded everything else in his life. Not the least of which was his love for my mother, Mary Elaine. Married for over sixty odd years, they traveled through a period which saw the rise and fall of the small town and the ruination of the family farm.

Most of Joe's life story takes place in a small rural Iowa town. Ironically, the life span of the town mirrors somewhat Joe's own life. The story I'm going to tell is about growth, expansion, change, and inevitable decline of both the town, the surrounding 'family' farms, and its native son. We will go back to the beginning of Sumner because, as James Joyce wrote, 'we are what we were'. Though Joe was a creature of the twentieth century his roots extended back to an era of immigrants and the settlement of the great prairie. This era saw one of the last great migrations to 'unsettled' land the earth will probably ever see, and it also brought together groups that for hundreds of years had been separated by borders but now were separated only by a small yard or field.

This story tells of a journey taken by Joe Sexton through a segment of time. Every generation finds a unique set of events layered upon their lives, and whether we wish to accept them or not, these events form the guard rails on our trip. Our families, too, have a binding influence on our progression. In Joe's case, the road he would take wouldn't be the scenic route of youthful imagination but a pedestrian path, one which a son instinctively vows never to take.

It's common for all of us to look upon old photographs of people we vaguely knew or didn't know at all and see only lifeless eyes looking back at us, but in their time these were people with triumphs and failures, gains and losses, and loves and despair. In these few brief pages, those eyes you see in pictures will possibly be animated again.

Part One

Dr. Wilson

The tin type is hazy, but you can make out who the people are in the picture of Sumner in 1877. In the center is a man unloading something from a wagon. This man is D.R. Little, the meat man. He butchered at night and made his deliveries during the following day from his double boarded wagon. The man standing near the horse pictured there is Lew Head. The wagon parked on what would be present day Main Street Sumner has behind it a long building, the Randall Drug Store. To the right of the wagon are buildings that appear to be oversized outhouses randomly placed in the open field to the east of the drug store. These are actually houses, temporary structures for settlers until something larger could be built. Two men are standing together at the back end of Little's wagon. The man in the derby hat is Chauncy Carpenter. He owns most of the land surrounding the pictured group, and standing beside him is Dr. J.N. Wilson. Tall and straight with a stove pipe hat, Dr. Wilson is Sumner's first doctor and a figure pivotal in Joseph West Sexton's future.

Son of a doctor from Troy Mills, Iowa, J.N. had received a medical degree after just two years of study, one year of actual class study at the School of Physicians and Surgeons in Keokuk, Iowa and one year as an intern, presumably with his father. At the time, Dr. Wilson had just relocated his medical practice to Sumner from a place called Cassville. After the Civil War the prairie west of the Mississippi River saw hundreds of small communities pop up like mushrooms. Cassville was one such town. More a hamlet than a town, it was the product of one man, Stephen Cass. The twenty-seven–year-old had made a sizable fortune clearing brush and grub land in Wisconsin. A true entrepreneur, by the time he sold his business he had under his employment several teams of men and oxen. Successful but restless, he planned to move his family to Iowa. We don't know exactly what his plans were but we know his path, the Military Road, which would hold several options along its route for a man of his foresight.

The Military Road was a government road extending from Prairie du Chien, Wisconsin to Boone, Iowa, which at the time was a coal mining area essential for the burgeoning railroad industry in the west. Traversing the state to Boone, the dirt road passed through the river towns like Waverly and Eldora, and interspersed along the entire route were stage stops necessary for a change of fresh horses and an opportunity for weary travelers to stretch their legs.

At one of these stops, Stephen, his wife and two sons found their trip interrupted. Thirty miles east of Waverly on the eastern branch of the Little Wapsie River, Cass and his family disembarked from the stage. His eldest son was sick. His parents, concerned for their son's health, decided to let him recuperate before moving on. The exact length of their stay is not known, but during this period Stephen fell upon an idea. Obviously, a man of vision, Stephen saw an opportunity. Not a merchant by trade, he envisioned a store to capture trade on the busy road. Traveling alone on to Waverly he purchased from the government a plot of land which adjoined the stage stop. Initially just a simple frame structure to serve as his store, the edifice would increase in size within two years to hold a post office and a hotel. The nucleus of a town started to take shape. The name Cassville was assigned to the small cache of shops either by Cass himself or by the sparse surrounding local population. Stephen's enterprise soon attracted other ambitious entrepreneurs. Flanking the dirt Military Road which ran through Cassville more businesses sprang up. Two blacksmiths, a shoe maker, and Dr. Wilson threw in their lot with Cass and the future of

Cassville. Dr. Wilson erected a two story building, serving as both a medical office and his bachelor's quarters.

By 1869, Cassville was already a viable village, when an Illinois man purchased a quarter section of land just over three miles to its south. Tucked in between two branches of the Little Wapsie River and bordered on the east by a thick wooded band extending several miles to the north, the property had all the essentials of an ideal prairie settlement, namely access to both timber and water, which were crucial elements for any successful habitation. The owner of the land, Chauncy Carpenter, initially wasn't interested in living on the land. As an absentee owner, he aspired to raise wheat. Rumor had it that he had paid for the land in gold; he had mined the precious mineral in California during the Gold Rush of 1849. As a young man, he had left Illinois, joining the stream of daring people heading out across the Great Plains and Rocky Mountains, as they would say "to see the elephant." This arduous three month journey by wagon or on foot would claim the lives of a fair number of adventurers. Injuries and disease rather than Indians, as is often imagined, would claim the majority of those lost. Chauncey, an odd little man with a peculiar beard which only protruded below the angle of his jaw, survived the overland trail and went on to become one of the few to find enough gold to be classified as rich. He did not, however, retrace his steps back to Illinois but instead took the ocean route home. It was a long trip with its own dangers; the ships left San Francisco, sailing down the west coast of South America. Some would then pass through the perilous Straits of Magellan, but most Forty-niners took the route which skirted along the coast of Mexico and dropping anchor off the edge of Panama. Then after walking across the malaria infested isthmus they would hop a north bound ship destined for New York harbor. From New York trains carried Chauncy back to Illinois, a relatively comfortable ride for a man with enough money. After a few years of wheat farming, Carpenter still lived in Illinois but saw a way to get a greater return on his investment in Iowa farm land through land speculation. Transportation was the key to maximizing

his profits, and in that era, transportation meant the railroads. After the
Civil War, railroads spread like spider webs across the plains west of the
Mississippi River. They were like major highways of their day bringing
increased traffic and population to cities and towns. When Chauncy
received word that his property was adjoined on its edge by the proposed Iowa and Pacific railroad he saw his opportunity. The purpose of
the line would be to connect Belmond, Iowa with the Cedar Northern
Rail Line which ran north and south, passing through Randalia which
was a mere ten miles from his land. Carpenter now got into the land
development business. His ultimate goal was to plot an entire community. There was more money in plots than sections of land. Chauncey
had the land surveyed and laid out in grids for streets, housing, and
commercial lots. He christened his town Sumner, after Senator Charles
Sumner of Massachusetts. Obviously enamored by the famous senator's
abolitionist history, Carpenter may have overlooked some of Charles
Sumner's less than laudable accomplishments. After he leveled a vicious
verbal attack against Senator Andrew Butler of South Carolina, Charles
Sumner, a large humorless man with flowing ringlets of hair, was pum-
meled by a cane. The man wielding the walking stick happened to be
a friend of Butler's, Congressman Preston Brooks. Supposedly several
senators stood by and watched without coming to his aid as Sumner
was beaten almost into unconsciousness.

One of the first houses built in Sumner belonged to Chauncey. (It
still sits just east of the present firehouse.) This was a time brimming
with optimism. One had to only envision the flood of individuals on
the move and desiring to gamble everything on small nascent towns
springing up across the grasslands. As with Cassville, the mere mention of a makeshift town brought in new business. Within twenty-four
months Sumner boasted two grocery stores, a blacksmith shop, a meat
market, and an "elegant" log hotel, called the Pacific House. (It is odd
the Pacific was such a popular name, considering that the ocean was
2000 miles away!) To be viable, all these businesses needed customers. That problem was easily accommodated by the endless flow of

immigrants and in Sumner's case they were chiefly Germans settlers. Telling was the fact that for nearly fifty years after their initial arrival some hymnals in the Lutheran churches in the Sumner area still were printed in German.

At this time Carpenter suffered the fate of many such developers: his plan fell apart. The Iowa-Pacific Railroad went bankrupt. No tracks were going to be laid beyond Tripoli, another nascent village eleven miles to the west. The grading that had been finished from Tripoli to Randalia was abandoned. Chauncey Carpenter refused to accept defeat, however, so he formulated a new plan. His idea, which stretched the limits of imagination, was to merge Sumner with another community, and he set his sights on Cassville.

A spring day in 1875, roughly a month before George Armstrong Custer had his fateful meeting with the Sioux and Cheyenne on the Little Big Horn, Chauncey, with a delegation of businessmen from Sumner, rode north on the dirt road to Cassville. They had concocted an absurd plan to have Stephen Cass move to Sumner and bring his village with him. There is no record of the negotiations, but there must have been something in them that enticed Stephen to move an entire village. Either Stephen Cass saw value in the scheme, or Chauncy was a convincing salesman. Stephen was by 1870 standards already a wealthy man, and he would need a sizeable perceived gain to persuade him to go along with this bizarre arrangement. A deal was struck. In the coming winter, Cassville, the entire village, all its buildings would be jacked up and moved to Sumner. It's entirely feasible to think some discussion had to revolve around the expenses of moving the structures and the cost for the designated lots in Sumner. As both Cass and Carpenter were astute businessmen, the expenses of the move were probably buried in the deal.

The laborious work commenced that winter after the ground had frozen. The buildings were hoisted onto skids and pulled painstakingly into Sumner. The buildings were moved one by one, each pulled by a team of forty horses. Behind each building, teams of oxen were yoked, acting like a braking system for wood framed buildings as they slid down the frozen hills. It must have been quite a sight, forty horses, their breath issuing in clouds of vapor in the frigid air, oxen lumbering behind with the heads lowered, and men, bundled up against the cold, walking beside the teams with long whips snapping above the beasts, and all the time the buildings inching painstakingly over the bumpy, rough, frozen roads, with drifting snow and bitter cold slowing their progress.

Spring found all the buildings seated on their new foundations in Sumner. Cass cut a favorable deal securing promising spots in the Sumner business district for his relocated edifices. The shoe store ended up on the southwest corner of Main and Carpenter Street. The hotel and post office owned by Cass got the prime corner right across the street. Dr. J.N. Wilson's office shared that same street corner in the center of the town, and J.N. took full advantage of his new location. He expanded his building and business by taking in a partner, a pharmacist, and opened a drug store. Banking on his reputation as a jovial, good-natured man, he grew to be universally liked and rapidly built his practice.

Although professionally trained, Dr. Wilson always looked to advancing his medical skills. He was known to return periodically to the medical school in Iowa City for further training. The route from Sumner to Iowa City passed directly through Center Point, Iowa, and it was here, possibly on one of these excursions, that he met his future wife, Katherine West. The eldest of four orphaned children, she would move to Sumner as Dr. Wilson's bride. Along with his new wife, Wilson inherited her two sisters and one brother, all of whom also moved in with him in Sumner. The hybrid family had been living together for nearly a decade when Katherine was suddenly widowed. In 1889, while on a routine house call, the unsuspecting doctor was bitten by a dog. The dog proved to be rabid, and poor Dr. Wilson suffered a horrible lingering death. Seventy five carriages and wagons formed the funeral cortege, with Katherine, her sisters Sarah and Stella and her brother Franklin West riding right behind the hearse as it wound its way through the streets of Sumner. Even with Dr. Wilson's untimely death, all the West family members had incorporated themselves into the social fabric of Sumner and would ultimately remain there.

George Sexton

It was April 10, 1910, and the brown, dormant of grass was giving way to the first green shoots of spring. The dirt streets of Sumner were quiet that Sunday. The first days of spring brought a fresh smell to everything, and windows thrown open to catch the breeze allowed the distinctive odor of the essential Sunday fried chicken to waft through the town.

The town's new veterinarian had just arrived with his meager possessions. He'd be the third vet to set up practice in Sumner in as many years. Dr. F.R. Mosler had come and gone in 1908, and Dr. R. Scothorn had followed the same pattern in 1909. Recently graduating from Chicago Veterinary School as valedictorian, George Sexton, a handsome man with dark wavy hair, had traveled to Sumner, passing through Independence, Iowa where his parents John and Elecia farmed. He'd' come to fill the void left by Dr. Scothorn's departure. Exactly how George came to hear of the available opening isn't known, but surely word of mouth could travel the short distance between Sumner and Independence.

Sumner had a lot to recommend it at this time. It had all the signs of a prosperous community. Clauncey's dream of connecting his city to a railroad had come to fruition. The Minnesota and Northeastern (later called the Chicago and Great Western) had laid tracks directly through town. This was not a trunk line but a major line, comparable to an interstate highway of today. The M and N Railroad during this time was the major connecting line for the entire upper Midwest, joining the largest cities in that area of the country. Besides Chicago and Minneapolis, the line also "hubbed" in Oelwein, with a separate line running from there to Kansas City. Due to the cities it connected, the railroad was busiest line in the state.

With six trains stopping daily in Sumner, the Jarvis livery service, which shared the building with George Sexton, maintained a busy schedule transporting salesmen back and forth the four blocks from the squat little depot to the local hotels.

A second rail line connected with the depot and the M and N from the west. The unfinished line from Tripoli, started by the bankrupt Iowa and Pacific, had been taken over by the Dubuque and Dakota Railroad. It never ran between the Dakotas and Dubuque, but only from Waverly to Sumner. The train's erratic schedule earned the D and D the nickname "damned doubtful." When on time, it ran a couple of times daily into Sumner. At the turn of the century a local family, the Wescotts, had established a race track just south of town where the present sewage treatment plant now sits. The horse track was capable of holding over five hundred spectators on the days the horses ran, and during race days the D and D would put on extra trains to bring in eager gamblers from as far away as Waverly. By the time George arrived in town the track had seen its last race, but a less impressive facility had been built just east of Sumner With a college degree, Dr. Sexton became a member of an elite group in Sumner, as a sizable segment of the population never progressed past the eighth grade. Within George's family, two sisters would also receive degrees; both Claira and Calista, were nurses. Calista had also married a man much her senior who had a law degree from Georgetown University. His older brother, John would move to Waterloo to work for the railroad. His departure presented a dilemma for George, because both boys were assumed to be the next generation to work the farm. But George had other plans which didn't involve farming. His parents, Elecia and John, must have been surprised when he pulled up stakes turning his back on agrarian lifestyle and enrolled in vet school. This left only three sisters at home, and they'd soon move on, with Margaret and Josephine marrying local farmers and Mary Ellen marrying a carpenter.

His Irish parents were one generation removed from the home island, but they fervently retained their Irish roots and their faith. Elecia's maiden name was Gorman and members of her family had taken religious vows; her brother Daniel becoming a Bishop and her sister a nun, oddly enough taking the name Sister Daniel. A story was told of Elecia on her death bed, with Sister Daniel pouring holy water on her head and questioning whether Elecia was fully aware of the gravity of the situation. The nun asked "do you know what I am doing?" In full possession of her faculties Elisha replied "Yes, but you don't need to drown me!'

George, a product of this Irish environment, now found himself in Sumner surrounded by Germans, who were the predominant settlers of the area. George may have found himself outnumbered by his German neighbors, but during this time that wasn't an uncommon occurrence, since most immigrants seemed to congregate together according to their nationalities. Not unlike the Amish of today, migrants settled en masse in certain areas. A common language and common customs obviously made resettlement in the new country less traumatic.

George found lodging at the "bachelor hotel" which was conveniently located on the same corner as his future office. His new home, the Central House, stood on the corner of Second and Carpenter Streets, and directly across the street to the north stood the long wooden framed livery barn stretching back nearly half a block. To the east of the livery, a small room served as Dr. Sexton's office. Also sharing that corner of the city was the Opera House and the burnt out shell of the Clifton House. The Opera House held mainly concerts and plays preformed either by itinerant actors or by locals. In the 1890's, Joseph Cass ran the Opera House which was owned by his father Stephen. Joseph had married an east coast socialite who used her influence to bring in famous actors from as far away as New York City. Across the street the Clifton House, after suffering a fire in the winter before George arrived, was in the process of being remodeled when George first set up practice.

An unknown dray-man is capture in front of the livery with George Sexton's flat-roofed office to the right.

The imposing livery in which Dr. Sexton had his office was capable of holding a large number of horses. George owned just one horse and rented others when he needed a team. Not all the horses he rented proved to be totally satisfactory. One winter evening he needed a team to run a farm call. Where he arrived at the farm, the son of the farmer asked if George wanted to have blankets thrown over his horses due to the cold. George replied, "Sure, cover that one, but not that son of a bitch," pointing to the rented horse. George loved his own horse. Long after buying a car with which to run calls, he paid for his horse's upkeep, even though the animal was now out of service. Married at the time he bought the car, he refused to sell the horse despite his wife's persistent nagging about the ongoing expense. When the horse finally died, George still could not part with him and had a blanket made from his hide.

On Saturday evenings, George was fortunate enough to have his clients come to him. After chores on Saturday, the town would swell with farmers. Horse drawn wagons would flood into town bearing the farm families. Businesses would stay open late into the night. While the wives did their weekly shopping the men would frequent the taverns. The livery stable would function much like a city parking garage. All the stalls would be filled. While the farmers entertained themselves, George worked.

On those Saturday nights, with each stall containing a horse George did a brisk business 'floating' teeth. Grain and grasses naturally harbor grit, which over time wears down the enamel of the horse's teeth, but the attrition is never uniform. Irregular edges develop on the teeth, many of which are sharp and serrated. These edges can catch and lacerate the soft mucosa in the horse's mouth and could become infected or painful enough to limit the horse's diet. Smoothing these edges, floating, was a demanding job. The float, a long rasp on a handle, was used to run over the top of the horse's teeth. Some horses remain calm during the procedure while others require more manhandling. Besides trying to restrain the head of a half ton beast, George needed to be alert, as some horses would strike out with the front hooves. Overall, the physical exertion was the most demanding part. Just the strength needed to force the file back and forth on the enamel was demanding enough but the long evening working down the row of horses must certainly have left George exhausted.

There was nothing easy about practicing vet medicine: the long hours on the road running calls, mud in the spring, dust in the summer, and cold and unforgiving bitter days of winter. Treating animals in lantern-lit barns with very few of the medicines available today added to the raw experience. Then there was the physical toll on George, who was forced to wrestle reluctant clients. Given the long hours and exhausting work it would seem impossible for George to have much a social life, but he did.

Meanwhile, the orphaned boy from Center Point, Franklin West, had made a life for himself in Sumner. He'd married a woman from Tripoli,

Phoebe Moment, and after living for a short period in Tripoli, Franklin returned to Sumner and bought a restaurant. The West Restaurant Hall, situated on a prime location right in the middle of Main Street, was well established by the spring of 1910. The business afforded Franklin a comfortable living for his family, and by the spring of that year two of his four children were grown and out on their own.

Perry West, the oldest of those children, had moved to Cedar Rapids to pursue a career in business. The second oldest, Inez, was teaching school in Sumner. The two youngest children of Franklin and Phoebe, Truman or "True" as he was called and the baby Dorothy remained at home.

Sumner claimed a population of 1400 when George started his practice and this lively populace found entertainment mainly in social events. There were silent movies like 'The Great Train Robbery' and 'Uncle Tom's Cabin,' but these novelties lasted only about 15 minutes. Church dinners, quilting bees, sleigh rides, bicycling, and wedding parties offered young men and women the best courting opportunities. Somewhere, at one of these happenings George met Inez.

The young teacher was slender and attractive, with fine features. She wore her long dark hair pulled back and built up, framing her face in the fashion of the day. She was intelligent, loved music, and wrote poetry. She did have, however, one blemish. By carefully watching her, one could discern a slight limp. During her first year of teaching she'd had an accident, a mishap in the buggy. She was riding in the rig when it flipped, causing Inez to tumble onto the road. Her most serious injury was a severe gash on her knee, deep enough to allow a subsequent infection to spread to her knee joint. Without antibiotics the course of treatment for the infection was to drain the area, hopefully this allowing normal healing. In Inez's case the infection, once inside the bursa of the knee, permitted the bacteria to ravage the tissues, leaving permanently scarred ligaments. The knee did heal but left Inez with limited mobility of the joint. By "breaking" the joint, a local physician thought he could tear loose the scarred tissue and return the freedom of movement. But after performing this excruciating procedure, the physician saw no improvement in Inez's knee. His advice was to do the procedure again. The second attempt must have been worse for Inez, for now she knew what was going to happen, but she still consented. The second endeavor, however, proved to be just as fruitless as the first.

The two young adults, George and Inez somehow found each other. Young love is blind love, and for George and Inez this was the case. Along with George, Inez got a dog, his bulldog "Doc." The man and his dog were inseparable: Doc ran calls with George and when George would visit the West's home, Doc would wait patiently on the front porch for his master. The dog was even rumored to have ridden on the running board of George's car when he drove around town.

George and Inez were dating in 1912 when her father and mother sold the restaurant. Franklin had been offered a position as the manager of the foremost hotel in town. The Clifton House, which had suffered the chimney fire in the winter of 1910, gutting its interior, had been purchased by Charles Pennington. Mr. Pennington was one of the wealthier men in town, on par with the Casses and Carpenters. Charles rebuilt the Clifton turning it into a show place. He took enough pride in the hotel that he put his own name on it. Now Charles had owned half the real estate on that corner, as the livery building in which George had his office was jointly owned by Carpenter and Pennington.

A brick two story building with tall windows curved on the top, the Hotel Charles had a clean appearance. A large, three pillared porch extended over the entryway and ran to the edge of the sidewalk. Mature deciduous trees sheltered the entire northern wall, and all of this produced as sense of opulence that Pennington wished to project in Sumner. The hotel soon became a favorite with traveling salesmen and even the local inhabitants.

A local farm is shown heading north on Carpenter Street. He is passing in front Tibbits' Pool Hall and the Hotel Charles on the corner. Further down the street the Cass Opera House is discernible.

The hotel did its best to cater to salesmen who were its main occupants during this period. During the week the livery service was kept busy making the run from the porch outside the hotel lobby to the depot. Men in three-piece suits and leather sample cases filled the halls of the Hotel Charles. On the ground floor, just off the lobby, the hotel management designated a small room for the salesmen's use called "the writing room." Fitted with a desk, a lamp and chairs, the room provided a space where the salesmen could fill out their order books in the evening after making their calls around town.

Charles Pennington was an astute businessman. He realized part of his hotel's attraction needed to be its food. This is why he had approached Franklin West. Also called "Uk" or "Uncle", Franklin for years had run a thriving restaurant in town, serving such delicacies as "seaship" oysters. The restaurant in the hotel already had elite status. Tables were covered with white, pressed, linen tablecloths, and waitresses in crisp dresses with white aprons gave the dining room an air of elegance. On holidays when most salesmen were gone, the restaurant filled with locals expecting a special meal, which was famous through out the town. In the winter of 1912, the Wests moved into the Hotel Charles as managers.

In June of the same year, the eldest daughter was to be married. Monday morning, June 17th was a clear and warm day. Inez West busied herself with preparing for the wedding that day, and her groom, George Sexton, laid out his suit and double checked his list, as he would be leaving his practice for the next ten days. He and his bride would be honeymooning in Chicago, but there would be a full day before catching the east bound train. The wedding mass officiated by Fr. Leen at the Immaculate Conception Catholic Church was only the beginning. Weddings demanded a chevaree, a barn dance open to one and all, and there would be no shortage of food and drink.

Early the next morning Dr. and Mrs. George Sexton stood on the wooden platform in front of Sumner's depot. Weeks prior to leaving, George had purchased a home on Division Street within a rock's throw from the back of the Catholic Church. Separating the two buildings were the tracks to the D and D railroad. The young couple moved in immediately after the honeymoon, and after the birth of their daughter, Donna Mary, they would spend seven years in the house before Joe came along. The day young Donna learned she was gaining a baby brother she happened to be walking next to the D and D tracks with her friend Martha, the girls discussing her new baby brother when Donna questioned whether Martha should get a baby brother also. Shortly after the second child arrived, George moved the family a block away to an unpretentious house on Main Street.

George and Inez, while possibly still dating, are pictured with George's ever present dog, Doc.

In this modest two story clapboard house, the Sextons would remain for the next twenty-five years. The quaint structure had a truncated front porch and matching construction behind. The downstairs living room monopolized the front of the house with the kitchen the back. In the center of the house above the stove, the single source of heat, grates in the ceiling allowed heat to filter upstairs. The Sextons' home was close enough to downtown that when standing on their front porch, they could read the time off the clock on Sumner's most dominant structure, the Bank of Sumner building. Steven Cass had built the brick bank building fifteen years before, capping the corner with a clock tower. It was undeniably the tallest structure in town. The two story building would house the bank and the post office on the first level and a medical office and the Masonic Lodge on the second. Ironically, the Masonic Lodge, which didn't allow Catholics, was started in Sumner by Dr. Wilson, Inez's uncle –in –law.

Downtown Sumner extended only two blocks but was the hub of activity in the town. Wooden sidewalks had yet to be replaced by cement. On a typical summer day, the awning on the store fronts would be cranked out, shielding shoppers from the summer's sun. With only ice cut from the ice pond down by the Little Wapsie to serve as refrigeration, shopping was at best done every couple of days. Inez, strolling the elevated wooden walkway in front of the stores with their large plate glass windows, would do her shopping dressed in the fashion of the day: full-length dresses, gloves, and possibly an umbrella. The expectations of dignity and style may have been more rigid than practiced today but they might be seen as lessons eroded by laziness that could still teach us something today.

Bancroft

One hundred and fifty miles due west was another town that had just sprung up from prairie grass. The very same year George rode into Sumner to start his vet practice, a physician entered this western town to start his medical practice. The town was Bancroft, Iowa. It was only thirty years old and showing its virility. Unlike Sumner, which had to wait for connection to a railroad, Bancroft was actually the product of a railroad. The Toledo and Northwestern Railroad had plans to lay tracks connecting Des Moines, Iowa and Minneapolis, and by the spring of 1881, the grading had almost been completed through Kossuth County, which at one time was part of a larger county called Bancroft. To defray construction costs most railroads were given land on both sides of the proposed track by the government and the sale of this land made railroad construction a very lucrative business. Between 1870 and 1890, given all the railroad construction, the United States' Congress donated to the railroad companies in Iowa 4,069,942 acres of government land. This would comprise one ninth of all the land in Iowa.

The Toledo and Northwestern had an interesting business model with which to maximize their profits: along the line which ran through long stretches of prairie, the railroad laid out, at defined intervals, new towns. Besides profiting from the sale of the lots of the programmed towns, the company could, in this way, create their own passengers and cargo traffic. Assigned to survey and plot the towns for the railroad was a man named Ambrose Call. He was nearing completion on his latest town which the railroad company had already decided to name Burt when Ambrose lobbied to rename the town Bancroft. With more towns to be plotted, his superiors did accept the proposed name change and assigned the name Burt to the next town on the line.

By 1910 Ambrose's town was a going concern. The lots had sold off and were now occupied by thriving businesses and newly constructed houses. To this vibrant community came a new physician, John Andrew Devine. He had already practiced for one year in eastern Iowa in the small town of Elma and had a lot in common with his counterpart across the state in Sumner. He had been valedictorian of his medical school class and he was also from a large family. His parents farmed near Sigourney, where his brothers Jim, Joe, Tom and Dan would remain and continue farming. Only his sister Mary would move away to marry a man from Carroll, Iowa.

John was a large man, 6'3 ½," but he had started life as premature baby. The first month of his existence he was kept in a shoe box with fruit jars filled with hot water wedged into the box beside him. Surviving his first precarious year, he had grown into manhood and started his professional career as a country school teacher, but after three years he abandoned that to study medicine. Always a religious man, he left a Catholic hospital in Cedar Rapids for practice in Elma, evidently because he couldn't tolerate the nuns who ran the hospital.

John went to Bancroft when it already boasted of having three physicians. For a town of 830 people, this was quite a feat. Dr. Devine had consented to go into practice with one of the already established physicians, Dr. Walter. Twelve months into the partnership, Dr. Walter abruptly departed for California. At almost exactly the same time the other two physicians also moved on, with Dr. Guilde starting a practice in the neighboring town of Titonka and Dr. Sartos moving north to St. Cloud, Minnesota. In one short year Bancroft had gone from four physicians to a single doctor and that situation wouldn't change for years.

When Dr. Walter left for California, John purchased his house. A large showy structure just half a block off the business district, its location satisfied the housing rule of that era: the closer to the center of the city the better. For two years following the transfer of ownership, the bachelor doctor rattled around the house by himself. This was about to change.

A successful businessman in town had a daughter who had recently graduated from high school. Despite the age difference, romance blossomed between John in his late 20's and Lillian Murray 19. By the winter of 1913 they were planning to be married in June. Lillian, an attractive woman, came from Irish stock. Her father was a relative newcomer, having arrived in Bancroft only fifteen years before. He originally came from Wisconsin where he had been the postmaster, but the allure of land to the west prompted him to uproot his family, his wife and four children and head to a new town in Iowa called Bancroft, where the family settled on forty acres due west of town. Joe, a large, dark haired man with a majestic mustache, probably suspected that he could not provide for his growing family on 40 acres of ground, so he started a feed and grain elevator, farming the farmers. His endeavor proved quite successful, and by the time of Dr. Devine's appearance he had amassed, by Bancroft's standards, a sizable wealth.

Though the family prospered it wasn't without tragedy. Lillian's mother Mary would die in childbirth at forty years of age, and Lillian would need to help raise her young sisters. Taken far too young Mary (Holt) Murray had already had a full compliment of life's travails. Orphaned, she and her sister were separated to be raised by relatives, one in Kansas City and one in Dubuque.

This is the wedding picture of John Devine and Lillian Murray.

Bancroft like Sumner had been settled by Germans. But the Germans of Bancroft were southern Germans, Catholic, unlike Sumner's Protestant northern Germans. In Bancroft over 90% of the residents were Catholic, and the size of their church reflected that fact. St. John the Baptist Catholic Church was already an impressive structure in 1910, but it was nothing compared to the proposed new church, which would be a massive yellow brick building with three tall, arched doors at the top of the front steps, and surmounting the doors was an eighteen foot circular stained glass window. All together these features made an imposing entrance. Protruding from the south side of the church was a 94-foot tall bell tower that could rival any tower from a Tuscan walled city.

Lillian and John were married in the old church on Wednesday, June 18, and the newlyweds immediately set up housekeeping in Doc's home. An elegant porch wrapped around two sides of the house and on the inside, opposite the foyer, an open staircase flowed to the second story. A spacious dining room, and three parlors, each separated by pocket doors, occupied the center of the house. The kitchen in the back comprised almost a third of the length of the house and was enhanced by a tall ceiling. Within the kitchen a distinctive aroma arose from the connected sun porch. Facing to the south the sun porch was a storage facility for fruits and vegetables, the source of smell which permeated the kitchen. The upstairs had only two bedrooms, which seemed out of character for the house given the size of the ground floor. There was one small bedroom on the landing at the top of the stairs which was a few steps lower than the master bedroom. The largest of the bedrooms abutted an abnormally spacious bathroom, which showcased a grand cast iron tub supported by four, clawed legs. Out the back, past the sun porch, sat the barn Doc had constructed just after he took possession. This wasn't an abnormality for the times. Those wealthy enough had barns, even in town, to house their horses and carriages. Doc's barn functioned to board his horses (it could hold four horses) on one side, with room left to accommodate both a two seated buggy and a sleigh. There was a loft above, a hay mow, with a track running down the central beam, terminating at an oversized wooden door that opened to load the hay into the barn.

In 1913, John still made some house calls with a horse and wagon in the summer and a sleigh in the winter. He had a driver to accompany him on his house calls, a colorful man named Punk Sprank. The man with such a sensational name had a life style to match it. Punk had a great and renowned fondness for drink. A town of less than 900 people, Bancroft claimed more than its share of taverns and a fair number of its good citizens shared Punk's proclivity for alcohol, but he stood out among them.

Doc and Lillian were alone in their home for the first three years, but over the next ten years, six children would be born: John Emmett, Kenneth, Margaret, Mary Elaine, Thomas and Arthur. Several years later the baby John came along. As the children grew, they didn't refer to John as father but adopted the name by which the rest of the community called him, Doc. His closest friends, however, called him Jack. Even as adults his children continued to refer to him as Doc.

Doc evidently treated his sons with a firm hand, and his daughters with a gentler bearing. Stories told by the Devine children would bear out this a distinct dichotomy. Margaret and Mary Elaine always expressed fond memories of Doc; and their youngest brother John, didn't remember him much, but the older boys viewed him something of a tyrant.

One story the boys told took place while Doc was serving as mayor of Bancroft. In this position he also was justice of the peace, ruling on minor municipal legal infractions. One day his two eldest sons, Emmett and Kenneth were brought before him by the local constable. The two had been apprehended after "tipping over outhouses." The seven- to eight-foot wooden boxes were normally situated some distance behind the houses, as indoor plumbing would not become typical until after the rural electrification. Without the electricity necessary to pump water, those families living on the outskirts of town still had a need for outhouses. This made a sizable number of flimsy shacks available for vandalizing by young miscreants. Caught red handed, the Devine boys had no defense and Doc, as the duly elected officer of the court, passed sentence: a night in jail. After the culprits were led away to their cell and his legal responsibility was completed for the day, Doc returned home to inform Lillian that her sons wouldn't be coming home till morning.

The Devine family: (the back row from the left) Kenneth, Emmett, and Margaret, (the center row) Doc, Lillian, and Thomas, (the front row) Arthur, infant John, and Mary Elaine.

The two youngest, Tom and Art, also ran afoul of their father. In possession of a cigar, the two young men sneaked behind the barn one day and while attempting to light their pilfered stogy were discovered by their father. Doc could be called inventive in his punishment that day; he brought the two boys to the house and ushered them into one of the parlors. Two chairs were removed from the dining room and positioned back to back. Tom and Art were ordered to be seated and each was given his own cigar. Doc lit the cigars after the entire family was called together to witness the boys punishment. Doc then told each to smoke the entire cigar. Neither boy made it to the end, each becoming "green" within a few minutes.

His children's perspective of Doc was limited. Even Joe Sexton, his eventual son-in-law, would refer to Doc as a 'benevolent dictator' and in his writings would point out Doc's finer qualities. He was known to have a great sense of humor and he dearly loved music, religion, and his family. A farmer at heart like his brothers, his idea of retirement was to build a home on a farm and live out his days separated from the demands of his medical practice and civic responsibilities. Every summer Doc would ship his family off to Sigourney to the Devine farm and when time allowed he would slip away from his practice, riding the train to join them. Doc never seemed to abandon his love for the 'simpler' farm life, an understandable sentiment, given the pressure of being the lone doctor in a small town.

When compared to a modern medical practice, Doc's practice might seem light years behind. First, prior to vaccines for diseases like small pox, which made its appearance in 1922, and for polio in the 50's, Doc had only rudimentary treatments for such diseases as diphtheria, whooping cough, rubella, polio, tuberculosis, syphilis, and gangrene. And chronic diseases like heart disease and cancer were essentially death sentences. Besides the everyday medical issues, Doc also faced epidemics like the Spanish flu which was thought to have spread from a mutated virus incubated in the trenches of World War I. The disease spread over the entire globe and in Iowa alone claimed eight thousand people between 1918 and 1920. The virus had a profound virulence, though the mortality rate was only 2.5%, those unlucky enough to fall in that category died quickly. There was very little Doc could do for these patients. Sometimes within hours of the first symptoms the patient would suffocate from the frothing bloody fluid that filled the lungs.

The second hurdle Doc had to overcome was that Bancroft didn't have a hospital. If the gravity of the illness or injury required, and time allowed, patients could be transferred to neighboring hospitals.

However, if treatment was needed urgently or the surgery necessary fell within Doc's capabilities, he performed it either at home or in his office. For minor operations Doc did the surgery right on his kitchen table, performing 'outpatient surgery' long before it came into vogue. For a procedure like a tonsillectomy that could be performed right in his office above Carmen's Drug Store, Doc would not hesitate to proceed. One morning Lillian summoned Art and told him to run a bundle of clean linens the two blocks down the street to his father's office. This task was just a ruse. Poor Art, unknown to him, was going to have his tonsils removed that day. Delivering the bundle of linens, he was abruptly shepherded into an examination room and anesthetized.

Doc delivered all the babies in town with many being delivered in their own homes, but a fair number took advantage of the services of one of Doc's nurses, who functioned as the town's midwife. Her house contained a delivery room and a bedroom for mother and baby. Very common for the period most mothers would stay with her from 7 to10 days after delivery.

All these services were performed on a very personal basis. Doc had an intimate relationship with his patients, without insurance companies and government agencies wedged in between them.

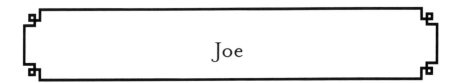

Joe

Lillian was already four months along. She and Doc were expecting their third child while clear across the state, George and Inez just had delivered their second child, a boy they named Joseph West Sexton. Two days before, America had celebrated the fourth of July, the day being muted by the fact that the nation had entered the First World War the year before. The Sextons already had a five year old daughter, Donna. Some children are spitting images of one of the parents, and so it was with Donna, who looked exactly like her mother. Donna, for years the princess of the family, now had to share her realm with this infant interloper. Every new addition to the Sexton's neighborhood was keenly realized. With only small yards separating the houses and warm summer nights which demanded all the windows be thrown open to catch any breeze, any late night disturbance, like a baby crying, echoed freely through the quiet of the evening. From an early age, Joe made his presence known.

Shortly after Joe's birth the family had moved to their second home. Now only two blocks from Joe's maternal grandparents living in the Hotel Charles, they were in easy walking distance. Just up to the corner, past the Cass bank building then turning east past the Overton Chemical building, a brisk stroll would bring them to the back door of the hotel. This was a frequent trip for Inez and her children. Of the two grandparents, Phoebe was every inch the doting grandmother. Short and plump, while hugging her grandchildren, she seemed to envelope them. As the children grew, they would make the journey to their grandma's on of their own. At four years old, Joe made such a journey.

Donna, Inez and Joe Sexton 1918

Seated on the lawn, Inez is pictured with her new-born son, Joe, and her daughter Donna.

He had been to see his father in his office in the back of the livery stable. To see his grandmother, he had only had to cross Second Street to get to the hotel. Oblivious, the toddler darted out into the street right into the path of a Model T Ford. The driver never saw the boy. His car passed right over him, but a combination of a soft dirt street and the narrow tires of the Model T left Joe only frightened and bawling. His grandmother happened to see the entire episode and flew into the street to Joe's aid. Finding him unhurt, she picked up her grandson and whisked him into the hotel.

Phoebe's answer to any trauma was a hot bath and food. This

remedy could cure anything. With Joe safely in her arms and in the hotel, Phoebe drew a hot bath. By the time Joe's frantic mother had heard the news and arrived at the hotel, Joe had already been scrubbed and was sitting at a table, eating ice cream. Phoebe's cure had been a total success.

Phoebe may have spoiled her grandchildren but their father George couldn't be accused of the same. When Joe was seven or eight, George bought him a horse. Through the early 1920's horses were still prevalent. They were still the power source on most farms, and young boys still rode them for sport, a remnant of a time when horsemanship was a necessary skill. Already Joe's buddies, Max Bowling and Ben Winks had their own ponies, which may have been the impetus behind George's purchase for his son a Shetland pony named Daisy. Shetlands are short, stocky animals, not initially bred for riding. Native to the Shetland Islands, these sturdy creatures were employed to work the local coal mines when children labor was outlawed there in the 1840's. After that period Shetlands were deemed to be draft animals, and the idea of using them as riding stock didn't occur until after the 1890's, when they were beginning to be exported to the US.

The beasts were stubborn and cantankerous. Daisy, true to her breed, was more than a match for young Joe Sexton. Frustrated that the horse fought his every command, Joe sought out his father for help. George listened expressionless while his son laid out his case against the horse. Unsympathetic, George gave his boy this advice, "You'll be able to ride that pony when you know more than she does." This wasn't the response Joe was looking for, but he'd just had his first lesson. George wasn't going to run to his aid and solve all of his problems; he'd better learn to rely on himself. Joe did win mastery over Daisy and would spend long afternoons out riding with friends, but the lesson was well learned.

Daisy's care and maintenance also fell to Joe. Currying the horse, cleaning her stable, and feeding and watering her were his responsibilities. George had made it perfectly clear; failure to care for the horse would result in the horse being sold, and Joe had no reason to doubt his father's resolve.

George's sternness and seeming lack of interest in their activities didn't mean he didn't love his children. He was a complex man. His sternness arose from his desire to have his children be self-reliant, and his apathy toward their activities was due to his notion that their activities were for their enjoyment not his entertainment. One exception to that was Donna's theatrical career. While in high school, Donna performed in several plays. Most were held at the opera house where the community plays attracted packed houses. George did make an effort to attend the plays Donna performed in.

George had his own interests, baseball and politics. Baseball was the national pastime, played in every town, big and small. George attended local games but the professional teams were also his passion especially the New York Yankees. With the advent of radio broadcasts in the late 20's, people then had access to live baseball. Car radios installed into the dash would not make an appearance until the 40's, but prior to that a home radio could be placed on the car's seat and connected to its battery, and with the antenna tilted in the right direction it was possible to pick up a radio signal. This is exactly what George loved to do. Out on a secluded patch of road, by himself, he would while away a couple hours listening to a baseball game.

Politics also were one of his passions. An ardent Democrat, he had a picture of Franklin Delano Roosevelt prominently hanging above his desk. We also know he had some dealing with the state party. On November 13, 1913, the *Sumner Gazette* ran an announcement about George: "Dr. G.J. Sexton of this city has been appointed Assistant State Veterinarian. An appointment that is merited from a professional as well as a political stand point." What is intriguing is that during this time the governor of Iowa was a Republican. The only plausible explanation could be that the State Veterinarian was probably a Democrat. The exact nature of his appointment may never be determined, but

George for years proudly advertised in the local paper always taking pains to add the phrase 'Assistant State Veterinarian' to his name.

Throughout the community George Sexton was reputed to be a man of a generous and kind nature, a man to be respected. Though well received publicly, in private his life had some rough edges. His marriage had two acknowledgeable points of conflict, notably money and drinking. Joe as a boy was exposed to the domestic discord which he would later characterize in his writings, describing his father as a "poor businessman." It is true that George would forgive accounts due of widowed wives of clients and he would extend terms to farmers who fell on hard times, but the exact nature of his books can't be known. One thing was true and known that the agricultural economy during the majority of his vet career would work against him.

In the first years of his practice George did prosper. Even in the first part of the century more prairie land yielded to the plow opening up more land for farms. As a young man Joe can remember riding with his father in the country. Patches of prairie were still interspersed between existing farms, and George driving in the country with his son would point out to Joe the prairie chickens strutting in the open areas. These birds, now gone from the area, were remnants of the days of unbroken prairie. In the first years after George arrived farming boomed around Sumner. Every farm had livestock and horses, which were still necessary for work and transport. These were the years just prior to the First World War, which would profoundly affect the farm economy.

The eruption of the war in Europe brought a great demand for agricultural products. As the war evolved year after year, commodity prices almost doubled by 1916, and then almost doubled again after 1917. Some of that cash found its way to Sumner and into George's pockets. As profits increased in farming the human ailment of speculation surfaced. Those who viewed the increase as the 'the new normal' refused to see the bubble in commodity prices that was developing.

One group who did see the bubble was the Federal Reserve, the product of a secret meeting held in 1912 at J. Pierpont Morgan's Jekyll Island Club, where twelve national bank officials united to regulate America's entire banking system. In 1913, Congress put their stamp of approval on the scheme, passing the Federal Reserve Act. With the end of the First World War, inflation took off and reached 20%. A bushel of corn rose to $1.50 and hogs to $20 a hundred weight. The sudden rise in commodities attracted the attention of speculators. Today this would not be alarming, but in relation to annual farm incomes, which at the time were less than $1,000 a year, this added income was a great windfall. As farm incomes increased, so did land values. Land prices increased from an average $150 to nearly $500 an acre. The Federal Reserve in lock step with the Congress decided to act. From 1920-1921 federal spending decreased from 18.5 billion to 6.4 billion, a 65% reduction in an effort to stifle the increase in liquidity. But the real culprit was the Federal Reserve. In June 1920 the Fed raised the discount rate (the cost of money to banks) to 7%. Immediately banks were forced to raise their loan rates above that mark. Money dried up and depression ensued. Deflation (the drop in the value of commodities) reached 15.8% and unemployment exploded to 11.7%.

Around Sumner prices for farm goods tanked, with corn dropping to 30 cents a bushel and other commodities fell in lock step with it. It didn't take long for George and his family to feel the pain.

By 1922, most of the nation had experienced a rapid economic recovery from the economic downturn. Unemployment by then was halved in industrial zones, but the same can't be said for the farm sector. Farming refused to recover and farm prices remained depressed. In 1924 Senators McNary of Oregon and Hansen of Iowa proposed a bill that would establish a federal farm board to buy up surplus farm production to stimulate an increase in prices. Even with backing from President Coolidge's Secretary of Agriculture, Henry Wallace, repeated efforts to move the bill through Congress all failed. The fear of increased food prices caused the political argument to become a battleground between consumers and producers. The consumer won. Farm commodity prices would limp through the 20's until 1929 when they finally fell in a dark hole.

These two decades would also be dark times for George and his family. A story was told of George returning home after running farm calls all day. Entering through the back kitchen door, George holding two live chickens by their legs announced to his wife that these were payment for one of his calls. George actually saw nothing wrong with a client making an honest effort to pay his bills when it was painfully obvious that the man had no money, but Inez took an entirely different view of the situation. Visibly upset with her husband, she berated him for accepting such a gesture. She made it perfectly clear she didn't need any chickens, she needed money.

Both Joe and his sister Donna vividly recalled this period, with George struggling to supply the family with monetary resources and Inez constantly chiding his efforts. Inez's criticism was vocal and persistent enough to influence Joe's young mind. He soon took up his mother's denouncement of his own fathers efforts. Like most injured relationships, once the flood gate of criticism opened, even the edges washed away. So it was that other parts of George's personality came under pressure, namely his drinking.

In this case, Joe would come to his father's defense. Later he would contend that his father was never a "drunk," but George did drink. This fact may have been filtered and changed by cultural differences and perceptions held by the bickering couple. George was Irish Catholic, and his background found drinking alcohol an acceptable behavior for a man. The fact he would go to the country and listen to baseball game on the radio and drink a couple beers probably wouldn't even raise an eyebrow among his brothers and sisters, but Inez had a contrary opinion. She had been raised as a Methodist and as such did not find value in drinking. Overlaying this differing opinion at the time was the

Eighteenth Amendment. In June 1920 the amendment forbade the sale of alcohol, giving rise to Prohibition. A driving force behind Prohibition had been the Women's Christian Temperance Union, for years at the national forefront against alcohol. Even back in the late 1880's it fought the evils of demon rum with a Methodist women, Frances Willard, as its president. On the subject of drink, George and Inez were like oil and water. There would never be a unified solution and it would always remain one more point of conflict.

Siblings

Joe was already six when his brother James Franklin was born. The difference in their ages had a profound effect not just on Joe and Jim but on all three of the siblings, who were separated by five and six years respectively. They may all have grown up in the same house, but each had a distinctly different life and personality. Donna liked music and cultural activities. She had her mother's cultural bent. When she was in high school because of their age difference her brothers were only in grade school and junior high. She had no reason to be interested in her brothers' activities. Joe was the athlete and so he naturally gravitated toward sports. Jim, the youngest, found his forte in socializing. Initially short in stature, Jim enjoyed sports but his size precluded his starring in any. But maybe because of his size he developed a magnetic personality and was able to gather people around him.

A prime example is his childhood boxing promotion. The following article appeared in the *Sumner Gazette*: "Signs posted Tuesday noon for a big-value boxing show to be staged in Jim Sexton's basement this Saturday at 1:30 o'clock. The admission is two cents and promoters are guaranteeing the public their 'money's worth.' Clayton O'Brien and Ray Schwerin are slated to go eight rounds while Jim Sexton and Harold Warries will fight it out in a six round match."

In an era before "personal devices," fun was made not from downloading games but from dreaming up entertainment for themselves, and parents were not needed as spectators. In fact, adults might have destroyed the entire experience of the boys. Fight promotion was only one of Jim's schemes. On the corner of Main and Carpenter right below a protruded turret, a doorway led in to a popular hang out for adolescents. In front of the marble countertop, round stools formed a neat line. Protruding behind the counter a bank of goose necked soda spouts dispensed carbonated drinks in a variety of flavors. Juke boxes and pinball machines were years away but a device called the pin game had gained popularity. For a penny the operator got 5-7 balls to shoot into the 'field.' It was all manual and required players to keep their own scores. Though only a penny a play and a nickel a soda even these trivial pleasures expensive for a young man during the Depression Jim found a way around this problem. His good friend, Jim Heyer, happened to have access to a stamping machine for lead slugs. Relying on their natural ingenuity, the boys figured out a way to make slugs in the shape of coins. The plan seemed to be working like a charm until the soda shop's owner started noticing their 'coins' in his nightly tally.

Days later Mrs. Sexton was interrupted one afternoon by a neatly dressed gentleman at the front door. As Inez opened the door, the man identified himself as an FBI agent. His next question stunned her even more, "Was she the mother of Jim Sexton?" After the shop owner reported the 'slug coins' to the local cop, he assigned the crime to the category of counterfeiting, bringing the boys' nefarious activities to the attention of the federal authorities. The shop owner and officials had laid a trap and swept up the desperados that afternoon. At the time of the agent's visit, Jim Heyer and Jim Sexton were safely behind bars in the Sumner jail. Both boys gained release from incarceration when their parents assured the officials that their crime spree was over.

Jim had other interests beside petty crime and sports promotion. He was actually quite gifted artistically. He loved to draw, and one of his favorite subjects was planes. His fascination with airplanes would stay with him throughout his life and dramatically influence its path.

All the Sexton children developed their own personalities. Joe's revolved around golf. In 1926, a group of Sumner men had bought 50 acres of pasture land just north of town, and there they laid out routing for nine golf holes and carved out round depressions suitable to be filled in to construct sand greens. After mowing the projected fairways and planting trees, the group of enthusiasts who had constructed Sumner's golf course named their club, Meadowbrook. By the 1920's golf was having a metamorphosis. Once restricted to the affluent, with the advent of Bobby Jones in the early 20's, the sport gained widespread popularity. The original club house for Meadowbrook sat between the present day holes 5 and 6. The course featured a par 6 measuring more than 600 yards with the hole running along the entire western boundary of the course and ending in a sand green not far from the Chicago and Great Western tracks, which delineated the course's northern edge. Meandering through the center of the course was a small feeder stream for the Little Wapsie. This was the only water for the course. It would be years before an irrigation system for the greens could be trenched in. Without water, sand greens were the only viable option the club had. The surface for these greens was actually composed of oiled sand. A unique surface it demanded a unique putting method. Each green had a roller and a rake placed beside it. The roller leveled the sand from the ball to the hole and after putting the rake returned the surface of the green to its pre-rolled condition.

At an early age, Joe became acquainted with the sport. As is the case with most sports among the young we played the sport with friends. From a young age, Ben Winks and Joe were friends and Ben's uncle Pat was an ardent golfer who watched young Sexton embrace the game and show constantly increasing talent. One day Pat who was going to Waterloo to take a golf lesson asked if Joe would like to accompany him. Joe couldn't pass up the opportunity. Both men, however, were disappointed when they arrived at the golf course in Waterloo. The pro who was to give them the lesson had been called away. The lesson then might have helped the young golfer, but as time would show, Joe developed a great game through his own efforts.

Joe's talents really started to blossom in his early teens. By the time he was fourteen years old he already held the course record at Meadowbrook, scoring a 30 for nine holes, a record which would stand for years. His success brought him recognition from fellow members of the club, many of whom were prominent men and women in Sumner. There were the Winks who were in the produce business, the Heyers who were in lumber and banking, the Karstens, a father and son who were both dentists and the Wilharms who were also in the produce business. Throughout his life, his relationships with these men would serve Joe well. Affirming this point later, Joe wrote "through golf I have met many fine people and the ability to be an above average player has been very advantageous to me."

Beside his athletic skill, Joe's maturity was recognized by the club members. In June 1935, at the age of 17, he was elected to represent the club at the founding of the Northeast Iowa Golf Association. An organizational meeting for the newly launched association was due to be held in Oelwein, Iowa. Each club was asked to send two representatives. Meadowbrook scheduled a meeting of the membership to choose their delegates and form a list of issues the club desired to be advanced. Ed Bonovsky, manager of the train depot and one of Sumner's better golfers and the young Sexton boy were chosen. (Ed quite possibly may have spent too much time on his golf game, as the following year he sued an Oelwein man, Richard McCue, for $7,000 claiming Richard had had an affair with his wife.)

Popular at this time were area club golf matches for men and women. Before the era of the "best shot tournament," throughout the summer medal and match play tournaments were played on most weekends in Sumner or on golf courses in the surrounding towns. The best players in the area regularly competed against one another, and Joe's name could always be found among the leaders. Besides offering local honors, some tournaments were qualifiers for regional and state tournaments. In September 1935, the *Gazette* sports column reported that "golfers from 20 towns competed in a tourney Sunday. Harold Smith, Oelwein professional qualified Wednesday by equaling a course record

with a 30. Joe Sexton shot a 34 and E.A. Bonovsky recorded a 40."
Another headline a year later reported, "Joe Sexton only entry from
here in State Golf Tourney."

That year the state tournament was played at the Cedar Rapids
Country Club where Joe possibly had a slight advantage. He had played
the course multiple times with his uncle Perry West who was a member
there, and young Joe had often been a guest. That week in Cedar Rapids
he would play well but would be bested by another young golfer named
Johnny Jacobs. Joe would have no reason to hang his head. Johnny
would go on to prove himself by having a very successful golfing career,
claiming five state amateur championships.

Golf was and would be Joe's passion, but in high school he also
played all the sports. He played basketball for all four years, football for
three years and track and baseball for two years. When later he wrote
about playing in so many sports he humbled himself saying, "I was
competing in a group without a lot of competition." Humility aside, he
did excel in every sport.

Black Tuesday

In one day alone, sixteen million shares of stock were traded on the New York Stock Exchange. This was only unusual because it was many times the average volume of shares traded during a normal day in 1929. That Tuesday, October 29th, the huge volume of shares came onto the market mostly all on the sell side. Panic ensued. At a time when a million was considered prodigious, in one session of the exchange billions of dollars were wiped out. A perfect storm of events had contributed to this day: speculation, ill liquid bank assets and a chronic struggling agriculture sector all joined together to foment disaster.

Back on the farms around Iowa the economy cratered. A bushel of corn, which a decade before had brought $1.50, now leveled out at 8-10 cents. It was cheaper to burn corn for fuel than coal. Cash, hard currency, became almost non existent. Farmers would hoard their cash. If they had any cash they would need it for taxes and to pay on their loans. George soon discovered the vet bill wasn't a great priority for any farmer. In fact, considering the demands of taxes, loans, food, and other nonessentials George's vet statements probably were near the bottom of every farmer's budget. Ravaged by this sudden turn of events, the Sexton family needed to prioritize their expenses also.

Poor Donna was first to fall victim to this change in fortune. In 1931 she had graduated from high school and had been accepted into Iowa State Teachers College in Cedar Falls for the fall semester. Per quarter the tuition there was $75 plus room and board. Assuming George's income was average for that time, about $1300 annually, this would comprise about 5% of the family's yearly budget, but these weren't average times. Her freshman year George scraped together enough for the tuition. Possibly aware of her tenuous college stay, Donna immersed herself in the experience. She joined a sorority, Delta Phi Delta, and by all accounts was a typical college freshman. By her sophomore year the financial strain was beginning to show, and bad as things were for her father, they were about to get worse.

A farmer's strike facilitated an even deeper depression. A firebrand by the name of Milo Reno had successfully organized a large block of farmers in Iowa and Nebraska. Hoping to cause an increase in crop prices, Milo's organization voted to initiate the farm strike in 1932. They carried as their slogan, "Stay home, buy nothing and sell nothing." Reno and his organization failed to affect prices, but they did succeed in causing widespread chaos.

By the end of Donna's sophomore year the handwriting was on the wall. There would be no more money for her education. Logically she understood why it had to be; emotionally she resented it, and she would carry her resentment with her the rest of her life. It would hang like a cloud over her relationship with her brother Joe and her future husband. Joe, who would finish school, would be accused of receiving some preferential treatment.

With two years of college Donna could find some employment positions available to her; one of those was as a school teacher. At a time when jobs were at a premium, Donna luckily secured employment in the Sumner school district, not to teach "in town" but rather in one of the country schools. Of all the schools spread throughout the rural area, she was fortunate to be assigned to one near town. Ray School, Sumner #2 was only two miles from her home. Just northwest of town, over the Little Wapsie bridge, the schooled bordered the southern edge of what was known locally as the Northwoods, a heavily timbered area extending northward past Wilson Grove. Like all the rural schools, Sumner #2 was strategically situated within walking distance of a certain number of farms. A single school housed all the classes from first to eighth grade and was under the supervision of only one teacher. After eighth grade any student wishing to go on to "higher education" would need to attend Sumner High School. For a majority of students graduating from eighth grade meant graduating from school.

That first fall Donna would have had as her first job to open the windows of her assigned school. She would need a breeze to clear out the stale smell from months of dormancy. It was the fall of 1933 when Donna saw her school room for the first time. Here she would be sequestered with her students for the next nine months. Today it would be hard to find someone to take such a job. Donna didn't own a car so either she walked or she finagled a ride to school everyday. Charged with writing lessons for eight separate grades and maintaining discipline, she also needed to be able to do any nursing or building repairs. The winter presented even more tasks. The pot belly stove needed to be started on cold mornings and the kerosene lamps had to be filled, since it would be a couple more years before electrification of the rural area. One more discomfort due to the lack of electricity was the absence of indoor plumbing. An outhouse served the school, and this could be a very grim prospect on very warm or very cold days.

About the same time as Donna started teaching, Joe took a job. He was just finishing his sophomore year of high school, and his first employment was a summer job at Wescott and Winks, a large produce company run by Leo Winks, father of Joe's friend Ben. This produce company was not involved in the distribution of fruits and vegetables, but rather, they sold eggs, ducklings, and poultry which at the time were big business. Every farm had chickens, and on each farm the care and income from the chickens belonged to the farm wife. This is how the wives made 'their money.' Daily feeding of the chickens and the collection of the eggs were sizable tasks, since the typical farm could have well over a hundred birds. Once collected, the eggs were carefully stacked in cardboard boxes comprised of several separated layers. Each layer could hold 3-4 dozen eggs set on to a cardboard sheet which very much likened the bottom half of a modern day egg carton. Much like milk routes for creameries, the produce company had egg routes. Drivers had assigned stops on the routes every day to gather the eggs from the farms. With a number of produce firms grappling for eggs, these routes were highly sought after.

Firms like Wescott and Winks did sell some whole eggs but most were processed, meaning the white was separated from the yoke, before that could happen each egg had to be "candled." In a darkened room women would take each layer of eggs from the delivery box and expose it to a bright light. What they were looking for was any darkness in the yoke, an indication that an embryo was already forming. This egg needed to be discarded (aborted). Careful attention was paid to where these discarded eggs came from. If too many eggs needed to be destroyed from one farm, that farm wife's check would be docked. When candling was finished all the clear eggs were sent to the cracking room. There sheets of eggs were loaded onto a conveyer belt which carried them to a row of metal cups each lifting the egg to a knife which split open the shell. The egg white and egg shell fell to a screen separating these two. The yoke then was carried up further by the cup and fell on to a trough. The whites which were filtered through the screen were then piped to a huge cooling vat. The yolks were piped to a tank to be measured into 25-pound tins to be then moved into a freezer.

Joe's job was quite simple but not pleasant. Early in the day he carted cases of eggs to the candling room, then moved the same cases back down the wooden ramp to the cracking room. Once enough egg crates were stacked for the day's cracking, he dressed to move the yoke canisters into the freezer. Just outside the freezer door someone senior to Joe would open the spigot on the yoke tank and load each 25-pound canister. Protected against the freezer's cold by coat, gloves and hat, Joe loaded a dozen tins on a push cart and entered the freezer. There he aligned each canister separating the rows by wooden slats so they wouldn't freeze together. He would empty his cart and go back for more. Once the freezer was filled, Joe reversed the process, removing each frozen container of yokes and loading them onto a refrigerated railroad car. At the end of the day the women went home, the office staff went home, but not Joe. Now the cracking machines had to be cleaned. All the piping from the machine to the vats needed to be disassembled and scrubbed with long soapy brushes on poles and left to dry over night. Now Joe could walk home, his clothes wet and caked with egg albumin. For his efforts he earned 15 cents/hour.

To augment this princely sum, Joe could work certain nights loading live birds onto train cars that Westcott and Winks would send to Chicago. Live chickens were brought to the train by truck. Each bird would then need to be manhandled into a cage on the boxcar for the overnight run to Chicago. These evening, Joe could make extra money catching chickens by their legs and loading them into cages, some of which were above his head. One of the drawbacks of loading chickens is that they are indiscreet about where and when they defecate. On more than one occasion, Joe returned home with chicken feces on this clothing.

It wasn't surprising that the following summer when a different job opportunity presented itself working for the new light plant, and Joe jumped on it. In 1933, Sumner voted to build its own municipal light plant to supply electricity to the town. At this time Central States Power and Light along with some members of the business community, F. Bartels, H. Nieman, F. Oltrogge and Charles Pennington challenged the vote in court in an effort to stop the plant's construction. The case went all the way to the Supreme Court of Iowa, which ruled on March 1934 that the town needed to hold another election. In May the town voted again to build their own plant, passing the proposal for second time. Later that year construction commenced.

Central State refused, however, to throw in the towel. The poles and electric lines in Sumner belonged to the company, and they contended that the lines and poles couldn't be used by the new power plant.

Sumner would therefore need to install power lines for their customers. Starting in the summer of 1935, the local light plant would need men to dig post holes and erect the line. There would be a limited number of positions available for the 'locals,' since the majority of the jobs were mandated by the federal government to go to WPA workers. As part of President Roosevelt's new deal, the Works Progress Administration had 8.5 million men and women to put to work, and some would need to come to Sumner.

Though only a limited number of job openings were available, Joe somehow secured one. At the time people referred to such a job as a 'ringer.' The slang term referred to a job with exceptionally good pay. Joe's crew dug post holes. Digging with shovels and two handed post-hole diggers, each man was required to reach a depth of six feet. The digger was a simple device with two shovels hinged together which could be rammed into the hole repeatedly until enough soil was loosened: then, forcing the handles apart to close the end enabled the load to be lifted to the surface. Foot after foot, dirt and rocks were excavated until the depth and width was reached to accommodate the wooden pole. Scoop after scoop, load after load, hour after hour for 10 hours a day, for six days a week, the men worked to earn 40 cents an hour. By the end of the week Joe could make twenty four dollars. Given that the average WPS worker made only $40 a month, Joe's salary was a 'ringer.'

Though he might still be considered a boy, Joe that summer worked with men. By far the youngest man on the crew, he found himself befriended by a more worldly local man, Al Cosby. Al could easily be categorized as 'colorful.' He was a bootlegger by trade and was not ashamed to admit it. Once brought before a judge, he was asked his occupation, and Al answered without wavering, "I'm a bootlegger." On Saturday nights after he finished his day job, Al plied his true vocation. Community dances were common on Saturday nights, and that is when Al sought out his clientele. He wore bib overalls, not an uncommon sight but his overalls were quite different from everyone else's. On the inside of the overalls were sewn multiple pockets, each capable of holding a pint of alcohol. At 50 cents a flask, Crosby could stock his moveable store with enough booze to make quite a sum in one evening.

That same summer Joe's maternal grandfather, Franklin West, died. He had been living with the Sextons in their crowded little house on Main Street. A few years before, Grandma Phoebe had died in Strawberry Point, long after Franklin and Phoebe had left the Hotel Charles for a good position managing the hotel in that town. Even before his wife passed away, Franklin had been in ill health but subsequently as a widower he needed care that could only be supplied by one of the family members. After discussion among the siblings as to who would care for their father, it became apparent that the job would fall to Inez. Dorothy, the youngest had moved away, and her husband was suspected of being an alcoholic. True, convinced by George to go into vet medicine, had earned his vet degree and moved to California. And Perry, who had a top management position with Collins Insurance in Cedar Rapids, and was also childless, wealthy and living in a big home, was by all appearances the ideal candidate to care for Franklin, but Perry's wife would not hear of it. A selfish woman, she had no time for her father-in-law. That left only Inez. To his credit, George, even though he was financially strapped, welcomed his father –in-law into his home and never once voiced a complaint.

In May 1936, Joe Sexton graduated from high school. Along with his buddies, like Ben Winks, he had thoughts of one last summer in Sumner before heading off to college. Before deciding where to go, however, he would need to talk to his father. The conversation did not go as Joe had planned. George was totally up front with his son. He told Joe he could start school but as with Donna, George didn't know how long he could support Joe's education. His finances weren't predictable and the family didn't have adequate savings to fall back on. Joe took the news surprisingly well, appreciating his father's honesty. After a few days, he settled on a plan of action. He would put off college for a year or so until he could manage to earn enough to support his own college expenses. Once committed to his plan, Joe didn't lose much time before landing a job.

Fortune and Misfortune

While all recollections of the Depression were ones of hardship for the Sextons, off in Bancroft the Devines managed the national economic disaster in a more comfortable fashion. The Depression left its imprint on every corner of the country but Doc Devine's was able to gain from the economic turmoil. There is no doubt that Dr. Devine was a hard-working and very intelligent man, but a fair degree of his financial success during this era came from his brother – in – law, Art Murray.

In 1916 the Murray elevator changed hands. Joe Murray, its founder, was forced to retire due to ill health, and his eldest son, Art, bought the business. Art would prove to be a dexterous businessman. The Murray elevator initially had competition in Bancroft from the Farmer's Elevator, but after a few years with Art at the helm, the Murray Elevator absorbed their competitor. Through skillful buying and selling of grain, the Murray Elevator expanded in the 20's, building a third elevator. In spite of the dismal agricultural economy, Art Murray managed to accumulate a tidy sum of money.

For those with cash, the Depression offered opportunities. Between 1930 and 1935, 750,000 acres were lost through bankruptcy and fore-closure. From 1921 to the middle of the Depression in 1933, farm values plunged 69%, and in 1922 the average acre brought $244, but by 1933 the same acre went for $66. With cash as king, Art Murray started buy-ing up Iowa black dirt. During this period he would amass seven farms to his net worth. During this period, Art convinced his brother-in-law to also purchase land, and with Art's help, Doc secured three farms just outside Bancroft.

It would have been entirely understandable to see a wave of resentment rise up against Art and Doc for profiting from the misfortunes of others, but that doesn't appear to have happened. Doc still held the respect of the community, and Art was very much admired. Years later, people would still refer to Art as a "really good man."

One story about Art deserves retelling. A local farmer down on his luck had his hay mower break. He was in need of thirty-five dollars to purchase a new mower to cut the crop for his winter fodder. The only asset he had to sell was that years' oats, and without them his horses would need to go without the supplemental oats in their diet. Loading the oats into his wagon he made for the elevator. Art met him at the scales. Interested in why the farmer thought about selling oats at that time of year Art pressed the question. The farmer answered explaining his circumstances and said he hoped the load of oats would bring close to the amount he needed for his new hay sickle bar. Standing with his hands in his pockets and wearing his typical straw hat, Art listened intently to the farmer's story. With the farmer's final word, Art pulled out cash from his pocket and carefully counted out $35. "Here take the money and your oats. Pay me when you can."

Given that Doc had enough financial stability to be able to purchase farm land, he also had the means to send his children to college. The three oldest were already enrolled at the time of Joe Sexton's graduation; Emmett was a junior at Trinity College in Sioux City and the next in line, Kenneth had started his sophomore year at Iowa State. And finally, Margaret had just left for Winona, Minnesota, where she would be a freshman at St. Theresa's. This left Mary Elaine for the first time with a bedroom of her own albeit the little bedroom on the landing. Her brothers Thomas, Art, and John weren't so lucky. They still shared the second upstairs bedroom.

It was a pleasant enough September day; the heat of August was over and the cool northern breezes of fall had commenced. Mary Elaine had just come home from the Sheridan house next door where she had been with her friends, and Art and Tom were still shooting baskets in the barn loft when Doc was arriving for dinner. Dinner, however, would be a sullen occasion. That day Doc had called the Mayo Clinic in Rochester. He had made an appointment to examine a lesion on his leg. For the last couple weeks, Doc had noticed a swelling on his ankle. Its persistence had caused him alarm. He may have concluded the diagnosis already or at least suspected it, but for the time being he shielded his children from his fears. Lillian, however, knew her husband. If he was going to Mayo's, Doc already suspected the worst.

As Doc pulled up, the Mayo Clinic building loomed in front of him. Fairly new, the fifteen story brick building had been finished in 1930. It towered over Rochester in tandem with the new Kohler Hotel only a block away. Now subjected to being the patient, Doc was x-rayed and examined by Mayo specialists. From the tests and symptoms the doctors reached their diagnosis. It was osteoscarcoma. Doc's ankle swelling was a bone cancer. (Today the diagnosis might be more accurately attributed to non-Hodgkin's lymphoma, a cancer of the bone marrow) The scope of treatment available to the doctors treating Doc remained limited, and amputation was the treatment recommended. At this point, they could only hope to eliminate the spread of cancer. The entire infected leg was removed the next day and Doc, after recuperating, was released to return to Bancroft.

A letter from the treating physicians at Mayo followed him home. They wanted to alert him to a second problem discovered just after his release. The x-rays of his lungs showed a spot. The doctors concluded the amputation had been performed too late, the cancer had already metastasized. The letter didn't go into detail but it didn't need to Doc understood completely. His prognosis was poor.

Of the three parlors in their home, the one nearest the kitchen had been remodeled as Doc and Lillian's bedroom, since the seven children upstairs left no room in the house. This downstairs bedroom became Doc's hospice room and a makeshift reception area. Almost immediately upon his return from Mayo's, a steady flow of clients and friends came to see their beloved doctor, most to say thank you and good bye.

October leaked into November and Doc's condition perceptibly worsened. All of the family members left at home were forced to watch their father suffer through those months and were not left unaffected by the trauma. Everyone had stories about the experience. Art, in particular, only eleven at the time, remembered nights when his father would be "moaning and crying out" as the children tucked in their beds heard his plaintive cries echoing up the stairway. Pneumonia attacked his weakened lungs in the beginning of December. Now with his bed enclosed in an oxygen tent, Doc sensed his own worsening condition. Aware that fluid was filling his lungs and would soon take him, he motioned Lillian to his side, possibly preparing her for the end. She immediately said she would call the three oldest children home but Doc would not have it. A proud man, he felt it was bad enough that some family members were forced to endure his decline, and he saw no need to subject the other children to this too. Concerning the three still at school he was reputed to have said, "I don't want them to see me suffer."

Tuesday morning, with one last ephemeral breath, John Andrew Devine died. It was December 10, 1935. That Friday morning Main Street Bancroft was all but deserted. All the shops had the front doors locked, and the only traffic to be seen was moving toward the Catholic Church where all the pews of St. John's were filled. It was nearly 9:30 AM and Garry's funeral home had the casket waiting in the vestibule of the church. Earlier that morning the funeral home reunited Doc and his amputated leg. The appendage had been returned home from Mayo's with its owner months before. A religious man, Doc was well aware of the church's dogma: for the Resurrection the entire body needed to be present. That cold Friday morning, all of John Devine would be laid to rest in the treeless cemetery south of Bancroft. John Devine was only 55 years old.

Columbia College

The summer right after high school graduation Joe resolutely started work at the local bakery. Conveniently located in the back of Cass building on the corner his workplace wasn't more than half a block away from his home. Once occupied by the post office, which had moved a block away, the space now emitted the intoxicating odor of baking bread. Since fresh baked goods needed to be ready each morning, the shop's baking was done at night. Joe started work at 1:00 AM six days a week. Normally, he and his co-workers finished by ten in the morning, except on Saturday, the busiest shopping day. Then the crew might not finish till noon. This job would give Joe an education in 'work' and employment. The hours were bad, the pay was poor, and his boss, as he would put it, was "a contemptible man."

His boss was W.R. Heiseman, known locally as Hizzie. He wasn't a very well respected man. There was loose talk that he had fled to Canada during the First World War to avoid the draft. Whether a coward or not, Hizzie had other obvious character flaws. At the end of work on Saturday the employees received their pay. Joe hadn't worked long before he came face to face with the real Hizzie. After paying Joe and his young co-worker, Carlos Dirks, Hizzie invited the boys to join him in playing pool. New to the job, the boys thought it impolite to refuse their boss. Out the back door and down the alley the three went to Tibbits Brother's Saloon and Pool Hall, a long narrow tavern next to the Hotel Charles. The front half of Tibbits was the bar, which extended almost the entire length of the room, and the back half was occupied by two pool tables and a snooker table.

While calking his billiard cue, Hizzie enticed his two young employees into playing for some money. The boys were being hustled, and if they weren't aware of it at the time, they would soon be. Hizzie was a good pool player and surely his intent was to relieve both of them of part of their pay. Hizzie persisted after that morning in requesting another game of billiards, but neither boy again fell for his hustle. Hizzie, truly was an unscrupulous man, but the head baker was a tyrant. Joe and Carlos were forced to deal daily with mad Bill Pickering. As a bully he loved to torment his young underlings. Gifted with a violent temper, Bill was subject to outbursts that entailed throwing bakery utensils and verbally abusing Joe and Carlos. Both boys grew to fear these volcanic eruptions. (Ironically, years later Bill would have his own grocery store and the Sextons would maintain an account there.)

After 12 months of enduring Hizzie and Bill, Joe finally found relief in the form of a new job. His new boss, in contrast to the contemptible Hizzie, would become a life-long friend. Sumner Produce, a competitor of Westcott and Winks, was in need of a new truck driver, and Joe jumped at the job. Besides a better work environment, the job offered better pay. At eighteen dollars a week, Joe's paycheck would be a third more than he'd made at the bakery.

His new boss was Paul Wilharm, called Poodle. Paul unlike Hizzie was a highly respected businessman in town. And even as a young man Paul had gained some local notoriety. In a town that was baseball crazy, Paul had been an outstanding catcher for the local team, the Sumner Cubs. He had played alongside his brother Claude and nephew Les Tietge; both men had been outstanding players in their own right. Claude's talents had been good enough for him to try out for the majors. Though he never made it, Les did and would go on to pitch for the Chicago White Soxs, where he made pitching debut against the powerful New York Yankees. Pitching to fabled players Babe Ruth and Lou Gehrig, Les would survive nine innings and go on to win the game

4 to O. He would pitch four seasons with the White Soxs and become celebrated in Sumner lore.

Joe's assessment of Paul was much kinder than that of Hizzie. He called him "a guy of class and moxie." He always thought Paul treated him like a man. Sometimes when Joe finished his route, Paul would invite him to share a beer, and on the week-ends the two frequently would play golf together. Paul was also an avid golfer and the two men would develop a genuine friendship.

As much as he enjoyed working at Sumner Produce, thoughts of college were always in back of Joe's mind. Late in the summer of his year at the Produce Joe was compelled to tell Paul that he was quitting. He had been accepted to Columbia College for the fall semester. His good friend, Ben Winks, had been there already for two years and after hearing stories of college, Joe couldn't wait to attend. The two buddies even planned to room together once Joe was accepted.

Columbia, later to be called Loras College, sat high on a bluff over-looking downtown Dubuque. The all male Catholic school was com-prised of a small collection of buildings dominated by the five-story Keane Hall perched on the very crest of the bluff. The bottom floor of Keane held the administrative office and class-rooms. The floors above were dorm rooms. The building had wings buttressing both ends the dorm, and it was here that the priests who taught at the college lived. Separating the wings from the dorm floors was a winding open stair-case from the basement to the fifth floor. The staircase stood open in the center, and the five-story drop proved too great an enticement to young miscreants fascinated by the thrill of dropping items down to the basement. The numbered dorm floors basically corresponded to class rank, freshmen on the fifth floor and seniors on the second. Though technically a freshman, Joe benefited from his roommate's status as a junior. He didn't have to experience the 'jungle' which was the name given the fifth floor. With high ceilings and four men to a room, many of them indulging in aberrant freshman behavior, this wasn't the place a mature individual would care to live. Because Ben was a junior and popular, Joe's social status as Ben's friend brought him instant social elevation. Another bonus was that Ben had money and was generous. Leo, Ben's father, was one of the wealthier men in Sumner and to Ben's credit he never flaunted the fact or was haughty but was more then willing to share what he had with Joe.

Besides the two roommates, one other young man from Sumner was enrolled at Columbia, a true freshman by the name of Lawrence Murphy. He was the eldest of four sons of the local attorney. Joe's brother, Jim, probably knew the family better since he chummed around with Lawrence's brother, Tom.

The faculty priests who resided in the wings of Keane were by and large a colorful lot. Some were gifted and well regarded by the students, and some weren't. Father Brean fell into the latter group. He was dean of students. A man large in girth and height, he was known both for his sadistic treatment of students and the effeminate fragrance he exuded. The students all snickered behind his back, amused by his proclivity to perfume himself, but they were not as amused by Father Brean's harsh discipline. Probably held in highest regard by the student body from among the facility was Father 'Shakes' Rowan. An English professor who specialized in Shakespeare (hence the nickname) Father Rowan expressed a sincere concern for students, and they returned the sentiment. A small quiet man, he did have one very large memorable feature, a bulbous red nose. Shakes Rowan was reputed to have a large capacity for beer consumption. Whether the nose and the beer were interconnected was open to debate.

Rumor had it on campus that one day two young priests who had heard of Shakes' quick wit decided to put it to the test. The two young clerics broached the issue of the true nature of Shake's reddish nose, alluding to his love of beer. Calmly disarming his young colleagues he replied, referring to his proboscis, "young men it is blushing with pride for its ability to keep itself out of other people's business."

When first enrolling in school Joe needed to give his desired course of study, and he had put down pre-dentistry. Whether this was a spur of the moment decision or a serious pursuit at the time, he would later contend that he really had a desire to attend medical school. Only speculation is left to explain Joe's thinking on his career choices, but there is one certainty: at the completion of his sophomore year, Joe applied to the Iowa State University for admittance to its Veterinary College.

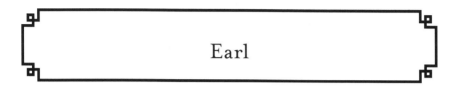

Earl

"Veterinarian Locates Here" the front page of the *Sumner Gazette* proclaimed on June 23, 1938. Following the headline, the paper printed a short article about the man:

"Dr. E.C. Ritter has opened an office in the Munger building south of the post office and will practice veterinary medicine in the community. Dr. Ritter is a graduate of Iowa State College and decided to locate here after considerable investigation. His home is Sac City."

For twenty eight years George Sexton had a solo practice in town, and after eighteen years of struggle he was finally seeing light at the end of the tunnel. Now for the first time he faced the anxiety of competition. In light of this turn of events there were two responses George could choose from, one being hostility and the other being acceptance. He took the high road. Earl and his wife Dori had no more than stepped foot in town when George issued a dictate to his family, "No one in this house will utter anything derogatory about him." Looking past his nagging doubts about financial failure, George proved to the most gracious of competitors.

Ambitious and likable, Dr. Ritter settled easily into his new practice. He made every effort to involve himself in the town. He joined service clubs like the Rotary and the Community Club. An avid golfer, he sought a membership at Meadowbrook Country Club, and he embedded his family in the church, accepting positions on church boards. Socially active, Earl and Dori soon became a popular couple in Sumner. Faced with a vibrant competitor, George could no longer feel complacent about his practice; he needed to devote more attention to the details of his business. While this occurred, Joe was home for summer break from Columbia and was again working for Sumner Produce. George's change in attitude didn't escape his son's notice. Joe saw that his father tended to business more assiduously, and Earl's presence gave George an incentive to try and practice harder. Joe had always assumed his father kept sloppy books and took an indifferent attitude toward paying his bills. It's truly ironic that Joe adopted such an unforgiving posture toward his father, since years later he was more pardoning toward one of Joe's friends, Ike Hayes(Woody's brother). Ike had been a classmate of Earl in vet school and had called his friend complaining about his dismal financial situation. At the time Joe knew Ike and his pathetic business practices, but would completely exonerate him of any fault. It's odd that Joe never gave his father the same credit.

George was a very generous man both with clients and friends, and that same generosity extended to Dr. Ritter. Earl was just settling into his office when George walked in. Extending a hand he welcomed Earl to town and offered him any assistance he might need. It was more than a mere gesture; George followed it with actions. This gracious deed would have a lasting effect on the relationship between Joe and Earl. George wouldn't ever be able to see all the repercussions of his simple act of grace. Fate would reward Dr. Sexton's for his magnanimous behavior.

Shortly after Earl set up practice an epidemic of equine encephalomyletis spread through the area. Known as sleeping sickness, it affected only horses. Even though the tractor was starting to make an appearance on some farms, the horse was still prevalent on many farms. Transmitted by mosquitoes, sleeping sickness was a warm weather phenomenon in Iowa. There were basically two separate strains of the virus, a Western strain with a 20-50% mortality rate and the more lethal

Eastern strain claiming 75-90% of its victims. The disease's first symptom generally showed itself as a high fever which caused the affected horse to appear blind or nervous. Then came the muscle tremors and finally complete muscle paralysis. At the time of the outbreak in 1931, there weren't any drugs with which to treat this disease, only rudimentary treatments were available. Earl and George usually placed ice packs on the horses head if the disease was in its primary stages. They could also give the animal dextrose injections for dehydration. And if they were dealing with a well developed case they would place the horse in a sling if its muscles gave out, keeping the animal elevated.

During that summer both vets had their hands full. With enough work for everyone, Earl's practice got off the ground and George could feel more secure in his struggling practice. After that summer the two men achieved a comfort level with one another. While George was relieved, Joe that summer took his first steps toward opening a friendship with Earl. Golf was their connection. Both found common ground on the fairways and greens of Meadowbrook, playing together on multiple occasions.

There is evidence that the relationship between Earl and George became a trusting one. Early the 30's, the Sextons received a puppy from an area farmer. Though dogs had come and gone in the household, this dog was special. Intelligent and lovable, the terrier-like pooch was named Jitters. The short-white-haired dog was not only a pet for the children, she endeared herself to Inez. When Inez went shopping, Jitters would go along. The dog especially enjoyed stopping at the grocery store. There the butcher, Ralph Jones, always presented the canine a bone. Proudly clinching the prize in her teeth, Jitters, would prance behind Inez all the way home.

Always a favorite with the boys and Donna, Jitters would join in the fray when ever Jim and Joe wrestled on the living room floor. Of all the family members, George, alone, outwardly presented a detached attitude toward the dog. However, that façade was shattered when George was discovered feeding Jitters ice-cream cones at his office.

As Jitters grew older, she became more protective of the family, and sadly, one day she bit Vera Karsten, the wife of the local dentist. George couldn't tolerate a dog that would bite, so he declared that Jitters must be put to sleep. Under the guise that he didn't have the proper materials, George asked Earl to please carry out the necessary task.

Joe, though he was in college at the time, made note of the event and the loss the family had incurred, stating, "It was a sad day for the Sexton household."

Jitters, however, wasn't the only thing on Joe's mind. Before coming home from Columbia for the summer, Joe had sent in his application to Iowa State for vet school. With Earl's arrival, work, and golf, he, during that summer, hadn't paid much attention to the mail. But as July slipped toward August, he expected a letter any day from Iowa State. His future plans depended upon that slip of paper. Then the first days of August passed by and still no word. With only weeks before the start of the fall term his anxiety increased with each passing day as news from the school failed to arrive in his mailbox.

Saint Theresa's

A year and a half had passed since the day December day when her father had died. Mary Elaine Devine, nearing eighteen years of age, looked forward to a change in her life. It was time to leave Bancroft. With the coming fall she'd be departing for St. Theresa's College where her sister was already a sophomore. With life insurance and the farms Doc had purchased, he had left the family financially secure. Money for college wasn't going to be an issue for Mary Elaine.

College would broaden Mary Elaine's world. No longer restricted to discussion of boys and clothes with the Sheridan girls next door, she found that in college the talked expanded to encompass world events. And the world during this time was ripe with drama. Though insulated by two oceans, America still had the daily paper peppered with stories of turmoil in Asia and Europe. Germany had a new leader challenging the treatment his country had endured since the signing of the Versailles Treaty, and the leader, Adolph Hitler, set his sites on remilitarizing the Rhineland in direct violation of that treaty. In Spain, a bloody civil war was grinding into a second year, and Japan had just opened an undeclared war with China. But for Mary Elaine these were just curious distractions from life at school.

Like Joe at Columbia College, Mary Elaine had an upper classman to show her the ropes at St. Theresa's. Her older sister Margaret took her under her wing, but they would not room together. Possibly because they'd shared a room all the time they were growing up, it was time for change. Uncle Art Murray's daughter Eileen would be her roommate.

Either Mary Elaine was following her sister's lead attending St. Theresa's, or Lillian had been the driving force behind sending both girls to the 'safe' all girl's school. No matter the reason for her enrollment, Mary Elaine's personality did not quite fit the school's regime. Run by the sisters of St. Francis, the small girl's school reflected the nun's more conservative approach to acceptable behavior. Charged with protection of their students' virtues along with their education, the nuns laid out a list of rules designed to meet that goal. Blocks away from St. Theresa's stood St. Mary's, an all-boy's school. The two schools did hold events like dances together but not without patrols of black and white habits moving about the perimeter of the dance floor. Dating was allowed but there were caveats. Any underclassman wishing to go on a date needed to be chaperoned by a senior. The senior could either double date or just go along as a third wheel. The arrangement probably made for some very interesting evenings.

There was also a rigid dress code. Any girl leaving St. Theresa's campus needed to wear a dress, a hat, and gloves. Wearing a hat could be understandable as a common practice of Catholic women, who were required to cover their heads for mass, but gloves would have been a throwback to the turn of the century and quite possibly made the coeds stand out visually from the local population.

In every restrictive culture there are those who test the limits, and the prudish environment cultivated by the nuns proved to be fertile ground for headstrong 18- and 19-year olds. Just to the north of the campus lay a defunct nine hole golf course, Meadowbrook, (now Cotter Athletic Field). Acquired by the nuns as a possible site for future expansion, they had only found need at the time for ground comprising the nearest three holes. They named the area St. Michael's Field. In the center of the green expanse the nuns built an open-air Greek theatre. The unused portion of the property lay dormant and overgrown but retained the distinctive features of the old golf course. Its deep sand traps fringed by tall grass ready to go to seed lay beside the vague outlines of what had once been greens. The inventive young co-eds would find those partially hidden sand bunkers highly useful.

Mary Elaine (kneeling on the right) is pictured, along with her classmates at St. Theresa's, deriving enjoyment from breaking the rules.

St. Theresa's rules and regulations contained a lot of does and don'ts. Among the don'ts was smoking, but Mary Elaine had her own ideas about this behavior, as smoking was something she enjoyed. Even living back in Bancroft, she and Margaret would smoke in the little bedroom with the window open in some vain attempt to hide the smell. It is safe to assume Mary Elaine could have joined the small cadre of coeds who would steal out past the Greek theatre and find shelter from the nuns in those overgrown bunkers. Crouching behind the bunker wall, the young ladies would puff away on Lucky Strikes or Camels, most likely with smoke billowing from the hole.

One incident has been recorded where Mary Elaine bested the nuns. For some reason she wished to leave the campus for the week-end and the good nuns refused her request. There was no reason given for her desire to leave for the week end, but it must have been something the nuns did not have condone. To get her way, she pulled off a ruse with the aid of her brother Emmett. He sent a Western Union telegram to the administration informing them that Mary Elaine's father had died and that she should come immediately. It wasn't a lie, her father had died, but three years before. The nuns should have been smart enough to figure out the scheme, but it appears Mary Elaine pulled it off. A little too restrictive for the likes of Mary Elaine, St. Theresa's would only have her as a student for one year; the rest of her college career wouldn't be spent in Winona.

Vet School

It was mid August of 1938 at ISU, and the campus was showing the first signs of life after dormant summer break, but back in Sumner Joe had already established a daily routine. After driving all day for Wilharm's Produce, he'd walk around the block to his house on Main Street and anxiously check the day's mail. Iowa State had to send word soon! This process had gone on for well over a week without any word from the school, but then the envelope finally arrived. Tearing it open, Joe read down the page. Before he reached the bottom, he felt a tightening in his gut. His hopes had been dashed. He wouldn't be part of the fall class at the vet school; their enrollment was full at present, but to soften the blow the administration had offered to entertain his application for the next year.

That night was long and sleepless. What was he going to do? He really couldn't tolerate returning to Columbia, especially since he had already said his good-byes to all his friends there. Morning arrived and still mentally dazed he wandered back to work. Paul Wilharm immediately noticed something was troubling Joe. When he confronted him as to the problem, Joe almost broke down crying. Listening to Joe's tale of woe, Paul patiently let him finish and then stood up and said, "come with me." Paul walked to the office followed closely by Joe. Behind his desk he started looking for a phone number. Armed finally with the number, he got the operator and asked for long distance, Marion, Iowa. After waiting for the trunk connections, he finally said hello and after small talk with the answering party he described to him his young friend's plight.

Always politically active and at one time holding high office in the state political organization, Paul had accumulated an extensive political network. Now he was tapping into it. His contact was a 'connected' veterinarian, Dr. Herman Strader. At one time Dr. Strader had been a state "regulator" and had developed his own network of state veterinarian officials. The conversation between the two men didn't last long. Paul put the phone down and told Joe he wouldn't be working tomorrow. He and Paul would need to drive to Ames. They were going there to meet with Dr. Strader at the vet school.

Showing up unannounced the next morning, a nervous Joe Sexton followed behind Paul and Herman through the hallways of the school. Dr. Strader, familiar with the school, set about looking up contacts to button hole. He progressed up the academic ladder till he thought he had the attention of someone who could help. After several hours of campaigning, the threesome broke up, Herman having done all he could. Dr. Strader may have felt confident of Joe's chances, but Joe was not quite so sure. But two days later Joe received a second letter from Iowa State. They welcomed into the incoming freshman class in September. The clouds parted and left only brilliant sunshine. For the rest of his life, Joe would be indebted to Paul Wilharm.

Of the 5400 students enrolled for the fall semester, two students had divergent reasons for being at Iowa State. One was fleeing from restrictive nuns and one was just happy to be there. The first one, Mary Elaine Devine, checked into student housing, settling into Oak Hall on the eastern edge of the campus where the female housing was pooled together. And the second, Joe Sexton entertained "rushing" a fraternity. Several frat houses rushed Joe. Earl Ritter and Joe had become friends and Earl advised Joe to join his fraternity, Sigma Alpha Epsilon (SAE). There were also other SAE members Joe knew from Sumner; Wilson

Heyer, Wilbur Bethel and even the McGuiness brothers had belonged. Besides SAE, a Catholic fraternity, Alpha Zeta and Alpha Sigma were on Joe's radar. Alpha Sigma was of interest since Joe's new brother- in-law, Erwin Mardorf had been a member and was encouraging him to give the fraternity a look.

Married to Donna the previous summer, Erwin, who went by the name Mardy, still had one semester left in his senior year. The union of Marty and Donna that summer had some commonality with George and Inez's. It was an inter faith marriage with a twist. The previous year while the two had started dating, Donna was still teaching school. The two may have only started dating but they had known each other a long time. Two years her senior, Marty was nearing the end of his engineering degree at Iowa State when he proposed. She was a Catholic and he was the son of the Lutheran minister in the largest church in Sumner. Even in the 1930's there was an unspoken distrust between faiths. A remnant of the Reformation hundreds of years before there were still ideas preached against the differing faiths. There were still Catholics, for example, who believed all Protestants were doomed to go to Hell. Carl and Olga, to their credit, rose above the whispering of small minds in the community and gave their blessing to their child to marry. If they had misgivings about their son marrying a Catholic, Carl or Olga, never voiced any doubts. Dignified to the last, they walked up the steps of the Immaculate Conception Church and down the center isle to one of the front pews, where they sat erect while Father Fischer officiated over the wedding mass. It was Thursday evening July 28, 1938.

The caption on this picture of Donna and Mardy is incorrect. This is most likely from the mid-1930's.

Shortly after the wedding in August, Marty's parents did, however, inject themselves into the life of the young couple. The fall semester was only weeks away and Marty still had one semester left to complete his engineering degree. Carl or Olga realized it was advantageous for their son to complete his schooling. Though now a married man and for all appearances on his own, they wanted to help him finish. They offered to pay for his final semester, but there was a problem. Donna had a new job working for the Sumner Gazette and had no intention of moving to Ames. Marty now was caught between his degree and Donna. He opted to stay in Sumner. He was "too much in love." Even though love won battle, this fateful decision would follow the couple for years. Young love masks most problems, this was certainly true in Donna's case. For years she'd carried the resentment of having to cut short her education; now she saw her groom willing to do the same for her. Her dilemma was that he did it for love of her. The bright light of young love would dim in time, however, allowing a darker side of this issue to become more recognizable.

In every restrictive culture there are those who test the limits, and the prudish environment cultivated by the nuns proved to be fertile ground for headstrong 18- and 19-year olds. Just to the north of the campus lay a defunct nine hole golf course, Meadowbrook, (now Cotter Athletic Field). Acquired by the nuns as a possible site for future expansion, they had only found need at the time for ground comprising the nearest three holes. They named the area St. Michael's Field. In the center of the green expanse the nuns built an open-air Greek theatre. The unused portion of the property lay dormant and overgrown but retained the distinctive features of the old golf course. Its deep sand traps fringed by tall grass ready to go to seed lay beside the vague outlines of what had once been greens. The inventive young co-eds would find those partially hidden sand bunkers highly useful.

Though Marty spoke glowingly about his fraternity, Joe in the end chose SAE. Now a member of a pledge class, he found himself one of its older members. More mature than the other young pledges, he inevitably found some of the pledging behavior quite silly but endured it with silent tolerance. Even when men his junior confronted him during pledging with absurd requests, he bit his lip. All this didn't go unnoticed. Nearing the end of the process the pledge class elected him their president.

Barring the initial phase, Joe took to fraternity life. He would be forever impressed by the social graces practiced in the house. Enhancing the experience, a house mother lived with them. Usually this was an older widowed lady, and her mere presence forced the young men to moderate their behavior. A prescribed set of manners was required of all the house residents. Dinner wasn't a hit and miss affair. Served nightly at a set time, it was presided over by the SAE house mother, Mrs. Boone.

A coat and tie were required dress, and with Mrs. Boone's entrance the young men would rise from their seats. Residing over the head of the table Mrs. Boone moderated any unruly conversation. Dinner was adjourned with Mrs. Boone's departure, the men once again standing.

The cultural experience fed Joe's developing sense of the complete man, studied and mannered. Lest we think that the fraternity was totally prim and proper, Joe related a story about a horse and the SAE house. The facts are sketchy, but during Joe's college years or near them, an old horse from the pens at the vet school was found dead in the SAE house's living room, supposedly electrocuted. The culprits and the grizzly details failed to be passed down, but the fragmented story is evidence enough that young men aren't easily tamed.

Luckily for Joe and the horse murderers the SAE house wasn't very far from the vet school. The house, on north-south running Lynn Avenue and only a ten-minute walk from the vet school. was located directly south of the Union, which was in the center of the campus. An imposing yellow brick structure with the look of a French manor house, the fraternity house had a steeply slanted slate roof punctuated by round port hole windows. Set back from the road, it could easily be mistaken for a grand mansion from a by- gone era.

In early September, with the rush over, Joe would get a second look at the vet school, the first being nearly a month earlier with Paul Wilharm. There had to have been anxiety and exhilaration mixed to- gether on that morning as he walked Lynn Avenue's tree lined side walks. Up over Lincoln Way, Joe then rounded the Union, passing right next to Lake LaVerne, which was actually an elongated bean shaped pond. That warm morning even though the vet school lay due north, he needed to scurry around the grassy oval surrounding the central bell tower. Just beyond the horticultural green house was the Quad, the oldest building of the vet school, now separated by Pammel Road from the Strang Clinics, the school's most recent addition. Arriving at the front door and not knowing anyone, Joe was initially bombarded by new sights and the cautious smiles of other freshmen. These two buildings would be where Joe would spend the next four years. But to make it all four years, he would have to make it through the first year.

Within days of starting classes, word had already spread about the freshman winnowing process. Rumor had it that at least 10% of the freshmen class would be sent packing. The class that everyone would fear was the freshman anatomy class. There the academic henchmen lay waiting. Two professors were to happily accept their role as 'guardians' of the vet profession; Drs. Calhoun and Forest. Dr. Calhoun was a masculine looking woman who transferred most of her responsibilities to paid upper classmen while withholding final grading as part of her fiefdom. She was an onerous human being but as far as the freshmen were concerned, the heart and soul of evil resided in Dr. Forest. It was whispered among freshmen that he was a professor of some academic renown but that could just have been idle gossip. Joe did refer to Dr. Forest, however, as "a dedicated and talented horse's-ass." Of the two professors, Dr. Forest held god like power over his students, reserving the right to determine who should be vets and who should not. He had a very subjective set of criteria, which weren't restricted to academic performance. Should a poor student, for whatever reason, incur Forest's erratic wrath, the student's fate was likely doomed. If Dr. Forest wanted a student gone, his fate was sealed.

Joe told a story about the anatomy exam, which like all the exams was oral. Outside the anatomy lab the students would form a line awaiting their turn, before entering one at a time for the inquisition. Inside, the lab tables were littered with dissected animals' limbs and individual organs. The gory flesh, reeking of formaldehyde, was marked by colored pins poked into blood vessels, muscles, nerves and connective tissue. Escorted by Dr. Forest, the nervous students would move from specimen to specimen answering questions about identification and tissue function. The day of the particular exam, Joe was still queued outside the lab when a friend emerged from just taking the test. He stopped to talk to Joe on his way out. The student was mad. In his fury he had to tell Joe about Dr. Forest. "That bastard asked me how many tonsils a

horse had and of course, I didn't know. Then he really chewed me out."
Now with his anxiety level increased, Joe fanatically started thumbing
through his anatomy book, looking for any reference to horse tonsils. It
wasn't long before Joe took his turn in Forest's little chamber of horrors.
With his palms sweating and the smell of formaldehyde filling his nose,
Joe stepped into the lab. There to greet him was one sober Dr. Forest –
armed with a clip board and a pen. Gradually the twosome moved
from table to table and specimen to specimen, all the time, Joe awaiting
the "question." Finally at the specimen table holding the horse's head,
Forest sprung his trap. With sense of smugness he asked Joe the tonsil
question. Almost in a hurry to blurt it out, Joe shot back "five". It was
obviously a trick question, and Forest was surprised to get an answer.
Hoping to avoid Forest's outburst, Joe was disappointed. Even the fact
someone knew the answer made the doctor angry. He barked at Joe,
"how did you know that?" No one was going to deny him the pleasure
of intimating any poor students.

The rumored 10% failure rate prayed on Joe's mind. Anxiety was
his constant companion for the first semester. It didn't help when he received a D on one of his mid-terms. Was he going to be one of the 10%?
What would he do if he failed? He wrote later about "being chronically
tired, chronically bored and chronically unaware."

The trees were barren of leaves and a blanket of snow covered
everything. After several frigid months, finally the warm spring sun
caused the snow to retreat. The first green shoots of spring found Joe
still in school. He'd survived. The worst was over. Now he could relax
and plan on at least three more years of school, and he didn't have to
worry about summer work; the job at Sumner Produce was always there
if he wanted it.

His finals done, and with the campus slowly clearing out, Joe
packed his meager possessions. It was going to be great seeing his
friends, playing some golf, driving truck for the Wilharms, and getting
some home cooking. And, of course, he could spend some time with his
father now that he could start to talk shop with him. George, as well as

discussing vet medicine, loved to talk about baseball and politics. He also followed the news and cautioned his son about the looming storm clouds gathering around the world. Japan was already deeply involved in an undeclared war in China. Russia, with a hungry eye on its neighbors had invaded Finland. Italy, under the control of the pompous strutting Benito Mussolini, with imperialist hunger eagerly consumed Albania, and the psychopathic Adolph Hitler had Germany swallowing parts of Czechoslovakia. All of this didn't go unnoticed, even in remote Sumner, Iowa. America had quietly reinstituted the draft. There was also a portion of the country, much like before the First World War, who wanted the nation to stay out of the coming conflicts. Groups like the America First Committee, which would not fully organize for another year preached a hard isolationist's line. During that summer Joe may have listened to his father but his world was centered in his small section of Iowa. He had more localized desires and concerns.

Like every Iowa summer, the time passed much too quickly. All too soon it was the first of September and time to return for his sophomore year. The sophomore year would prove to be easier that the first; if nothing else it would be less nerve racking. The routine would be familiar and the atmosphere more relaxed. Joe's class which was all male, now had shared an entire academic year together, and the men bonded by the experiences of that time, both good and bad. Through the freshmen test of fire Joe forged several friendships which would last a lifetime. Among that group was Ray Tobola, a Nebraska farm boy, large and kindly. A very intelligent man, he was also part of the class which was married. Joe remembered Ray's wife as a large person with a large heart to match. Ray sat next to Joe in most classes and on his other side sat Bill Sessions. Probably Joe's best friend, though, was Joe Graham.

Joe wasn't very tall, only coming to 5'2" but he didn't have the short man's syndrome. He was blessed with a great sense of humor, and the two Joes bonded easily. During their sophomore year, Joe Sexton had moved out of the SAE house and the two shared a room in the basement of the home of a classmate, Darrol White. They roomed together for only one year, since in the spring his second year, Joe Sexton was elected president of his fraternity. Joe, with good reason, thought this to be quite an honor since most fraternity presidents were seniors, and Joe was just a sophomore. But the position of president came with some strings attached. Most importantly, Joe was required to live in the house. But unlike the "open aired" dormitory where most members were forced to sleep, Joe and two others shared the prime bedroom well away from the crowded dorm room.

The sophomore year passed without incident, so with spring and another year of school under his belt, Joe returned home. As usual, his job at Sumner Produce awaited him, as the Wilharms were always willing to find work for him to do. His summer was also uneventful, with work and golf consuming the majority of his time. Older now, he found that Sumner didn't have much to offer him. His friends like Ben Winks had graduated college and moved on, he pursuing work away from Sumner, but Joe made the best of what he thought would be one of the last summers he would spend in Sumner.

Of all the four years of vet school, the third year was deemed the easiest by the students. The class schedule in comparison to that of the first two years was remarkably light. Clinics were held every day but only from 10-12AM. And the lecture classes restricted to just Monday, Wednesday, and Friday, were short and scheduled only from 1-2 in the afternoon. Given the light load, Joe had almost a perfunctory attitude toward life, but the events of the next twelve months would change all that.

Given that Joe now actually had free time, he considered a "try out" for the University golf team. The university golf course called Veenker lay was just north of the vet school on the other side of the railroad tracks. Any student was entitled to try out for the team. Qualifiers were selected from players with the lowest scores of all the players competing for three rounds at Veenker. Joe made the team on his first attempt, which was quite a feat, given the skill level of the other golfers. The Iowa State Golf team was restricted to a five man roster. Anchoring the team and by far the best players were the Hall brothers, Bill and Max. Both were seasoned members of the team, having played the two previous years for Iowa State. Both would go on to have distinguished amateur careers as well as collegiate careers. The year before Joe made the golf team, Bill Hall had been conference tournament medalist, averaging the lowest score of all the golfers in the meets. Once he qualified for the college team, Joe was good enough to play third man behind the Hall boys. Playing behind Joe were two fine players, Bucky Walters and Bob Thompson. The 1940 team would have big shoes to fill; the prior year Iowa State had won the Big Six title in golf. That same year they went on to play in the National College tournament held in Manchester, Vermont and finished 7th. The new team with Joe on it, though, would valiantly defend that title. They did have a slight advantage, however, since the conference tournament in 1940 would be held on their home turf, the relatively new Veenker course.

The course was just two years old, having been designed by the architect Perry Maxwell who was already associated with a strong port-folio of golf courses. He had designed and renovated a distinguished list of courses, confining most of his work to the Midwest and eastern half of the country. In Oklahoma he had laid out South Hill Country Club, which is still considered one of the best courses in the United States. Out East he renovated such courses as Pine Valley, Augusta National, Hope Valley and Merion, most of which were household names among golfers. In Texas he worked on Colonial Country Club, famous as the home course for Ben Hogan.

When designing Veenker, Maxwell took advantage of the natural terrain of the central Iowa river bottom. The Raccoon River flowed through the center course, forcing golfers to cross it with several of their shots. And above the river the bluffs offered Perry a prefect op-portunity to challenge golfers by allowing them only the center of the ridge as the landing spot for their shots. Any errant shot would most likely run down into the trees that lined the fairway. The course proved to be a test for even the most skilled of players. That season when they attempted to defend the Big Six title at Veenker, they were coached by

Hugo Otopalik(The Big Six was comprised of Missouri, Oklahoma, Nebraska, Kansas, Kansas State and Iowa State).

The golf team didn't have the same elevated status as the football and basketball teams, so the university saw no reason to hire a real "golf coach." The team's coach was the head wrestling coach, who just happened to be free since wrestling season had ended. Hugo, a man of medium build and receding hair line, had the look and demeanor, not surprisingly, of a wrestler. He had served with General Pershing during the First World War and with his return to Nebraska after the war had made a name for himself in wrestling. Iowa State had spirited him away from the University of Nebraska to help build the floundering Iowa State wrestling program and along the way someone convinced him to be the golf coach. He seems to have embraced the situation and grew to be a very good coach and leader.

Seated together on the Veenker Golf Course, the Iowa State golf team posed for university year book picture. On the left, Coach Otopalik is next to Joe, with the blonde Hall brothers and Bucky Walters filling out the bench.

Wrestling like golf is an individualistic sport. In both, a man has only his own skills to fall back on while he is competing, and though they are classified as team sports, the players don't comprise teams in the full sense of the word. A player can't hand the club off to some other player or have someone called in to play a few holes when things aren't going well. Actually, Hugo's wrestler's philosophy fit well with golfers: be aggressive. Coach Otopalik was hard nosed man but very popular with his players. Joe, in fact, would have a long standing relationship with Hugo. Even after his college career, Joe still corresponding with him right up to the time of Hugo's death in 1953.

The two years of college golf would be forever a great source of pride for Joe. The Hall brothers became legendary through Joe's telling and retelling of their exploits. Though he never boasted about playing college golf, he more than likely enjoyed his friends introducing him as a former Iowa State golf team member.

The very same year Joe was earning accolades on the golf course he experienced a pivotal moment which would forever change his life. Late fall in his junior year when Joe was president of his fraternity and third man on a winning golf team, he had the wind of life blowing at his back, but something was missing: a woman in his life. In January 1941, when the winter formal ball was held, Joe was lined up with a blind date. His fraternity brother, John Fischer, had a girl friend who just happened to know a girl who was right for Joe.

As on any college week-end night, an expectant air filtered through the campus and on this particular night it was especially felt at the S.A.E. house and President Sexton. Groomed and attired in a rented tuxedo, Joe excitedly prepared for his blind date. Meanwhile Mary Elaine Devine had already been filled in by her roommate on this guy from Sumner, Iowa, but she wanted to see firsthand if the advertisement fit the product. With the nervous tinge of a first date, Joe climbed into the passenger's seat of John's 1929 Ford roadster for the short drive to the girl's dorm to pick up their dates. If Joe's fraternity brother and his girl friend envisioned sparks flying, they were to be disappointed. What looked good on paper didn't seem to be working out in real life.

As Joe confided later about the evening, "it didn't go especially well." All the elements were there: a future vet, a college jock, the fraternity president, and the dark-haired attractive, intelligent young woman from a prominent family. What could go wrong? It's hard to say what did not work--whether it was the assured expectations of the matchmakers, or the awkwardness of the moment for the couple, but the two did not hit it off. He would attribute part of the problem to the fact that he wasn't a very good dancer. But Joe, in his youthful wisdom, had a keen sense that there was something good here and that this girl from Bancroft was the right person. Joe, fully aware that he had gotten off to a bad start, was determined to pursue this woman whom he knew as the one for him.

In truth this may have been a case of the fruit which is just out of reach looking the most delicious. For Joe, that fruit that was just past his finger tips was Marilane Devine. Marilane was Joe's pet name for her and the name over time would supplant Mary Elaine with friends and family. The next week, Joe started his pursuit in earnest. Through utter persistence he secured a date for the following week, meeting her for coke at the Union. That second date turned into a third and a fourth. Marilane swore that they had ten dates before Joe ever kissed her good night. By spring they were considered a couple. Every week they were seen together. To fill voids in between dates, phone calls would keep the ardor stoked. Joe was smitten. Life now couldn't be better. He was in love. He was in the junior year of vet school and the future was bright. He was totally consumed by the optimism of youth. If you had asked him, he would have said nothing could stand in his way.

Joe, still in his golf shoes is pictured with his new found love, Mary Elaine Devine.

Even when on the road for golf meets, Joe sent letters back to his sweetheart. One such letter was composed while seated on the bed in the Kentwood Arms Hotel in Springfield, Missouri, Joe's roommate Bucky Walters having already commandeered the only desk in their hotel room. The prior day the team had played a match in Columbia, Missouri against the university golf team there, losing narrowly by 9 1/2 to 8 1/2. Joe had won his match but his roommate hadn't fared so well. Bucky was still disgruntled since in his match he had been one hole ahead with two holes to play and had lost both the last two holes and his match. This proved to be pivotal to Missouri's win. There wasn't much time for self pity, however, the next morning the team would be off to Norman, Oklahoma and a date with the university golf team.

In the letter Joe wrote that evening he only briefly touched on golf. Mostly he concentrated on Marilane and descriptions of his trip. Leaving Iowa for the first time, Joe might have been considered very provincial. He was easily impressed by the Lake of the Ozarks as the team drove by, and he made special note that the diner where they stopped had windows overlooking the water and that he had ordered ham for lunch.

The letter might initially give the impression of having been written by a country bumpkin, but further reading revealed a more worldly man. While leaving Columbia one of the team members clandestinely purchased a bottle of Four Roses whiskey. The team had every intention of indulging themselves that Saturday night in the Kentwood Arms, but Coach Hugo, who the team called Otto, had booked into an adjoining room, dashing their planned party.

Whiskey wasn't the only distraction the young men had on these trips. Even under Otto's watchful eye the boys found time for another pursuit: women. Joe offered up a glimpse when he wrote to Marilane, "remind me to tell you of the Stevens girl club the boys were telling us about. Would tell you now but my vocabulary is too meager to tell you and still maintain the dignity which exists between us."

It might be inferred from the letter that Marilane might have had a 'wild side' to her. This may have been part of Joe's attraction to her in the letter he brought up Marilane's week-end plans. She evidently had gone out with her roommate, whom they called Badger, and Badger's date. Inquiring as to the night's outcome, Joe tipped his hand about Marilane's nature, "Am wondering if you and Badger and Bob had a bang-up time tonight. Kinda hope it was Badger."

Marilane and Joe were in the midst of finals week for the semester. Marilane would finish her finals first and soon would be leaving for Bancroft and from there on to a summer job. She'd secured a job as a cook at a girl scout camp in Mankato, Minnesota. Separated by one hundred and fifty miles, Joe wouldn't see her for nearly three months, but he would soon have other matters to occupy his mind.

The End of Youth

Summer was just commencing, the leaves on the trees and the grass on the ground still had that vibrant green color and glossy appearance, and Joe again had his standing job at the produce company. Returning home after work one day he walked in to find his father uncharacteristically prone on the couch. He was suffering from a case of "sciatic rheumatism" (today we would refer to the ailment as a ruptured disc). He was completely incapacitated with any movement bound to cause him excruciating pain. His only relief came from remaining recumbent on that well worn sofa. And so there George would stay, imprisoned on that couch confined to that small living room with his only relief from the summer's heat being the open windows which might just catch any slight breeze. His only distraction that summer understandably was the radio or something to read. His confinement would last for months.

Obviously unable to work, he was fortunate to have his son, the junior vet student, to call on for help. The family, with no vet fees being generated by George, needed money, so Joe, not a licensed veterinarian, quit his job at the Sumner Produce Company and started work in his father's place.

The fact that Joe didn't have a degree or license didn't seem to cause any concerns in the community. Even Earl Ritter, who had every right to object, never registered a complaint, but even without any verbal objections George's practice began to suffer loss of cliental. Only the most loyal and most desperate of clients would call the office for Joe's services. If on the job training is the best training, Joe had it. George did his best to advise his son on any difficult case and the fine art of dealing with clients, but by fall George was started to gingerly return to work, and Joe was more than ready to go back to school. He may have been mentally ready but there was one issue he had to deal with first.

All the money Joe made working his father's practice had to stay in Sumner to support the family. For that summer Joe had been the only bread winner. Jim, his younger brother, was fresh out of high school and not in a position to help, so all the money Joe had hoped to put aside for school wasn't going to be there. George certainly wasn't going to be able to help Joe, even once he got back on his feet, since he would need to spend all of his efforts just to rebuild his practice. So now Joe had to scramble to get money for his tuition.

Walter Heyer was president of the First National Bank. Joe had known him for years, since Walter was also an avid golfer. Just before leaving for Ames, Joe went to see Mr. Heyer. He was looking to borrow $200. A modest amount by today's values, it would now amount to about $3,400. The amount of the loan being about a sixth of a normal workman's yearly salary, it surely would require some form of collateral, of which Joe had none. Walter Heyer was a good banker, but to make a loan of $200 just on a hand shake was going to be a hard sell when Walter presented the arrangement to the board of directors of the bank. Walter, however, took a chance on his young friend, and Joe got his money. Now he had half the tuition for his final year of school. There was one more stop he thought he would make to secure the rest of his tuition: that would be to see his uncle Perry.

Perry still lived in Cedar Rapids and had moved up the ranks of the Equitable Insurance Company, now occupying a very well paying job. He had a comfortable living and being childless and an avid golfer had taken an especially keen interest in his nephew Joe. When Joe approached Perry for a loan, his uncle was more than happy to help. He scribbled out a perfunctory note on a piece of paper, both men signed it, and Perry gave Joe a check. Now armed with his finances for his senior year, Joe drove back to Sumner to pack his books and clothes.

All his ducks seemed to be in a row. School started, and everything was right with the world. Then came a call from home: Perry was dead. Uncle Perry traveled extensively for work and had just buttoned up some business affairs in Mississippi when outside Granada he had been involved in an auto accident. Initially he appeared to only be injured superficially, but this proved only to be a deception. The injuries would be fatal. His wife, Collete, the very same woman who was unwilling to take in her aged father in law, Franklin West, happened to discover, while cleaning her husband's desk, the note Joe had signed. Though the note itself made no reference as to a date of payment, the assumption had to have been that Joe would pay it off after graduation. Even though she knew that Joe was still in school, Collete called him and demanded immediate payment. Years later, Joe would freely admit he didn't know at that moment exactly how he could up with all the money, but he somehow scraped together the needed funds and paid off avaricious Collete. He would harbor intense dislike for her the rest of his life. But on the day he sent her the money, he realized he'd was right back where he started months ago. He still needed another $200.

A month after Perry's death, Joe still didn't have any idea where he would get the additional $200 he needed. Then, out of the blue, he received a letter from Clark Stewart. Clark was a veterinarian from Tripoli, Iowa, eleven miles east of Sumner, and he and George had been good friends for years. Joe and Dr. Stewart had talked a couple of times the previous summer about school and vet medicine while George was laid up and Joe was playing at being a vet. Clark had contacted him during that trying summer, offering his assistance to the Sextons. Dr. Steward, a large and brusque man, took a liking to the novice vet. Word had reached Clark that following fall through the small clique of area veterinarians of Joe's financial plight and his run in with his penurious Aunt Collete. Unsolicited, the Tripoli vet sent Joe money. Opening the letter from Tripoli, Joe found the check for $200 and a brief word simply saying "pay me when you can."

Late afternoon October 21st, in Ames, the broken cloud cover would only allow the temperature to struggle into the 60's. Joe was in the stands at the football game between Iowa State and the University of Missouri. The Cyclones never mounted much of an offense, losing 13 to 39, and the disappointed crowd started leaving Williams Stadium before the last snap, even though it was homecoming. Joe and Marilane shuffled in the stream of disgruntled fans down through one of the exits. They then headed past Lake LaVerne, no doubt grousing about State's poor play. Just past the lake, the couple was half way up the steps of the Union when Joe heard someone yelling his name. Turning around, he could see that it was a fraternity brother. He had been frantically looking for Joe in the mob leaving the game.

"Someone has been trying to call you on the phone all day" his friend shouted from the bottom of the steps. Like the phone call late at night or the sober tone of family member on the line, the implied urgency of the utterance gave Joe that uneasy feeling in the pit of his stomach. Hurrying the two blocks back to the fraternity house, he learned the calls had been coming from Sumner. Nervously dialing home he got his mother, Inez. Her voiced was subdued and quivering. His father had died.

Early that morning George had gone to his office. His rheumatism had subsided and he had just recently started back practicing full time. His small office was only half a block away from the family home, a gentle walk for a man who in the course of the last several months had gained weight. His humble office was just large enough for his desk and room for his vet supplies. George was already seated at his desk, possibly working on his books, when Oscar Bethel arrived. Like Doc Devine, George had a driver, and Oscar, besides driving, also probably proved to be quite helpful when it came time to manhandle a horse or a cow. The two men briefly greeted that morning and Oscar appeared ready to go. George pushed back from the desk and took a few strides toward the door. He hadn't even cleared the doorway when he turned back toward his desk. In a short gasping statement he told Oscar he wasn't feeling well and wanted to sit for a minute, collapsing on the floor as the last word left his lips. Oscar rushed to his side grabbing him under his arms and pulled him up to his chair. Oscar had managed to maneuver George into the chair, but when he released him George slouched forward, dead. George Sexton was only 57 years old.

In Ames, Joe was just about to hang up the phone when his mother told him to expect Earl Ritter to be there any minute, because Earl had already left Sumner sometime before and was driving directly to the SAE house to pick Joe up. In the time it took him to pack a few things, Marilane was already back at the fraternity. When Earl finally turned off Lynn Street and drove up to the house, he found the couple huddled together on the front steps. As Joe kissed Marilane good-bye and opened the passenger's door, the sun was just hovering above the horizon, shedding the last light of the day through the broken gray sky.

On Sunday and Monday the family gathered in the little house on Main Street. Arrangements needed to be made, and surely Joe, as eldest son, was called upon to be the face of the family during that tenebrous time. Tuesday morning the little Catholic Church down the street started to fill, with the families of George's brother and sisters quietly filling the front pews. Then friends, neighbors, and clients filtered into the remaining pews with their muffled conversation only interrupted by the occasional sound of a kneeler being turned down. Once everyone was seated, the crowd fell silent as the casket entered the church. Following the casket as it made its way down the aisle were four priests and a retinue of altar boys. Officiating the requiem mass were Father Fischer, the local priest, Father Daniel Gorman, George's cousin who one day would be named a bishop, Father Paul Maquire from Waverly and Monsignor E. Dougherty from Waterloo. It was quite a lofty assembly of clerics for a lowly country veterinarian. Bearing the pall were six of George's colleagues, Drs. Nygen and Finley from Waverly, Dr. Stewart from Tripoli, Dr. Willis from Waucoma, Dr, Wais from Oelwein, and Dr. Sperry from Fayette. George might not have been financially successful during his life, but his intellect and gentle personality had amassed a fortune in respect.

Though rich in friends, George hadn't left much of an estate to Inez, and his children were left to toil with their mother's financial future. Donna was married and still working for the local paper, *The Sumner Gazette*, and she could not really afford to aid in supporting her mother. Jim, recently graduated from high school, wasn't in any position to help either. This left only Joe. His dreams of going to exotic places like Panama went up in smoke that dismal week. Joe's future wasn't a dream to be pursued but rather a reality to be dealt with. His path now was laid out in front of him. To maintain what he could of his father's practice and to contribute to his mother income, he would spend the rest of his senior year driving home to Sumner on the week-ends and practicing vet medicine. As in the previous summer, he would be an un-licensed doctor doing part time work. And just like that summer, he wouldn't pose much of a threat to Earl or any surrounding vets. If questioned, most likely, the area vets didn't mind someone taking all the week-end work and clients who were difficult to work for.

Joe couldn't have been excited with the prospect of weekly trips home, especially given the fact he would be leaving Marilane, but his desires would have to be subjugated to his duty. Inez, living on the very edge of downtown, wasn't in need of the family car because church and shopping were only blocks away, so Joe took George's car to make the trip back and forth from Ames. For the next seven months Joe and the smelly old car made the boring three- hour drive religiously every week-end.(Quite possibly Inez didn't need the car because she might not have known how to drive. Even later there is no record of her ever driving a car.)

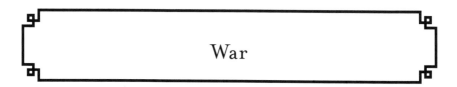

War

The fall had been unseasonably warm, and the ground was still bare that December. Late Sunday afternoon, Joe's black coupe sat parked behind the SAE house, the dreary drive back from Sumner completed for another week. It had been a month and a half since George's funeral, and the route back to Sumner was already getting stale and tedious. Marilane, though on infrequent week-ends she would ride home with Joe, had stayed in Ames and walked over that afternoon to spend a few minutes with Joe who had just returned. Both were sitting on the back steps of the fraternity talking when a fraternity brother poked his head out the backdoor with the look of someone who was bursting with something to say. He nervously wanted to know if the two had heard the news about the Japanese. He had just heard on the radio that the Japanese had bombed Pearl Harbor, ships had been sunk, and a lot of Americans had lost their lives. The couple, like most Americans that day, tried to process what exactly had just happened. The magnitude of the event was still beyond everyone's comprehension. Their lives and the lives of millions of Americans in a matter of 24 hours would be forever altered. Within the span of one day the United States entered the greatest war the globe had ever seen.

The tumultuous world events, however earth shaking, weren't among the young couple's most immediate concerns. Marilane was graduating the beginning of January and after the end of the first semester she would be moving to the northwestern part of Iowa. She'd landed a job in Cherokee, Iowa, working as a dietician in one of the state's mental institutions. Joe now would be alone, dividing his time between school and Sumner. Just prior to the end of the semester, Marilane had come to Sumner for a brief visit during the last week of Christmas break. Just having put his love on a bus in Waverly, Joe returned home and sent off a love letter.

My Darling,

Leaving you yesterday was no easy task. The thought of not knowing when I would see you again left me with an empty feeing in my stomach too. The ride home from Waverly was a cold one, but I got home about 7. Packed and left Sumner around 9. Got in at 2 and to bed by 3. Was cold, tired and dejected. Wondered about you getting home – imagined your mom had quite a wait in Algona. Hope she wasn't too unhappy about it.

Sunday completed one of the happiest weeks of my life – the happiest without a doubt. Just to have you near me all the time was a joy, honey. Words could not express. My entire future is planned with you in mind – don't wreck it honey. Being here at school without you seems dull. Now all is a process of marking time.

Our immediate future is also hanging time – in the outcome of a physical exam of my competitor. Nothing would be so swell as my being able to go back to Sumner to practice and have you as my charming, loving, and devoted wife. I could ask no more of life and were you happy and contented with it all. I'm sure you'll be married to the luckiest guy in the universe.

Give your mother my regards also John. I hope your

lengthy stay in Sumner met with your mother's approval. I know mom enjoyed having you as she said she did.

Love me always, darling, and do write.
Most lovingly,
Joe

Like millions of Americans at that time, they were swept along with the immensity of the war, the tide of events dictating the course of their lives for the next three to four years.

During this time it would be impossible to find any city or town, no matter how small, which did not have a son or daughter going off to serve. Earl Ritter would join the millions of Americans called up for active duty. Though Earl could be considered just one of the faceless masses being sent off, his enlistment would have a profound effect on Joe. Joe's fate would take a different path.

As a professional young man, Joe's status was different than the majority of servicemen. His fate rested with the Procurement and Assignment Commission, which had the complex tasks of balancing the needs of the service with the demands of the home front. All draft age physicians, dentists, and veterinarians were pooled together in their respective professions and from these groups the commission would decide who would be drafted and who would need to stay home. Dictatorial in their 'rulings,' the commission tried to balance the civilian needs and the ever increasing military demand, as the country ramped up to meet the challenges of war on two fronts.

Weeks before their graduation, Joe's entire senior vet class was bussed to a pre-enlistment physical. Thirty miles south of Ames the army had a medical facility at Fort Des Moines where all of Iowa's young men and women received their physicals. By early morning the sleepy eyed class members had gathered in Ames to be loaded on a bus bound for Des Moines. After the thirty-minute ride, they were dropped off inside the base. Joe and his classmates at that point became indistinguishable from the thousands of young men lined up and standing in their underwear anticipating the verdict as to who would pass and be going off to war. The exams, the poking and prodding, were administered mostly by recently drafted physicians. The physician who did Joe's examination had recently graduated from medical school and had been a classmate there with a man from Sumner, Maurice Murphy, Lawrence's brother. During the course of the physical the doctor noted that Joe did have a history of childhood asthma, but this alone did not disqualify him as eligible for the draft. At the end of the day he was 2-A, deferred but still eligible to be drafted.

A month after graduation, state veterinarian boards were administered in Iowa. After practicing for almost a year as a student, Joe would finally be a fully licensed veterinarian. Upon completion of his boards, he received a letter informing him he ranked first of all the men who took the boards. He had come a long way from the timid student who'd struggled to get through the first year of vet school. No doubt Joe was intelligent, but the year he spent actually practicing vet medicine went a long way toward focusing his intellect on the science. Though Joe did not finish as valedictorian like his father, George still would have been proud of his son's achievement.

The summer of 1942 saw Doctor Joe Sexton assume his role as a full time veterinarian. Building on what was left of George's practice, Joe soon made it his own. Dreams he had of traveling to distant lands were laid aside. The yearning to escape from the small world of Iowa had been dashed, but he still had Marilane, whom he desperately wanted to marry. One issue to be resolved before he could seriously think about marriage, however, concerned the question of his military service. He felt compelled to go and serve, as so many of his peers in Sumner were already committed to that end. With the war only a half year old, several young men were already actively engaged in the fight. A family who lived on the huge Cass farm north of town had two sons already away in the Pacific Theatre of the war. The first boy had been on the remote atoll, Wake Island. After a valiant struggle against overwhelming odds, he and his comrades had been captured by the Japanese, all this occurring shortly after the attack on Pearl Harbor. His brother was also captured and brutalized by his captors when the American and Philippine force surrendered on Bataan Peninsula in the Philippine Islands. General Douglas McArthur shortly before the capitulation had been spirited away on a submarine leaving General Wainwright in command. The Sumner boy would survive his captivity but a large percentage of his comrades would not be so fortunate.

Numerous others from Sumner had also enlisted, like Joe's close friend, Ben Winks, and his other college friend, Lawrence Murphy. Earl Ritter was also called up for duty. Earl's case was different. Prior to the outbreak of the war he had been a reservist, so there was little doubt as to his war time status. Joe, seeing friends and neighbors leaving for the service, though he felt a strong commitment to his mother, felt he should enlist, and so he did. Shortly after submitting his application for enlistment, he received a rejection letter from no less than the head of the Veterinary Corp, Colonel Crosby, who informed Joe that his services wouldn't be needed. Oddly enough, weeks after the Colonel's letter, the local draft board reclassified him as 1-A.

Even with Col. Crosby's letter, his reclassification by the local draft board meant there was a strong possibility of Joe being called up for service. In a small town even the most trivial of gossip spreads rapidly, and the news that Sumner could be without a vet became big news on the rumor hot line. With Earl already preparing to leave, the rural community flew into a panic. A petition got started, requesting that Joe Sexton remain in town. Signed by nearly everyone who was asked to sign it, the petition was delivered to the board in Waverly, the county seat. After its delivery, the following month the board met and rendered their decision. Joe Sexton's status changed, he wouldn't be drafted. For the duration of the war Joe would remain in Sumner.

Marriage

Marilane and Joe had every intention to marry, but Joe was now dragging his feet. First there was the issue of military service, which caused Joe to wonder if this was the appropriate time, and then there was his financial situation. He was basically starting from zero monetarily. He had no money, no assets, and he still felt compelled to aid his mother. How could he afford a wife? How could he subject Marilane to this shameful fiscal situation? He believed the correct course of action was to establish his practice first, then consider marriage.

Dr. J.W. Sexton opened his door officially on June 6, 1942. Ray Johnson from Norden Labs was more than happy to supply his new office with twenty dollars worth of vet supplies to get the practice started. Joe didn't have any cash but worked out a deal whereby he agreed to pay off the bill over time. The rent on his father's old office came to five dollars a month, and the light bill averaged $ 1.02 monthly, but even this meager amount pushed the limit on the young vet's budget. How could he be thinking about supporting a wife on this pauper's salary.

Joe may have considered that he was being responsible by delaying the marriage, but Marilane had her own take on the situation. If Joe had doubts, Marilane didn't. Joe had fallen in love with a much stronger woman than he knew. The military, the vet practice, the lack of money – none of these things mattered. Marilane was going to marry and soon.

By early July, the drama surrounding the draft board had been settled, and Marilane came to Sumner for a visit. She came with an agenda:

she was intent on planning a wedding. Joe used his best arguments to regain control, but he was hopelessly overmatched. Against the dictates of a commanding woman, the best he could do was push the wedding back until August.

Saturday evening, August 22, 1942, was mild, cooling into the 60's. It was an ideal summer evening and the perfect temperature for a bachelor's party. Claude and Mabel Wilharm prepared a party for their old employee, sparing no expense. Saturday nights were normally hopping anyway so with the added enticement of food and booze, quite a crowd was attracted to send off one of Sumner's favorite sons to be wed. Everyone there took full advantage of the Wilharms' largess, including the very person being feted, Joe Sexton.

The words "You smell terrible!" awakened Joe the next morning, with Inez standing beside his bed. She needed to rouse her debauched son. It would be a good four hour drive to Bancroft, and they couldn't wait for Joe to sleep it off. Today the Sextons were going meet the Devines for the first time, and at present Joe wasn't in any condition to meet his new in-laws, no doubt the idea of riding in a hot stuffy car four long hours seemed like torture to Joe. After gathering at the little white house on Main Street the Sexton's split up for the drive to Bancroft, with Marty and Donna driving their car and taking Inez with them, and Jim driving George's old work car with his hung-over brother riding shot gun. Joe certainly hoped he'd feel better once they reached Bancroft.

As they pulled onto the gravel drive on the south side of the Devine family home, Lillian walked down the steps of the sun porch to greet the Sextons. Introductions completed, Inez made a focused point to apologize for Joe, who still appeared to have the lingering effects of the previous night's overindulgence. Luckily for Joe the entire Devine family wasn't present. Besides Lillian and Marilane's little brother John,

Margaret came home to be the bride's maid, and Kenneth was there with his new bride Evelyn. That evening, fortunately, Joe was more himself when the local relatives came to inspect Marilane's new family. The Murrays and Clarks presented themselves, wishing the young couple well. After a more sedate evening than Joe had experienced the prior day, the household the next morning was up early since the wedding mass was set for 10 AM. A Monday morning wedding might seem odd today, but Marilane had made all the arrangements on such short notice that this may been the only appropriate time available. It wasn't going to be a large wedding. Marilane planned to be married not throw a gala.

Shortly after 10 AM the couple could be seen kneeling at the altar of St. John's, the voluminous interior sparingly used by the small wedding party. Stationed in the first few pews, the twenty-five celebrants were dwarfed by unused space. Adorned in a simple white dress with a single corsage, Marilane knelt by her groom, her black hair covered by a short veil. Joe, now cleaned and bright eyed, had on his best, and possibly only, suit. Both knelt before the altar while Father Schemmell officiated over the wedding mass, his words echoing in the nearly empty church.

Following the ceremony the Devine's neighbors, the Sheridans, entertained the wedding party with a wedding dinner in their home. Within a span of four hours the wedding ritual was over. Inez, Jim, Mardy and Donna needed to start for Sumner, and Doctor and Mrs. Sexton would be leaving on their honeymoon. Kissing her family good bye, Marilane opened the door and slid onto the bench seat next to Joe in the car. She was familiar with the car, a 1939 Chevy infused with lingering aroma of carbolic acid, iodine, and manure. It can only be surmised as to Marilane's thoughts driving away in a foul smelling car seated beside a poor country vet. The fact that they had no house and no money didn't seem to matter to Marilane. She had gotten what she wanted As the couple backed out the drive, waving to the small crowd sending them off, they were caught up in the moment; neither of them had any idea of the adventure they were setting off on.

In the backyard of Lillian Devine's house the newlyweds poised for pictures with Inez, Jim, Donna, and Mardy.

Heading east out of Bancroft, the Sextons followed the two lane roads toward the Minnesota border. Joe, once committed to the wedding, had done all the planning for their honeymoon. Their first night as husband and wife would be spent in Rochester, Minnesota. He'd booked a room at the Kohler Hotel, the fanciest hotel within one hundred miles from Sumner. After just one evening, Joe drove his bride southward. Barely across the Minnesota/Iowa border and forty five miles from Sumner, they stopped for the last night of their honeymoon in Decorah, Iowa. Hardly extravagant, this was all the time and the money that the destitute couple could afford. Joe needed to get back to work, and their finances were in an abysmal state. Four hundred ninety dollars comprised their entire net worth. Joe had made ninety dollars the previous week testing cattle, and Lillian had sent them off with a wedding gift of $200. Uncle Art Murray had also given his niece $200 as wedding gift. Besides that, they had George's car and their clothes.

Thursday morning found Joe up early and dressing in the small bedroom in Inez's house. After a cup of coffee he walked across the street to his office. He hadn't been there long when the siren went off. Attached to the water tower just south of Main Street, the siren served as an alarm clock for the town, going off at 7am when the work day started and at 12:00 and 1:00 and finally at 6:00pm when the day was done, except on Sunday. The howl of the siren four times daily usually gave order to Sumner's work days, but these weren't ordinary days. The war brought a whole new look to the community.

In his work overalls, Joe is just leaving his vet office on the corner of Main and Railroad.

The first thing some stranger would have noticed were stickers in all the car windows. Each placard boldly projected a letter corresponding to the occupation of the car's owner. "A" signified the car's driver worked at a job deemed non essential to the war effort, a gas station attendant pumping gas couldn't exceed four gallons a week in that car or he else he would be fired. Much of this had to have been on the honor system since documentation of every gallon pumped would have been a nightmare. Joe's car had a "C" in the window. As a veterinarian he joined physicians, ministers, and mail carriers, who all could get more than eight gallons a week since their professions fell into the essential category.

But gas wasn't the only commodity rationed. Sugar, meat, silk, shoes, nylon, and rubber were probably the most crucial items needing to be shared with the military, who required the bulk of these objects for rations, parachutes, and tires. With the Japanese dominating most rubber producing areas of the world, tires were valuable items to possess and almost impossible to purchase. Conserving this commodity became a national priority. Working on the theory that slower speeds would wear down tires at a retarded rate, the government mandated a 35-mph speed limit on all roads. Signs popped up next to American highways reading "keep it under 40," thereby hoping to encourage drivers to conserve precious rubber.

Signs and placards became regular fixtures on roads and homes. All over Sumner and every town across the nation star flags appeared on front windows of homes. A blue star in the window indicated that a son or daughter from that home was serving in the military. Some homes, like the Lawrence Murphy's, had three blue stars on the front door for Lawrence and his brothers, Tom and Maurice. There were also "gold" stars. These, however, announced the news that the family had lost a son or daughter in the war. Surely designed as a badge of honor, it only announced the grief within the house's walls.

A week prior to Joe's wedding a blue star appeared in the front window of the Ritter home. Earl called up already had packed off for a stateside base awaiting his deployment. By the time Joe returned from his honeymoon he found himself as the only vet in town. Within the span of a few weeks Joe had gone from a practice struggling for business to being inundated with calls for service.

Though it may seem ridiculous now, during Joe's first year back Sumner actually prepared for an air raid. In December of the first year of the war, the town scheduled a practiced black out. Programmed for a Monday night from 10:00-10:20, the event was to begin with the siren being sounded, whereupon everyone was directed to move inside and turn out their lights. Citizens were cautioned not to use the phones during that time, so as to keep phone lines available for emergency use, and they were also instructed not to smoke or use their radio; the theory being that light from the radio dial or from a cigarette could be seen by an enemy bomber from a great distance. There were surely those who scoffed at the idea of Japanese or German bombers flying over Iowa, but these were uncertain times and even the incredible seemed plausible.

Now busy, Joe recruited Marilane to be his receptionist. This also helped her to fill her days. Answering the phone from a secondary phone line installed in their home, dispensing chicken medicine, and doing book work for the fledgling practice afforded her an opportunity to remain busy and save Joe's practice the expense of office staff. This also gave Marilane and Inez some degree of separation, since during the first year of marriage the two women were often thrown together. Having two women sharing the same roof could have been seen as a problem, but during this time Inez also found work, which possibly took some of the strain off the situation.

As the war moved further into the first year, more and more men left the community, which caused a labor shortage to develop. Jobs which normally would have been filled by a man now were open to women, and Inez, who hadn't worked since her days as a school teacher, found her talents in need. The municipal light plant had an opening for a book keeper, which was an ideal position for Inez. The uncluttered looking brick building situated merely a block and a half from her front door was an easy walk every work day. The hours were good and the pay decent, and Inez enjoyed the job enough that she would continue working there for decades after the war.

The first months after his marriage, Joe made every effort to introduce his wife to friends around town either out of pride in his beautiful bride or to have her feel more comfortable in her new home, but didn't take long for Marilane to become acquainted with goodly number of the citizens. The young couple didn't take long to fall in with a lively social group. Once a month their circle of new friends gathered at someone's house with a bottle of booze, a deck of cards and a pot luck dish. They were a rather eclectic group however. There was Gilly and Ruby Wells who ran the local movie theater in the old opera house across from the Hotel Charles. Then there was the local priest Father Fischer. Jim and Virginia Whitmire were part of this group. He was the local physician who shared a practice with his father in an office above McAloon's store, which had once been Dr. Wilson's building. Jim's father had actually come to Sumner not many years after Wilson's death and after all those years had installed himself as one the town's characters. The older Whitmire was a cigar smoking, cantankerous man. People learned to watch out for him as he drove his Model-A around town, since he never stopped for stop signs, his rationale being that he had been here before they put up the sign, so it didn't really apply to him. Also prominent in this social group were Walter and Elda Berg; he ran the town's funeral home. A dignified and gracious man, he would pass the business along to his son who unfortunately didn't share his father's social skills. Walter Jr., while on the board of Meadowbrook Country Club years later, proposed to restrict membership to only people living in town, thereby excluding farmers from joining to "keep out the riff raff." In a rural community this was sure to alienate over half the citizens and earn Walter junior the reputation as an idiot from the other half. There was a dentist in the group, Horace Kartsten and his wife, Vera. Horace practiced with his father, and their office was above Ribbeck's Clothing Store on the south side of Main Street. A long dimly lit staircase lead up to their offices from the street's sidewalk. To their patients it must have looked like the stairs to the nun's office in *The Blues Brothers* movie, a grim climb to an unpleasant meeting. Horace and his dad's practice, for the times, was a modern form of dentistry. Belt driven dental drills whirling in front of the patient's eyes, chairs with spittoons to the side with water continually running around the bottom to catch the bits of filling and tooth mixed with saliva and the pervasive smell of eucalyptus oil permeating the dental operatory were the norms for the times. Neither, Horace nor his father put a lot of stock in anesthetics. While George was alive, one of the two dentists extracted a couple of teeth for him all without any form of novocaine. Rounding out the group was Walter 'Fats' and Coney Schultz. Walter ran one of the town's three grain elevators. Professionally they were a diverse cross section of the community.

By far the youngest members of this group, Joe and Marilane probably were at least ten years the junior of the other couples. The war had taken away all the couples in their age bracket. With his deferment Joe was one of the few twenty year olds left in Sumner.

Within this group Marilane would find friends and confidants, but first among them had to have been Virginia Whitmire. Prior to marrying Jim, she had divorced her first husband. A divorce had its own stigma in a small town, but the fact she was a doctor's wife applied another layer to her acceptance in the community. In small rural cities physicians were socially held apart from the rest of the populous, and the wives normally shared that different standing. Virginia was perceived by many in town as an uppish and waspish woman, especially by those who didn't know her well, but Marilane may have been uniquely qualified to see past that exterior because of her mother who had learned to tolerate the same small town prejudices. Virginia and Marilane would grow to be great friends.

Marilane also befriended a woman not part of the immediate group, Martha Woods (the girl Donna had thought should also have a baby brother). She was somewhat of an eccentric. A large woman, she was famous for expressing herself in "very colorful language." She could swear better than most men, but her demeanor did not seem to upset Marilane.

Late in the fall of the married couple's first year, Donna moved in briefly with Inez, Joe and Marilane. Mardy was away working as an engineer in Kansas, and Donna, pregnant at the time, sought the company of her mother. Marilane, ironically, found herself also pregnant at same time. Two women in a home were bad enough but three women could spell trouble. Donna, years later, commented that she and Marilane never really hit it off. In retrospect Marilane very likely felt like the odd woman out. Though everyone tried to make the best of the situation, Joe decided on his own, or maybe with enthusiastic prodding from his wife, that it was time to have a place of their own.

Pictured here, the Joe stands with his mother, Inez, and sister, Donna, on the sidewalk in front the family home. To the right, the white building on the corner is Joe's office. and across the street is the clock tower, the old Cass First National Bank building.

The Family Goes to War

By the one year anniversary of Pearl Harbor, four million American men and women were in the armed forces. The next few years would see that number balloon to twelve million, with the apparent effect being evenly spread across the country. It seemed like almost every family had someone gone. The Sextons and Devines were no exception.

Joe's younger brother Jim had enlisted. He left a job he'd secured with Mardy's help in Kansas City working construction, since his brother-in law at the time worked in the area around Kansas City for the Arm Corp of Engineers. During his youth he had spent hours drawing airplanes and Jim carried that fascination with flying into manhood. Now finally the war would give him that chance. He enlisted in the army air corps and was sent to Arizona for training. Now standing on the hot parade ground of Williams Field in Chandler, Arizona, the boyish looking Jim Sexton had finished his flight training and was now commissioned a second lieutenant. It was 1944, and pugnacious Lieutenant Sexton was only weeks away from seeing the war first hand.

Within half a day of the ceremony the young lieutenant stood on a train platform sweating in his wool dress uniform. Smartly attired in his new uniform with blue patches on each arm showing gold wings sewn above a star, the insignias proudly signifying him as a pilot, Jim Sexton was taking the train north to Iowa. He had only a week before he needed to report back to his unit. That unit, once united, would be shipping out for England.

While he was home on leave, Marilane couldn't get over the fact that this "boy" was going to fly planes. While standing in the kitchen smoking a cigarette, Jim, who was unusually short for his age, looked barely old enough to drive a car. The irony of the moment was even richer. Jim's unit was assigned to fly C-47's which were huge cargo planes nicknamed the "flying boxcars."

Once transported to England on one of the hundreds of ships making the dangerous Atlantic passage, Jim found himself stationed west of London at Ramsberry Field. This was the assigned home of the 84th squadron of the 437th troop carrier group. The name, however, was a misnomer. Their main purpose was essentially to fly cargo. They flew critical supplies to some of the pivotal events of the war. Probably the most well known was the Battle of the Bulge. During that conflict German armies had pushed through the Ardennes Forest in eastern Belgium on December 16, 1944, surprising the thin line of American troops spread across that sector. The Germans then pushed through Belgium, hoping to cut in half the American forces in the south and British forces to the north. Right in the center of the front sat the town of Bastogne a pivotal crossroads in central Belgium. Collapsing on the town, the Germans surrounded the 101st Airborne which held out even in the face of German armies vastly outnumbering them. With the 101st cut off and low on supplies, the 437th drew the assignment to drop supplies to the beleaguered troops. Fog and snow hampered their efforts until December 23rd when the sky cleared and lumbering C-47's took flight from England for Bastogne. Flying just above the tree tops, the huge planes dropped their 1446 bundles of food and ammunition close to where they assumed Americans to be. The flight wasn't without peril, not all the planes returned to England, as some were brought down by German anti-aircraft fire.

Two days after the drop, Patton's third army broke through German lines to relieve the city, spelling doom for the German's last major offensive of World War II. Months later the Allies pushed over the Rhine and advanced into the German homeland. As they progressed the Allies liberated prisoner of war camps. Now rebased in France, the 84th did become a troop carrier. Jim and his fellow pilots flew into Germany and after loading up the released prisoners would transport them back to France. On one of these flights Jim had his closest call of the war. After leaving German soil with a plane load of freed soldiers, he was forced to crash land in France. Assuming that it was a mechanical malfunction, Jim skillfully brought his damaged plane down in one piece. Jim and his no doubt anxious passengers all walked away.

During Jim's seven month overseas he would fly in eight combat supply missions and would altogether accumulate 525 hours of military flying time. The last four months of his service he would forego flying to be the aid to the unit's brigadier general. Though discharged from active service on January 13th, 1946, while stationed at base in Santa Ana, California, Jim would continue in the reserves, with rank of captain, till 1957.

Meanwhile Mardy was still working for the Army Corp of Engineers as a civilian and was never drafted. Though spared military service, Mardy had to accept a certain trade off. As long as he worked in that capacity he was subjected to frequent relocations as the corps moved from project to project. After Kansas, Mardy and Donna moved to Starksville, Mississippi, and from there they would move nine times in ten years. Pregnant in Sumner, Donna delivered her first child, Karl in October 1943 prior to their move to Mississippi. This was the start of the family odyssey. During their wandering, their second child, Chris, was born in 1947. A few years later in 1951 the family's journey brought them to Slidell just north of New Orleans. There six-year-old Karl contracted pneumonia. He was affected with Down's syndrome, and whether that contributed to a weakened immune system can't be known but after a few days of hospitalization, he succumbed to the disease. Both parents were devastated by the loss of their son, but Donna was especially troubled. Possibly in psychological denial of her son's condition she flew into a rage when a nurse attending Karl made mention that the boy suffered from Down's. Karl's death may also have augmented Donna's displeasure with their itinerant life style.

While Jim and Mardy experienced the war in their own ways, on the Devine side of the family, with the exception of John and Kenneth, everyone became involved in the war. John was still be in high school and his brother Kenneth, a surgeon at the Mayo Clinic, would find his fate tied to Joe's and remain undrafted. Allocated to civilian medical needs he would follow with keen interest his brother and brother-in-law's military service.

Margaret, when she served as maid of honor for Marilane's wedding, was already anticipating her own wedding two months later to a man she had met while at Iowa State. A native of Colo, Iowa, Ray Goodenow would wed Margaret that fall. Shortly after the ceremony, Ray, already enlisted in the army, shipped out. His regiment was being sent to an obscure corner of the war: India. Based on the border with Burma, the troops were assigned the task of pushing into the jungles of Burma. Earlier in the war the Japanese had swept the area of allied forces, forcing them into India. Now under the command of General Joe Stilwell (nicknamed Vinegar Joe) the allied forces would fight to reestablish the 700 mile dirt road connecting India with China, the Burma Road, which was necessary to supply Chinese forces. The jungle-covered mountains comprised the inhospitable terrain along almost the entire extent of the route to China. Fighting in this thick cover against the tenacious Japanese soldiers, Vinegar Joe pushed his troops ever further up the Burma Road. Hampered by monsoon rains, leeches, flies, ticks, mosquitoes carrying malaria, dysentery, typhus and encumbered by a Byzantine British military organization, Vinegar Joe drove his haggard army further north. Though we have no record of Ray's exact duties, it is hard to imagine any one in that theater of the war being spared its discomforts.

Ray's brother-in-law, Art, wasn't called to fight but was enlisted in the war effort on an academic stage. He enlisted as a pre-med student. During the war, medical schools "accelerated" their curriculum, compressing a four year course of study into three. (Art entered medical school at the tender age of nineteen. He had started his undergraduate studies at Iowa State when he was only sixteen and completed his degree in three years.) Enrolled then in medical school at the University of Iowa, Art would receive his degree just as the war was ending, but due to his "enlistment" in the accelerated program the army still demanded his time.

Art's brother, Tom, would also enlist but got to see the war up close. Of all the brothers growing up, Thomas would stand out as probably the best athlete. In high school he excelled in baseball and basketball, receiving enough acclaim to be recruited to play basketball for Iowa State. Even as a freshman on the team, he started for the Cyclones. His career would only span two years. In September 1943, in what would have been his junior year, Tom enlisted in the army air corp. Taking lessons from Hunter Flying School in Cedar Rapids, Iowa, Thomas was listed as a pilot by the army after only eleven lessons. Transferring to Fort Myers, Florida, he took advanced training in the gunnery school. Completing his first year of enlistment stateside, he finally shipped out for Italy in 1945. By this time, after months of bitter struggle through the mountains south of Rome, the allied forces had pushed into Rome itself and Italy had thrown off their strutting little dictator, Mussolini, killing him and his mistress and then hanging their bodies from meat hooks. With the departure of German forces from Italy, the Americans established airbases on Italian soil and by the time Thomas arrived were flying bombing missions into southern Europe.

In Italy, Tom was assigned to the 340th bomber group flying B-25 Mitcheles. Once on base, pilot Devine found that he was part of a surplus of pilots, but what the squadron lacked were tail gunners. The shortage was a result of the perilous nature of the duty. Now Tom became a tail gunner. The tail section of a B-25 looks like a huge "H," two vertical tail sections positioned on the side of the tail gunner's cockpit. The tail gunner sat in an enclosure with a canopy allowing him a clear view above, to the sides, and below. While manning a 50-caliber machine gun to protect the plane from enemy fighters from behind, the tail gunner's real danger came from the tortuous access to the cock-pit. To get to his position Tom had to pass by the bomb bay doors of the plane and crawl into the tail section. Besides being shot at, the tail gunner had a perilous escape route if his plane should become damaged. With the war winding down anti-aircraft flack was more of danger to the bombers than the German fighter planes which by that point in the war had had their numbers decimated.

Tom flew during the last 6 months of the war. By this time the German Luftwaffe, which had dominated the sky for years, was in retreat. Decimated but not defeated, the Germans could still put up a few planes, among them a new terrorizing threat, jet fighters. But the biggest danger came from anti-aircraft fire from 88mm flak guns. Death, as Thomas surely was quite aware, was still a very real possibility on every mission.

The story of Tom on one bombing mission with his squadron flying north from Italy into Nazi held positions bears telling. Isolated deep in the rear of the plane, he was nearing the end of the mission. It had to have been a harrowing experience for Tom and he became overcome by nausea. Unlacing his boot, Tom vomited into it and then put the boot back on. Embarrassed by being overwhelmed by fright, he hoped to hide the fact from his crew mates.

The oldest of the Devines, Emmett, remained state side during the entire war, but he had a ringside seat on events which would forever alter the world. When the war broke out Emmett was already in the service. His exact duties during the war were never spelled out, and there is probably a very good reason for that. After the war certain postings came to light that at the time were known to very few people. The event which would first find Emmett surfacing had to do with the atomic bomb. Early in the war Einstein and others warned the government that Germany was working on a new weapon harnessing the splitting of the atom. In secret the US instituted the Manhattan Project in a race to beat the Germans. With clandestine facilities spread around the US, the actual bomb would be designed in a secret complex in the desert of New Mexico: Los Alamos. Gathering the prominent nuclear physicists from across the county, the facility was under the leadership of Robert Oppenheimer. Uranium 235 was to be at the core of the new bomb. The element, while extremely rare could be painstakingly gathered in microscopic amounts from tons of soil. A threshold of material was necessary to achieve "critical mass" to set off the chemical reaction explosion. These facts all conspired to present a problem. The amount of uranium 235 available to them was barely enough to form a single bomb. The quantity would not be enough to test their theory of nuclear fission with an adequate amount left to achieve critical mass for the actual bomb. To solve this problem, the scientists decided to gamble on an untested idea; use plutonium with a conventional explosive surrounding the nuclear material. Their hope was that forceful compression of the radioactive plutonium would still cause a nuclear reaction.

On July 16, 1945 the scientists readied to test the devise they code named "Trinity." They scheduled the test to take place in a remote patch of white sand desert in southern New Mexico. High on a steel derrick, a metal ball several feet across dangled with a hundred wires running from it. In the orb's center was a soft-ball-sized mass of plutonium. Called the "gadget," the orb, now positioned high off the ground, was abandoned, all its handlers having gone to seek shelter.

Early that morning a rare rainstorm delayed the scheduled test but by 5:30 PM, the gadget was triggered. Just prior to that much awaited moment, speculation by the observers on the effect of the explosion ran from a perceived moderate flash to an uncontrollable igniting of the atmosphere, but most of the spectators understood the history changing event about to transpire. Once the device was detonated, an intense light brighter than the sun illuminated the New Mexico desert. In a split second the massive steel derrick supporting the device vaporized. The super heated air which obliterated the steel rolled out across the sand dunes like ripples on a pond. Following behind the heat wave, faster than the speed of sound, a blast flattened everything in its path.

Issuing upward from the point where the steel ball had hung, a great mass of fire and gas billowed, churning ever higher. Rolling towards the heavens the cloud assumed the distinctive mushroom form extending to 40,000 feet across. One woman observing the awe-inspiring sight commented that "the heavens were boiling." Secured in cement bunkers a safe distance from the blast, 425 souls were the first humans to witness the unleashing of energy stored within atoms, proving Einstein's theory that mass can be turned into energy. Huddled with this privileged small group who viewed the milestone in man's history was an officer from Bancroft, Iowa: Emmett Devine.

At the same moment Emmett was coming to grips with the enormity of the event, the new President Harry Truman sat in a room in Tehran, Iran with the leader of the Soviet Union, Joseph Stalin and the British Prime Minister, Winston Churchill. The leaders had gathered to discuss the fate of post war Europe and the distribution of their spheres of influence. The distrust and underlying tension between the east and west which had always been an unspoken part of their alliance was starting to bubble to the surface. Truman, fully aware of the Manhattan project since his assumption of the Presidency, was informed by an aide of the test's success. Compelled to share the news with his allies, Truman informed his allies of America's new weapon. Stalin surprised Truman with his sterile response. Unknown to Truman, the Soviet Union had two spies in Los Alamos the entire time of the bomb's design who were fully aware of America's progress. And the Soviets had already ignited their own atomic weapons program.

Not long after this meeting the war in Europe would draw to a close. As America and the Soviet Union pushed into Germany, the race was on between the two new super powers to seize as much of Germany's intellectual resources as they could lay their hands on. High on their list of scientists was Werner Von Braun. He was the mastermind behind the Nazi's jet propulsion program. Fathering the V-2 missiles and the first jet airplanes, Von Braun's capture would prove to be a coup for the US. His conveyance to America may have been fortunate for the west, but

Werner, near the end of the war, had his own fortunate turn of events. While working on the V-2 rocket, the first intercontinental ballistic missile, Von Braun, a Nazi party member, started to rethink his association with that party. He would later contend his interest in missiles had shifted from military use to possible "space ships." True or not, the Gestapo suspected Werner was drifting from the party line. He was arrested and would spend two very uncomfortable weeks in Gestapo custody. Too valuable to keep incarcerated he was finally released after confessing to have "seen the light."

After capture by the Americans, Von Braun was scurried to the US and at first he spent a short period in New York City, the army assessing exactly what they had and how amenable their guest was going to be to their needs. When they were satisfied with his compliance, Werner was transferred to Fort Bliss in El Paso, Texas. Since the beginning of the war the air force had been an extension of the army but gradually had developed its own personality as a separate entity, much like the navy, there now needed to be a liaison between the army and its detaching air wing. The man assigned the task was Emmett Devine. He would spend the next couple years in contact with Dr. Von Braun until he ultimately transferred him to Huntsville, Alabama, where Werner would lead the Ballistic Missile Agency.

Indirectly associated with the war and not nearly as high profile as Emmett, Joe's Uncle Truman served as a merchant seaman. Truman had taken a rather tainted route into the merchant marines. When George and Inez married, True was still in school. Influenced by his brother-in-law, he entered the vet program at Iowa State. With his veterinarian degree, and always a free spirit, True headed for California and there fell in with the horse racing industry. While in Los Angeles, True married a 23-year old Morman woman named Millie Lee and his life appeared quite stable. The couple had one child, Dorothy, who tragically died at the age of 12. After this time True's life's story becomes murky. He divorced and quit his vet practice. It's hard to say what drew him to be a merchant seaman when he apparently had never been at sea, but a sailor's life is the one he chose. All this happened just prior to the outbreak of the war. In 1943, Truman had just signed on with ELIAS HOWE. She was one of the Liberty ships being mass produced by industrialist Henry J. Kaiser on the first-of-its-kind ship's assembly line. The ELIAS HOWE was a fairly new ship, having been launched for use in July of the previous year.

Almost a year to the day, July 17, 1943, the ELIAS HOWE left Antofagastre, Chili with a crew of four-two seamen and eighteen armed servicemen. The hold was loaded with 9200 tons of nitrates, which could be used for fertilizer, but this load was destined for conversion into explosives. The ship intended to steam half way around the world, with its destination being Alexandria, Egypt. Heading south out of port, she headed for the turbulent Cape Horn passage and once through the passage steamed eastward across the Atlantic Ocean. Cruising past the Falklands and remote St. Helena, she beat a path for the Cape of Good Hope to round the southern tip of Africa, progressing up the coast of Africa and then through the inside passage of Madagascar before entering the Gulf of Aden. The ship now was within less than a days travel to their final port.

Traveling alone in these dangerous waters the ELIAS HOWE cruised to within 75 miles of the city of Aden on the tip of Yemen. She was making her turn the west for the run up the Red Sea when an explosion ripped open her side. For hours a Japanese submarine had been waiting for this prime opportunity when the ship's turn would expose its entire length. With the ELIAS HOWE's entire side to aim at, the captain of the Japanese sub ordered the firing of two torpedoes. The first torpedo hit near the engine's compartment, flooding the compartment and bringing the Liberty ship to a dead halt. Unprotected and motionless now, she was a sitting duck. Realizing his prey was immobilized, submarine I-10 surfaced to face the doomed ship, and fired off one more torpedo which administered the death blow. The men of the ELIAS HOWE quickly took the life boats. Their ship had just moments left above the waves when the Japanese culprit could be seen sailing away. It would be twenty four hours before a passing ship could rescue the crew floating in their lifeboats. Not a soul from the cargo ship was lost.

Even after the harrowing experience, True would remain in the merchant marines, but his life's tale would have a mysterious ending. Without a regular port of call and no permanent address, True sent his wages to his sister, Inez, to hold and to distribute back to him as he needed. He normally would call her and have money wired to him wherever he might be docked. One day in September 1946, Inez received a long distance call from New York City. The multiple connecting phone trunk lines caused less than clear reception on the phone. Long distance calls were achieved by routing through several hubs, each of which took a toll on the transmission quality of the sound. Though the voice Inez heard was slightly garbled, she sensed that this wasn't her brother who was asking for money to be sent. To verify his authenticity she asked the caller, "What is our mother's name?" The man on the other end said he couldn't make out what she was asking but she needed to send the money. Convinced that she wasn't talking with her brother, Inez hung up. She never received another call from Truman.

Years later a detective hired by Inez wasn't able to discovered Truman's fate. In 2016, the mystery was solved. Truman arrived in New York on September 26, 1946 from Montreal. The next record of his existence is a manifest from the *USS Gauntlet,* where he appears as the cook, but when the ship sailed for the Suez Canal Truman was listed as "failing to join." Two years later, a death certificate declared his demise by 'cerebral accident' while in Philadelphia prison.

Outside the family, several friends of Joe's from Sumner went into harms way. Earl Ritter's service during the war would be assumed to be elemental in its duties being that he was a veterinarian. Besides meat inspection, the army still maintained horses, mules and war dogs, so wherever these animals were sent, vets were needed, and this is exactly what happened to Earl. In the jungles of Burma, mules were ideal pack animals to carry equipment and supplies along the narrow trails, and here is where Dr. Ritter would spend his time during the war. In that pestilent environment, the mules were prone to the same jungle diseases as their handlers and also to lameness. But in that unique jungle environment, the vets needed to perform an obscure procedure on the army mules. Unlike horses, mules bray. This is a form of communication between mules, warning others of danger. Known for being stubborn, mules when presented with the unknown will stop, refusing to move until they feel safe to proceed; faced with what the animal perceives as danger, it will bray to its companions. The singular problem with the braying behavior had to do with the Burma's particular environs. In the jungle terrain the sound of a braying mule could carry for miles, thus alerting any Japanese in the area of the pack train's location. An ingenious operation eliminated this hazard, taking only a matter of minutes. Veterinarians could quickly sever the mule's vocal cords, rendering the poor animal mute.

Earl was just one of the one hundred and forty two men from the small town of Sumner to serve during those years. Of that number nearly 10% wouldn't make it home alive.

Among that unfortunate group were three individuals who had a bearing on Jim and Joe Sexton. Claire Benning was a man from nearby Readlyn who had worked just prior to the war in one of Sumner's gas stations. Falling in love with one of the local girls, Lavonne Korman, he eloped with her and the couple married in September, 1943. Not unlike thousands of other couples married just before the man entered service, Claire had enlisted in the navy and shipped out shortly after the wedding. He saw action through the numerous battles fought hopping from island to island, securing airfields across the small island chains of the western Pacific. With the war nearing its end, the American navy drew ever closer to Japan, and Claire's ship was one among the armada setting off the island of Okinawa at the tip of the Japanese home islands. During the struggle for the island the Japanese sent thousands of Kamikaze pilots towards American ships, these suicide pilots all attempting to fly their planes into the vessels of the fleet. One of the ships unlucky enough to be hit was Claire's. His ship went down with him. His young widow would marry again, this time a young airman returning from the war, Jim Sexton.

The other two men who were casualties of the war were good friends of Joe's, one being his best friends, Ben Winks. After graduating from Columbia, Ben enlisted in the air corps and was trained as a pilot. He flew gliders. His plane was a guided Waco C-G4A, a wood and canvas shoe box with wings. Nicknamed the "flying coffin" or "tow target," the moniker said it all. Its 85 foot wing span could support 30 men plus a pilot and co-pilot. The plane was essentially a throw away, a single-use plane. Men who piloted this deadly craft had a maverick's reputation. Their commander, General James Gaven, captured what it was like to fly a Waco saying "it is a chastening experience. It gives a man religion." Towed by C-47's, the flimsy Waco would reach its optimal glide speed of 70-90 mph. At that point the release would be at the discretion of the glider pilot. Altitude and position were crucial, since normally the flying bus had only a little over a mile of glide distance. The connection between the two planes was a one inch thick nylon rope. At the release, the pilot engaged a scissor like device on the nose to cut the cord, starting the plane's gradual descent. Then the most pressing problem became finding a place to land, made more difficult by the fact that most operations took place at night. Nearing the ground, with only limited maneuverability possible, the craft had trees, buildings, and walls to avoid. In occupied France the Germans also, in full anticipation of just this kind of operation, had embedded 10-foot poles in any open ground behind the beaches of the coast line. To make it even more lethal, the poles were capped with explosives. These poles earned the name "Rommel's asparagus."

In the pre-dawn of June 6, Officer Winks felt the tip of the nylon line hoisting his Waco airborne leaving English soil. It's hard to imagine the atmosphere within the glider being towed over the channel and the chilling silence seconds after Ben cut loose from his C-47. Ben did get his glider down but not without injuring himself. Alive but hurt, he was removed from his crumpled Waco. But fortune had one more cruel turn for him. Surviving a night landing, some time during the next twelve hours a sniper zeroed in on the injured pilot. Ben, along with thousands of others, lost his life that day.

Ben's body was sent to Sumner and a funeral was held at the Catholic Church. Joe, his best friend, was appalled by the meager attendance for one of Sumner's heroes. In retrospect, there may have been a couple reasons for the slight turnout. First, this wasn't Sumner's first funeral for a fallen son, so there may have been some weariness toward the war. Second, Ben's father Leo may have been one of the wealthiest men in Sumner; though he was a gracious and kind man, it seems that envy and jealousy are an inherent part of human nature and quite possibly contributed to the small funeral turnout.

The second serviceman Joe knew well was his classmate from Columbia, Lawrence Murphy. He had also joined the air corps to become a pilot, but he was assigned a more manageable plane, the B-24 Liberator, a bomber that was the most mass-produced plane of the war. The huge plane was flown by a crew of 10 and could carry as much as 8000 pounds of bombs. Powering this flying truck were four colossal 1200-horse powered engines. Murphy and his crew luckily had flown several missions and returned unscathed but, their luck couldn't hold.

The squadron was placed in line for a special mission. Thirty miles north of Bucharest, Romania lay the Ploiesti oil fields and refineries. Vital to the German war machine, the site had been a prime target for some time to the allies. The extensive complex supplied over 60% of the fuel and oil to keep German vessels and planes in motion. Winston Churchill called Ploiesti the "tap root of German might." Previously bombed from high altitudes, the great size of the oil complex proved problematic for the allies. The imprecision of the incursions seemed to be having little effect, so a new take was formulated: tree-top bombing. This untested strategy demanded an alternate bombing technique.

Flying out from their base in Libya, Lawrence and crew practiced for the mission, cruising fifty feet above the desert to the south of their base. The tree top height was crucial if the planes hoped to avoid German radar. One Sunday morning, August 1, 1943, their training complete, it was time for the real thing. 178 planes headed out of Benghazi, Libya, forming up after take off into their squadrons while flying over the Mediterranean. The cold air of the desert morning added lift to the planes loaded with bombs and the extra fuel needed for the long flight. With each plane's four massive engines at full throttle, the formation skimmed barely above the blue waters of the Mediterranean. It would take hours for the aerial armada to cover the 1000 miles to their target and hopefully return.

The weeks of training over the desert was intended to give the planes and the crews the element of surprise, but unknown to the airmen the Germans had cracked the communication code. Moments after they began lumbering skyward out of Benghazi, the Germans had picked up the chatter between the on coming planes. With ample time to prepare their defenses, the Germans had to simply wait for they prey. Setting the trap set for the 178 American bombers, the disastrous day would later be known as "Black Sunday". An integral part of the Germans' trap was the railroad lines running parallel to the entire oil complex. Positioned on these tracks were specially designed rail cars mounted with anti-aircraft weapons. Starting at the southern end of the oil field, the weapon trains steamed north, shadowing all the time the incoming bomber squadrons with devastating effect. These "flak trains" would prove the Americans' worst nightmare.

Lawrence and his fellow pilots had one other issue to deal with. Flying so low they needed to avoid the forest of smoke stacks arising from the refineries and cracking plants used for the initial breakdown of the raw oil's hydrocarbons. These spires reached 70-80 feet and needed to be flown around, and all the time black smoke was billowing up from below, obscuring the pilots' vision. Getting to their targets would be deadly enough but once they released their bombs the explosion and subsequent fire could reach well above their 50-foot flying height. Once free of its payload, each plane would throttle up pushing upward as fast as possible to escape the living hell they'd been flying in and to escape being consumed by fire produced by their bombs. On that day, one hundred twenty–eight planes of the 178 were able to make that climb and turn southward. Not all of the 128 planes, however, would safely return to base. Several of these planes stricken with extensive damage or with inadequate fuel would never make it to Benghazi. The fifty left never escaped the oil fields. Lawrence, his crew and plane were among that number. An eye witness in a nearby bomber saw Murphy's B-24 damaged and veering downward, ultimately crashing into a burning cracking plant.

Part Two

Children

Late Thursday morning Marilane phoned the farm of one of Joe's clients where she was hoping to find him still there on a call. Her contractions had started. She had already talked with Dr. Jim, and the no-nonsense country doctor had advised her and Joe to head to Oelwein, the nearest hospital. Now she just had to track down Joe. Though the hospital was only 25 miles away, this was their first child and no doubt this produced high anxiety. She did find Joe, and after he rushed home the couple headed to Oelwein. There had to have been nerve racking moments for Marilane, experiencing contractions while sitting in a smelly work car speeding south on the blacktop with its windows down on that warm morning. Thankfully, the baby decided to wait until they arrived at the hospital. It was August 19, 1943 when one very proud father would look down for the first time on a rumpled little dark-haired baby, Michael Joseph.

For the days after the delivery, Marilane and baby Mike remained in the hospital. There were no complications this--was the medical protocol of the day. Joe dutifully drove daily after work to see both Marilane and his infant son. He was completely enthralled by the boy, thinking him "such a good baby." In a truly ironic twist of fate, one day he announced to Marilane "even if we have more children, I don't think I will ever love another baby like I love him." After a week and a half, Joe brought his wife and son home to Sumner. They still shared the little house on Main Street with his mother. Now that they were a family, Marilane needed her own home and her own things. Joe may have felt the same way but Marilane definitely needed her own space and surely would have impressed that fact upon Joe. After a few well placed inquiries, Joe contacted Mr. Nieman, who was a local grocer. He had a little home he would happy to rent to them. The house sat just west of town and north of the D & D railroad tracks. Now it seems humorous, but at the time Marilane viewed their new home as living in the country. Marking the unofficial western edge of the town was the little stream which flowed through Meadowbrook golf course. Once it passed what is now the fifth green, the creek basically set a course directly south until it connected with the Little Wapsie in the middle of Meier's cow pasture just north of the Catholic Cemetery. Joe and Marilane's rental home was on highway 93 a block west of the bridge over the stream so officially the house was 'out of town'.

A proud father, Joe holds his first born, Mike.

Their first house bordered farm land, but though it was 'in the country,' it had a lot to recommend it. A small screened-in porch extended out the rear, protruding into an expansive back yard. That summer of 1944, with Mike nearly one year old, Marilane pregnant again and sweltering from the heat found refuge on the little screened in porch with just enough western exposure to pick up any breeze that might arise. Fruit trees dotted the yard, and an ample garden took up space in the back corner. Enthusiastic at having their own place, the couple took to gardening, which in the coming years would become a summer passion. Next to the patch of the turned earth they blocked off as their garden was a stand of mature horse-radish and asparagus planted by the previous renters.

The home's interior was rather spartan. Without furniture or kitchen appliances the young family needed to cobble together some meager belongings to make their place more livable. They first moved their clothing and wedding gifts in the back of Joe's Model A Ford. The limited space in the back seat would require a few trips up the street past the Catholic Church and over the bridge to their new house. Just days before this final move, Joe and Marilane had driven to Waterloo to buy their first furniture. A bedroom set and some modest living room furniture were their first purchases. For their elegant dining room, Joe found a second-hand, round, folding card table with matching folding chairs. To outfit the kitchen they found a used gas stove and pressed cardboard refrigerator without a condenser, so cooling was accomplished by a block of ice. Their refrigerator was actually the norm for the times.

Putting the Sextons on his regular route for blocks of ice was the local ice-man, Russ Beebe. Russ was well received in town. Like the milkman, he had access to all the homes on his route, casually walking in whether the owner was home or not. No one bothered to lock their doors. On that subject George Sexton had had unique take. He thought it foolish to lock the door because then any thief would have to break a window to get in, just causing more of a mess. With truly an 'open door policy,' local delivery men entered homes, leaving their slabs of ice or milk sometimes very early in the morning, and everyone seemed to accept it as just a way of life. But, in Russ's case it was better if you were home. He was outgoing and gregarious, and like a bee carrying pollen from flower to flower, Russ carried local news from house to house.

Their squat little home may have been humble, but there is always something special about anyone's first home. Missing many of the trappings that would be accumulated over the succeeding years, the austere house would lend itself to a certain sense of reflective pride. Years later, Joe and Marilane would talk about the house and how they "had some good times there." Marilane would have three children while living in the Neiman house. She was already almost six months pregnant with their second when they moved in August of 1944. This had to have been uncomfortable, since of all the months, August is usually the hottest in Iowa. It would be years before air conditioning would become even part of the lexicon for anyone in that part of the country.

Once settled in their home, they took in a high school farm girl. Country school ended at eighth grade, and at that point any rural student who wanted to attend high school had three options: walk daily to school, get a ride, or live in town during the week. We don't know how the young girl came to stay with them, but Alvina Grahlmann somehow made arrangements with the Sextons. We do know that in compensation for her room and board she helped out around the house and also with the children. It was a very symbiotic arrangement.

In October 1944, now nearing the end of her second pregnancy, Marilane consented to attend a wedding celebration for a local boy, Allen Kroblin, and his bride from Readlyn, Millie Mathias. It was Saturday night, and as usual Joe had kept his office open late. After locking up, Joe drove home to pick up Marilane for the party. The chivaree had already started. After leaving the church, the wedding party had fortified themselves at Allen's home with food and beer. Sustained with alcohol, the newlyweds, once loaded onto a horse-drawn buggy, were paraded through the streets of Sumner. The terminus of their route happened to be what Joe called "a soda shop." Here is where Joe and Marilane found the well oiled wedding party. The evening was just getting started and the beer continued to flow, with Joe stepping up to make sure he got his share. With the evening drawing late and the revelers slowly drifting away, Joe and Marilane made their way home. It seemed like only moments since his head hit the pillow that there came a knock on their front door.

It was two in the morning, and Joe was still afflicted by the night's intoxicants when he heard the familiar voice of one of his clients. Opening the door, he could clearly make out the face of Francis Meswarb in the moon light. With his heavy German accent Francis explained his reason for late night's interruption "I got a horse, Doc, that can break wind but can't make manure."

Overhearing the conversation from the front bedroom, Marilane nearly fell out of bed laughing. Joe, however, put on the best professional demeanor that he could muster at that hour and went back inside to dress. Leaving the house Joe walked to his car slipping into the driver's seat. The engine of his Model-A grumbled to life and he followed Francis to his farm.

Arriving at the farm he walked into the barn to see the horse in question, and without a doubt it was in distress. Even with the dim light of the kerosene lantern, he could make out the grotesquely swollen stomach. Earlier that day Francis had cut corn. Unlike picking corn, this process called for the cutting of the entire plant; the stems, the leaves, and the ears. The entire mass could then be chopped into silage. The horse somehow had been able to gain access to this green corn and proceeded to gorge itself. Once ingested, the fresh concoction caused a prolific gas production which distended the poor animal's stomach. Joe after inspecting the beast suspected that its stomach might have been ruptured. Compelled to try something to save the horse, the dreary-eyed vet injected fluids into the animal, protecting it from dehydrating. Then he had Francis walk the patient around the barn. Twice they went through that procedure; injecting fluids, and then, with the lantern in one hand and the horse's halter in the other, the farmer walked the afflicted animal around the farm yard. While Francis went for his walk Joe returned to the car and rested his head on the back of the seat.

Over an hour into the "treatment" Francis had just returned the horse to its stall but the stricken animal was still in distress. Joe once more filled his syringe and injected the horse. The syringe's plunger had no more reached its bottom and the needle was withdrawn for the horse's hide when the wide-eyed equine reared up on its back legs and lunged forward, falling on the weathered boards at the front of stall. Then there was silence. The thousand pound steed was dead and straddling the stall. Both men stood there in amazement for several seconds. But then Francis turned to Joe and asked, "Doc, did that shot kill the horse?".

Weary but maintaining a calm tone Joe replied, "No, Francis, he has been dying all night."

When the shock of the moment passed, the farmer grappled with a more pressing dilemma. He had half a ton of horse flesh draped over a stall, and within an hour it would become rigid with rigor mortis. Turning again to Joe who was by now packing up his grip, he asked "How am I going to get him off the manger?"

The night was already creeping toward morning, and Joe, with his enthusiasm all but exhausted, stopped half way through the barn door and answered in a firm voice, "Francis, I haven't the foggiest idea!".

Joe could definitely feel the predawn chill as he turned his 75-dollar Model-A around and headed for home and hopefully a few hours sleep.

During the next three years, Marilane would have two more children. After three years of renting, the couple now had three children all compressed into the little house. Each year had been punctuated by a new family member. Mike was an infant when the move was made from Inez's house. By November of that first year, Thomas James had joined them. The very next year Daniel John moved in with his brothers in the second bedroom. If this pace continued, the family would soon grow completely out of the house, and it was time for Joe and Marilane to own their own home.

The old Ribbeck house, a stout looking two story house on Division Street, came up for sale. The asking price was $7,500. The facts surrounding the purchase were inexact; there could have been a realtor, possibly Tom Bump who was a balding little man with an office on Main Street incongruously veneered to have a log cabin look. Whether negotiated through Tom Bump or not, the heart of the deal was the financing, and the bulk of that came from Lillian Devine with a loan of $5,000. In his heart Joe may have been reluctant to accept the loan from his mother-in-law because later he would express great pride in paying the loan off very quickly. Like all new home owners, they took a keener interest in the property than they had in their rental. Though beautiful in their eyes, the house wasn't without problems.

The back porch facing the driveway behind their house was falling down, the flooring and steps rotting away. This porch surrounded the back door exiting out of the kitchen which had been remodeled previously and quite bizarre; when the prior remodel was completed they had walled off a room completely without access. During the same remodeling, the upstairs bathroom had taken on a dysfunctional shape which Joe referred to only as "unique." To rectify the home's numerous problems Joe called on the Hammeters. An old family name in the area, the Hammeters had originally been farmers living out by the one-room school house where Inez had taught. The family had since left farming and moved into carpentry. Claire represented the second generation in this business. He had studied under his father. They were craftsmen, precise in their work, showing up early every day on the job to sharpen the handsaws and organize their tools. Claire may have been particular in work but the old German in him felt free to express his opinion even if it didn't agree with that of his clients. Claire assaulted the remodel. Always calling Marilane "Mary," he basically told her how he thought it should "best" be done. After several weeks of hammering and sawing, the house became quite livable.

Residing back in town now, the Sextons were part of a neighborhood infested with a horde of children all around the ages of the boys and the newest addition, Peggy. The whole neighborhood wasn't very large, running just two blocks from Main Street then south to the definitive edge of town. Leaving town, Division Street extended southward, passing between Meier's pasture and the old sewage treatment plant. Then once over the Little Wapsi, it went past the Catholic Cemetery, the remnants of the old horse track, and the Wescott farms. This small realm would comprise the center of the Sexton family's world for the next three decades.

The neighborhood held a diverse group of people. On one corner butting up against Main Street, sat the Potratz house, a new brick colonial. Its mere presence spruced up the area. Across the street was the little Murphy house. Lawrence's windowed mother lived there. No one really saw her that much, but she was a kindly lady. Just outside her side door was an apple tree just meant for climbing. When the apples were still green, the local kids could scramble up its low hanging branches and pluck the fruit. Mrs. Murphy surely was aware of the periodic swarm of youngsters climbing in her tree but she never seemed to mind. Next to the Potratz house was a much more modest home owned by the Whitefords. He was the local barber, and the children of the neighborhood were cautious passing this home, unlike Mrs. Murphy's should the Whiteford's cocker spaniel be out, they would take care, since the mutt would bite. At the end of the block lived the Whitmires, Doc and Virginia. It was a proper, well kept home and only one house removed from the Sextons'. It was a great arrangement for Marilane and Virginia, given their friendship. Also the Whitmires' youngest child, Bill, was Tom's age and they grew up together as best of friends. As years passed Bill, who was a good bit younger than his siblings, was accepted as a quasi member of the Sexton family. It would be impossible to calculate the number of meals he ate with the Sextons.

Across Division in a nondescript square, two-story home lived the Kroegers. Andy Kroger sold John Deere implements and tractors. He and his wife Emee had four children similar in age to the Sexton children. The ill-fated family would have more than their share of tragedy. Their third child was a girl named Sue who was diagnosed with degenerative muscle condition in both legs, which became shriveled and bent. To straighten her legs, both were broken and set. Sue would spend six months in a cast from her waist down. After she was confined the entire summer to a renovated bedroom downstairs just off their kitchen, when the cast was finally removed, her legs would not ever function again. By fall she had been outfitted with crutches and stainless steel braces for her legs. When she swung herself on the crutches, the screeching of the metal announced her presence. She had an indomitable spirit, however, and refused to accept that she was not a normal child. Probably because of that, all the other children seemed to accept her as such, giving little notice to her crutches.

Years later the black hand of fate would visit the Kroeger home again. Their eldest son, Wayne, somewhat of a free spirit, fell in with friends who had taken up the new sport of sky diving. On a pleasant Sunday afternoon Wayne, with some cursory training, went up with his friends in a small plane for his first "jump." After exiting the plane a couple thousand feet above Iowa farmland something went horribly wrong. Wayne's chute never opened.

Andy Kroeger sold green John Deere farm equipment, partnering with Bill DeHaven who operated a branch of the business in nearby Oelwein, Iowa. Bill had a wife and two sons who lived in Sumner, but Bill himself preferred to live in Oelwein. For a small town, this arrangement was a budding plant for the fruit of gossip. Ironically, Andy's major competitor, Adolph Miller, lived across the street from him and next door to the Sextons. He owned the implement dealership selling red Farmall Tractors, and at that time the red tractors were the most popular implement with farmers in the area. This fact may have been due to Adolph more than the quality of the equipment.

Adolph and Helen lived in a neat and tidy two story home which fit their personalities. The couple had three grown daughters, so when the Sextons moved in they assumed the personae of kindly grand parents. They rapidly befriended the young couple with their ever expanding family group. Adolph, a short stocky man, plain spoken and kind, was never without a cigar clinched between his teeth. He may have lit his cigars from time to time, but he mainly chewed them. Helen was a stout, large-bosomed woman who was quite affectionate. As surrogate family members they both helped out Joe and Marilane with now seven children. Helen, and even Adolph, would spend time down at the Sextons, Helen helping Marilane and Adolph reading to the children.

The garage was behind the house, and this where Joe usually parked. The last year they lived there, Dan was three years old and head strong even by that time. One day, convinced that he wanted to go with his father, Dan stood in the drive way crying as his father drove away. With a full view of the whole episode from her kitchen window, Helen watched as Dan threw himself on the gravel in a tantrum, sobbing uncontrollably. Lovingly Helen walked out her back door and picked up the sniffling toddler wiping the accumulated snot from the bottom half of his face and helping him back into the house.

The Farmall Dealership the Millers owned was an easy three block walk down Main Street from Division. Even as small children, the Sextons were free to wander the town, and the dealership was a popular destination when Helen was working there. She was always good for a warm greeting and a dime for each one of the kids. At a time when a movie ticket was fifteen cents, a dime was a great deal of money, enough to buy a pocket full of candy. The relationship with the Millers would be life long. The gentle duo would retain the pseudo grandparent status even after the children were grown. In fact they would be an intrinsic part of the Sexton Christmas tradition.

After a little less than two years the Sextons moved but just right next door. The Mathers' house came up for sale. A little larger than the Ribbeck home, it had been owned by Wade Mathers who lived with his sister, Julia. There was little doubt among the neighbors which of the siblings was the dominate individual. Her brother Wade often could be seen standing outside the house smoking, or restricted to the basement during inclement weather. Julia wouldn't tolerate smoking in the house, even though cigarette smoking was a prevalent habit indulged by a large percentage of adults. So Wade would have to suffer the indignity of standing outside the back door puffing on his cigarette with the neighbors passing by, no doubt chuckling to themselves.

The house had come up for sale with Wade's untimely death. When Joe bought the home for 8,500 dollars from Wade's estate in March of 1950, his college buddy, Lawrence Murphy's dad, J.P. Murphy handled the deal. Joe sold the Ribbeck house for tidy profit, receiving 7,800 dollars, 300 more than he paid for it two years before. This savvy transaction, assured Joe that he had slipped out from under his father's financially debilitated shadow.

Marilane is pictured holding Mary while seated on the front porch of the Mather's house. Also captured were Mark, Peggy, and Grandma Lillian who is standing beside her suit case, so she was just arriving or preparing to leave.

Post War Boom

At the time the Sextons moved into the Division Street property, the Second World War had ended and the thinking among the "great minds," who were half a country away from Iowa, was that there was chance American could slip back into a depression. With twelve million men coming back from the war, the labor market they thought would be flooded, and with a decrease in government spending the domestic consumption and private investment would certainly be depressed. Again these great minds were dead wrong; the consumption of goods rose by 22% in 1947, and private investments increased by 223%. The shift from a wartime economy to peacetime prosperity was breathtaking. America had a positive trade deficit with the rest of the world which the US would enjoy for the next decade. Price controls and government directives on consumption of certain products were finally lifted. Along with the GI bill and decreased taxes, the country experienced economic expansion. Americans saw their standard of living go up and experienced an increase in economic opportunities. The country, by and large, also felt its new status as a world power. The next 12-15 years would be the halcyon days for the country during the twentieth century.

The waves of economic good fortune which rolled across the country also washed through Sumner. By 1948 the town could boast nearly a hundred thriving businesses and even had an airport run by Ray Lauterback. By May the following year just west of the little rental house workmen were pouring cement footings for a twenty-two-bed community hospital. Donations from the town citizens paid for the construction of the entire edifice. The community was totally self-reliant, with no need to go begging to the government. On Main Street a tall eye catching marquee protruded from the new movie theatre Harry Pace built to replace the aging Opera House. Even the dining room of the Hotel Charles was upgraded, with booths installed against the walls. An enormous Coca Cola sign was painted the side wall of McAloons' dry goods store on the corner of Main and Carpenter. It covered the previously painted placard which carried the names of the men from Sumner who had served in the war. Across Main Street from Inez's house, a yellow glazed brick façade covered three new buildings. Murray Gissel had sold his implement dealership, which had previously occupied that site. Now DeHaven and Kroeger would move in with their green machinery. Beside them A.H. Huebner had his car dealership and showroom selling Chryslers and Plymouths. Next to that Dr. Sexton had a new 13 x 29 foot office with a small reception area, office and storage space.

During this era consumer goods and electronics proliferated. Most notable among them was the television. The TV actually had been around since 1939, developed by RCA with the help from a Russian born scientist, Vladimir Zworglien. It took a decade for the novel device to become commercially viable. Up to that time there weren't enough television stations to supply the signals, but once an area had a "reliable" signal, the television became a must-have device, and TV shows multiplied to meet the demand. Between 1949 and 1951, television shows like Milton Bearle, Howdy Doody, Amos and Andy, and Jack Benny became popular. By the early 50's 12 million homes owned TV sets. They grew in number every year, and by the mid fifties viewers would experience the golden age of TV. Besides live TV programs, there were crude attempts to cover sporting events. Most were broadcast from one fixed camera, which produced a picture a present day viewer would find prehistoric. With a grainy and myopic picture, announcers were necessary to describe the fuzzy-looking action on the tube.

Among the millions who had TV's in the fifties were the Sextons. Unlike today's flat screens, TV's then were called "sets" and for good reason. Encased in heavy wooden boxes, TV's were the size of a dresser. Housed in the box, the picture tube looked like a gigantic flood light. The front of the set had an array of knobs to control the channel and focus the picture, which was constantly moving in and out of focus. On top of the TV were the antennae or rabbit ears, usually two metal wires which needed to be carefully aligned to receive the signal. Many times the careful positioning of the antennae was more an art form than skill. Besides the knobs in front, there were buttons in the back near the forest of vacuum tubes. These buttons controlled the vertical and horizontal hold. The TV picture had an annoying tendency to flicker and roll but by very carefully turning these knobs the picture might be stabilized, at least for a while. A modern day TV viewer would probably find this process maddening.

Early TVs, just like AM radio, were also susceptible to any atmospheric change. Like the cracking noise on the radio, the picture on the set could be disrupted by even mild weather changes. If the problem couldn't be corrected manually, the issue probably resided in one of the vacuum tubes in the back of the television set. Like plumbers and carpenters, TV repair men did a brisk business going house to house to repair TVs, since the size and weight made it impractical to "take in" sets to be worked on. Sumner's repair man was Henry Fritz, a disagreeable little man who acted like his job was a major imposition. It's questionable how much talent was needed for his profession, since most service calls involved a large degree of trial and error, the exchanging vacuum tubes until the right combination was found and the picture restored.

Through the 50's, all TVs were black and white. Color wouldn't arrive until the next decade. In the neighborhood, however, a neighboring family, the Hilgendorf's, announced one day they had a color TV. The Hilgendorf boys bragged they now had a color TV, but when eager neighborhood kids went to their house what they saw wasn't exactly what they expected. The color wasn't from the TV tube but rather a shimmering color plastic film taped in front of the picture tube. The images produced had a bizarre and irritating hue.

Four children were added to the Sexton family while they resided in the Mathers house: Margaret Ann (called Peg), April 1948, Timothy Andrew, May 1949, Mark George, August 1950, and Mary Ellen, December 1951. It was at this time we see the first emergence of the bifurcation of the children into the "big kids" and the "little kids." The eldest four were grouped together as the "big kids" and the last four held the lesser title. This nomenclature would follow them into adulthood. The evidence of this occurred when Joe and Marilane took the three oldest to Cleveland, Ohio where Donna and Mardy had recently settled. Several things were noteworthy about this trip. It first set a pattern for family vacations. Never would the entire family travel together; only with fragments of the family would Joe and Marilane be brave enough to travel. Second, this would be the very first trip the family would take. And finally, Cleveland would be terminus of Donna and Marty's nomadic life style, but this wouldn't happen without difficulty.

In the years since both Marilane and Donna were both pregnant with the first children, the Mardorf's had relocated nine separate time. The combination of Karl's death and the gypsy life style forced Donna to demand a change. Mardy, for ten years, had moved from site to site in southern states, when a firm in Cleveland either through word of mouth or because of Marty's reputation contacted Mardy with a job proposal. The firm, Intrusion Prepacked, specialized in soil stabilization and was looking for an engineer who had worked in the field. Mardy, working for years in the Army Corp of engineers, had specialized in building and maintaining dikes along rivers and reservoirs. He was an ideal candidate for the Cleveland firm.

Donna and Mardy drove all the way to Cleveland to interview for the position. Parking in the lot in front of the firm, Mardy went in by himself, Donna preferring to stay in the car. After waiting for an anxious period of time, Donna couldn't wait to hear from Mardy as he returned to the car. Settling into the driver's seat, Marty casually related that he wasn't impressed by the interview and he didn't think the job was right for him. With the prospect of returning to their previous itinerant lifestyle, Donna's demeanor changed. Sternness could be read in her face and heard in her voice. "You'll go right back in there and tell them you'll take the job." Mardy knew the tone and though a man of great kindness, he couldn't stand up against his wife in her present state. It is doubtful whether he mounted a defense or not, but he did take the job and they would live for several years in Cleveland.

This is the first recorded case of Donna's intimidation of her husband, but it wouldn't be the last. The practice would become an imbedded part of their relationship, easily recognized by family members and friends. Through several memorable incidents, Marty never lost his temper even though observers would comment (but never to Mardy) that a profane verbal defense by Mardy would not have been out of line.

The Fifties

The mid point of the twentieth century was anything but mediocre. Opening the century with an industrial revolution on steroids and the accidental presidency of a man who would forever alter the office (Teddy Roosevelt), America was hoisted onto the world stage and drawn into a First World War which was renowned for its mechanized slaughter. The first attempt then to regulate the unpredictability of nations by the forming of a "league of nations," which failed in the United States Senate, was followed years later by an economic bubble that finally burst, spreading misery and chaos across the globe. From these events arose another conflict consuming millions of people and reorganizing the bases of power, leaving just two great world powers locked in a "cold war." The two nations were intractably separated by economic theories as diverse as oil and water.

Washing on shore out of this historical storm, obscure little Sumner, Iowa and the nation as a whole would actually see prosperous times and rapid technological development. The interstate system based on the Autobahn of Germany would be implemented by President Dwight Eisenhower; the rise of the suburbs allowing working men and women to escape from the inner cities, the pooling of stores in shopping malls, and the introduction of credit cards democratizing credit would all surface in this decade. Television, with iconic shows like "I Love Lucy," "Walt Disney," and the "Mickey Mouse Club," would be seen weekly by millions of Americans. Music would forever be changed by a new genre called rock and roll, with unlikely idols like Elvis Presley and Buddy Holly and the Crickets. In science, DNA was discovered, unlocking the template to life, and doctors for the first time had the audacity to transplant organs from one human being into another. Auto design entered a new era with such vehicles as the '57 Chevy and Ford Thunderbird. With jet planes, countries started to seriously consider new faster modes of transportation and a forever altered style of aerial warfare and Werner Von Braun's dream of voyaging into space became a reality. America's archrival, the Soviet Union, entered space first, placing into orbit a small satellite called Sputnik, a basket ball size object more symbolic than functional. Explorer I, launched shortly after Sputnik, was the US's entry into the space race.

Television left its imprint on sport expanding its exposure. Golf had new found popularity with telecasts of tournaments giving rise to new entities like Arnie's army, the ardent fans of swash buckling golfer Arnold Palmer. Football saw the NFL and AFL extend its fan base, and baseball, still America's pastime, served up live games no longer restricted to the radio broadcasts so familiar to George Sexton. George's team, the dynastic New York Yankees, claimed 8 out of 10 pennants in the decade and their team roster was a who's who of baseball, with Mickey Mantle, Roger Maris, Yogi Berra, Whitey Ford, Phil Rizzuto, Billy Martin, Hank Bauer, and Enos Slaughter. George, if he had lived, would have been thrilled by the team at the very apex of its power.

The cold war, a moniker first spelled out in the "Iron Curtain" speech delivered by Winston Churchill in Missouri, was a struggle for political spheres of influence between the communists and capitalists, played out across the surface of the entire earth. The friction between the two camps was bound to ignite a fire some place, and when it did it was in the small peninsula protruding from Manchuria: Korea. The war or "police action" was a test of the two wills and the limits of the nuclear age. When Douglas McArthur pushed the North Koreans to the Chinese border and it looked like China would enter the fray, McArthur contemplated using nuclear weapons, but Harry Truman, the first and so far the last president to authorize using atomic bombs, refused to allow it, and he sacked the general at the same time. The world then had its first taste of the new nuclear reality. In America, the nation came to grips with this reality. Part of the new lexicon included SAC (Strategic Air Command), fall-out shelters, and practice drills in schools for nuclear attack. Unthinkable just years before, these terms became part of the public psyche.

In small rural towns like Sumner, the residents were aware of the nuclear threat but as with any unrealized horrific situation their mind tended to deeply discount the danger in the face of pressing day-to-day events. Sumner and its civic leaders were more concerned with the town's newfound prosperity than with any distant crisis. Posting signs on the major roads leading to Sumner, the billboards read "Sumner City with a Future," giving voice to the citizen's enthusiastic view of their prospects. In 1950 and 1951 on Ray Lautterbach's airport just south of town, over 150 planes flew in for the annual "fly-in-meal." With so much perceived interest in the local airport, the city council passed a recommendation that Sumner should pursue the idea of becoming a hub for commercial air travel connecting to cities like Minneapolis and Chicago. The absurdity of the idea, when viewed in retrospect, did not occur to the city council who were obviously swept away by their grandiose vision of Sumner's potential. It was an era when something that far fetched might just seem possible. It was a grand time to be an American.

Sumner has a Makeover

It was five in the morning when sparks erupted from the old frayed wiring in the wall of the hotel. Mere moments later, room number 38, on the second floor of the Charles Hotel, was engulfed in flames. A gentleman guest from Joplin, Missouri sounded the alarm as the fire was already progressing into the hallway. Now awakened, the twenty-one occupants of the second floor had no escape but was the stairway, which had its access blocked by flames. Antiquated but functional, escape ropes stored in each room allowed all the guests to flee to safety in different degrees of dress. Within 30 minutes two volunteer fire departments were on site; both Tripoli and Sumner fire departments manned their thick fire hoses, pouring water onto the blaze that illuminated the entire block. Helping man the fire hoses was volunteer fireman, Joe Sexton, who knew the building intimately from his childhood.

The combined fire departments gained control of the conflagration, saving the front half of the hotel which contained the lobby, the Western Union office and the Bowling Brothers' office, which held a stack of tires and a ton for flaxseed stored inside. The blaze and commotion had awakened the surrounding residents, among them Mrs. Kroblin (Allen's mother), who opened their gas station located across Carpenter Street and busied herself brewing coffee for the firemen and gathering bystanders. The sun was already above the horizon when the fire finally appeared to be subdued. It was July 11, 1952.

The second fire in the corner hotel spelled its doom. It would be razed with only the stone foundation left in place. On its footprint, Dr. Jim Whitmire would construct a modern medical building. The one story facility encased in fashionable narrow red brick had with its construction only enhanced the community's optimistic perspective.

This same period saw the town raise money to build a swimming pool on top of the hill at then end of Pleasant Street. Again the city accomplished the feat without need of any government funds. Sumner also pursued plans for building new schools needed to handle the spike in population resulting from the post-war baby boom. And on the east side of town a new bowling alley went up. In the absence of automatic pin setters, young boys from town could secure work, which required them to be suspended above the bowling lanes manually setting pins. Right next to the bowling alley a new 50's phenomenon sprang up, the drive-in. Inventively named the "Drive-In," the restaurant experience was completed with car hops. Downtown, the Overton Chemical building which sat north of the back door of the bakery was razed to the ground, and Jim McAloon erected a modern super market with an interior spacious enough incorporate all the grocery shopper's needs from baked goods to the meat counter. The little corner groceries of which Sumner still had two and the butcher shop down by the light plant, all over time would be gradually phased out. Supermarkets were the new face of progress. Any truly modern town had one.

Modernization extended also to the school system. In 1948 the local school board hired Malcom M. Rogers as their new superintendent. A large man both in stature and personality, MM would shepherd, or more correctly, dictate the changes necessary for the school's metamorphosis. The baby boom had strained the present system. One room schools, like one where Inez had taught, were antiquated, and high school, which once had been an option, now was now considered the norm for all students. Prior to closing the network of rural schools, M.M. Rogers initiated a building program. The Durant Grade School previously built two blocks west of the old school (built in 1903) was only five years old when it was tripled in size, making it capable of holding three classrooms of each grade. A block and a half north of the Durant school, in 1959, a cornerstone was laid for a new high school on land basically confiscated from the Meadowbrook County Club. M.M. Rogers, his black hair parted down the middle, had approached the board of the golf club, bullying the poor members. He had eyed that property for his new school, and heaven help the man who might stand in his way. In retrospect, the changes instituted to Sumner schools were dramatic. Things needed to be decided promptly and with conviction. Decisions by committee are laborious and normally half hearted. Having a firm hand at the helm proved crucial even though like any community project there were just about as many opinions as there were citizens. M. M. proved to be the right man at the right time. One sad note: years later after he had retired he would commit suicide by running his car in a closed garage.

By the mid fifties, construction was complete on the two schools and consolidation could begin. Fall arrived and it was time to test the new system. All one-room schools were closed for the last time in the spring prior to the consolidation. It wasn't the case that the number of students couldn't support the number of one-room schools, there were still a multitude of 'farm kids.' In 1949 the total number of farms in the US peaked at 7 million, each one occupied by a family. There would be a gradual decline in family farms from that year on but in the fifties every section of land still had an average of three to four families living on the 640 acres. The majority of these farms had dairy cattle, hogs, chickens, and corn, beans, oats, and alfalfa fields. The work was very labor intensive; the more hands available the better. The basic economics dictated that more children produced more help on the farm, and all those little workers would need to go to school.

The advent of the school bus made country schools impractical and for Sumner's school system, buses would be in high demand. At its peak in 1960, Sumner schools owned fifteen school buses, each with its own route. Parked end to end they stretched for two city blocks. Boldly marked with numbers that corresponded to routes, they were easily identified by student.

Given today's enrollment the numbers during this period seem hard to imagine. Today, Sumner school, after combining with neighboring Fredericksburg, has only 852 students from kindergarten to the senior year, but in 1960 that number was 1706 students for Sumner alone. Today Sumner can function with only four bus routes, unlike the fleet of those by gone days. During those days the shear number of buses required a strong hand on the tiller, and M.M. Rogers was just the man. Today, fog, extreme cold or the hint of snow will either delay or close the school. But M.M. believed we were all are made of sterner stuff. Then, even impending blizzards could not sway M.M. to alter the school day. On two separate occasions busses were caught in raging snow storms and their passengers were forced to seek shelter in the nearest farm house. Driver and students would end up being uninvited guests for anywhere up to 24 hours until the roads could be cleared. For all the hand wringing no one was ever injured, and to this day students who found themselves marooned recall the experience as an adventure.

Cognizant of all the new business and the expanding schools, a growing number of local businessmen decided to put together a promotional film. Appearing now grainy and amateurish, it was only fifteen minutes long. Narrating the "documentary" chronicling Sumner's growth was Jim McAloon, who made a pointed effort to highlight the new hospital, the swimming pool, the two new schools, and the host of thriving businesses as selling points for any enterprising person wanting to expand or relocate. Jim's voice exuded the sincere optimism of his time. With great pride he also pointed to the fifty new houses built in the previous year as part of the town's trajectory.

One thing Jim failed to mention was that many of those homes were the result of one business in town, Kroblin Trucking. The company was the brain child of Allen Kroblin, the same man whose wedding Joe and Marilane had attended years before. Allen's trucking firm was an off shoot of his father Elmer's company. With a wagon and a team of horses Elmer started Kroblin Drag Line a few years after George Sexton came to town. He had a thriving business transporting materials in and around Sumner. By 1918 he had modernized his business, buying a square, snub-nosed truck with hard rubber wheels. Without power steering, truck driving then was hard work, demanding brute physical strength. Twenty years later, Elmer expanded again calling his firm Kroblin Transfer. By then he was carrying perishables and livestock on interstate routes. The new firm had only been in existence a few years when Elmer died, leaving his wife Olinda and high school son, Allen, to carry on in the business. Eight years later, in 1946, Olinda sold out. Allen then kicked around for two years until he decided to go back into the trucking business. Starting with only a pick-up truck and the mail route from the post office to the train depot, Allen gradually expanded. With Loyal Frisch (who would later buy the Ritz Café) as vice president, his single pick up truck by 1956 had grown into a fleet of eighteen wheelers. It had grown so fast and large enough that it warranted a much larger facility. Just west of town, past the Sunset Motel, Allen built a modern looking brick building on an acre of land. The facility had massive service bays for the semis and was fronted by an office complex large enough to accommodate the nearly twenty people necessary to run the business.

Now named Kroblin Refrigerated Xpress, the company's front office kept track of the several hundred trucks carrying goods across the county and its nearly 300 employees. On one side of each truck was the Kroblin emblem, the same one Elmer had once used on his snub nosed truck, a large circle with KROBLIN inscribed around its edge and a single feathered wing propelling the circle forward. Disappointedly Kroblin Trucking would outgrow Sumner and move to Waterloo then on to Tulsa, Oklahoma. Allen, ever the river boat gambler, would be hounded by different government agencies for years; prominent among them was the Internal Revenue Service.

Moving to the Farm

Wescott was a name that appeared among the eminent Sumner families at the turn of the century. The name was associated with the height of the horse racing craze and with the firm, Wescott and Winks. Though the family ultimately sold out to Leo Winks in the 20's, they remained large land owners with hundreds of acres just south of town. As with many family enterprises as the land passed from generation to generation bits and pieces were sold off and broken up among the descendents. One parcel which sat out past the Catholic Cemetery consisted of two farms remaining in the family hands. The original home place on the east side of the gravel road was owned by George Wescott who tinkered as a gunsmith and part time farmer. On the west side the farm was owned by his sister, Olive, a spinster second grade school teacher who had it worked by a ne'er-do-well live-in hired hand, David. George decided to put his farm on the market because he had his eye on buying the old Stephen Cass house.

There were two grand homes in Sumner both on Railroad Street. The one on the west side of the street was built by Stephen Cass, an imposing Victorian with a wrap around porch, situated on a large tree-shaded lot. Right across the street was an even more august home. That house, with a covered carriage entrance that led into an elegant foyer with a great curved stairway, was the mansion built by Stephen's son who was married to an actress from New York. The only way she would consent to live in Sumner was if her husband would erect the grandest home in town for her. It is not recorded how she adapted to Sumner's social environment, but conjecture would lead one to assume that she did poorly.

With his family swelling, Joe Sexton leapt at the opportunity to own a farm. In a very short time he closed the deal with George Westcott in March of 1954. It would prove to be an ideal purchase. Just ¾ of a mile outside the town, the family had the best of both worlds; the space and freedom of farm life and ready access to the town's activities.

The family farm George sold still exemplified the flamboyance of his ancestor's status of sixty years before. Very much a working farm at one time, the barn, the hog house, and the corn cribs were all neatly aligned north of the central driveway. To the south, the two story colonial sat in the middle of a spacious yard. Two side walks arched toward the side door by the kitchen. One sidewalk, stretching one hundred feet from drive to door, tastefully set the house back from the working segment of the farm. The other walk led to a long squat building tucked in the northeast corner of the yard. Here George had had his gun smithing shop. The building's roof sloped south to north, with a wide expanse of paned windows comprising the southern wall to help to illuminate the shop.

The yard, full of mature maple trees, was separated from the drive by a large hedge. And in the isolated confines of the yard were two cement fountains. The largest one sat between the arching sidewalks directly in front of the kitchen window. Of an oval shape nearly 12 feet across at its widest point, the cement pond had an ornate spout in its center. Behind the house, out the screen door of the small backporch, and under the branches of an elegantly spreading hard maple was a smaller fountain. Circular in shape, this fountain was only 5-6 feet across also with a central water jet. When Joe and Marilane moved in they disconnected both fountains. With several toddlers wondering the premises the risks outweighed any aesthetic value the fountains might impart to their home.

Joe had already finished the fence by the time this picture was taken, but Claire Hammeter hadn't commenced the addition. The southern porches were still intact.

The oval pond was the first to go, being broken up and buried, leaving only the outer ring noticeable during the dry months of summer. Elegant at one time, it was now just an eyesore. Joe had his own vision of what he wanted his farm to look like. Besides the pond, the hedges fronting the yard had to go. With the help of friends, he laboriously ripped out all the plants and leveled the ground. To add a touch of class he installed a wooden fence around the entire yard. Wooden square posts notched to receive three boards were set in the newly exposed ground, aligned perfectly so the fence ran straight and true. The painstaking work soon produced a tasteful addition to the farm, as the fence would be painted white to match all the other buildings on the farm. The major drawback to the oil-based paint used on the fence was inevitable yearly bubbling and chipping, which required repainting on a regular basis. Until all the children had grown and left home, painting would be an intrinsic part of summer life.

The exterior painting would need to wait because the house's interior needed immediate attention. Harold Minkel, the town's painter was called in to help. Harold was well into the task when one day Joe was home for lunch and walked over by the busy painter. Pulling up an empty paint pail to sit on, he mused for a minute and then presented Harold with a proposition. Joe hadn't sold the Mather's house yet, so he offered up the idea of having Mr. Minkel buy his house. Harold had never owned a house because he had never been able to secure financing. Joe threw up this plan; Harold would use the money Joe owed him for painting his house as the down payment, and then Joe would take a contract on the remainder. Harold gave it a little thought and accepted the deal. With a paint brush in his left hand and extending his right, he bought a house that afternoon. Later Harold would swear that it was the best deal he ever made.

The barn, which had not seen much use for many years, was jacked up, and the lower three feet of the rotting wood sill was cut away. Joe wasn't about to have crumbling building on his farm. To replace this section of the barn Joe had masons lay modern-looking, red glazed blocks, giving the building a clean appearance.

While the fence and barn took shape, Claire Hammeter commenced work on the house. The Sexton's eighth child was on the way, and the present home's three bedrooms would not be sufficient to house the growing family. The stairway to the second floor ascended from the north corner of the living room terminating in a tiny hallway that branched off to the four second story rooms: to a bathroom without a shower, just a tub, to the southeast a narrow bedroom overlooking the roof to the back porch, to the north a large bedroom truncated on its north wall by the attic stairs, and to the southeast a bedroom with two closets and panel glass door which opened onto a second story sun porch. The porch afforded a comfortable view over the countryside, but this porch and its twin below it would need to be sacrificed. Claire and his crew set to work removing both porches, since the only logical choice available was to expand the house in that direction. Increasing the length of the house by nearly a third, the addition which replaced the porch would hold only two bedrooms, but in this case two would be adequate.

Upstairs the spacious bedroom Claire built would be called the "dorm." Knotty pine siding covered the walls and ceiling. Two long closets with metal sliding doors consumed most of the west wall. Into the south wall, Claire built in four desks with bookshelves above. The room outfitted with bunk beds would be the "big boy's room."

Below the dorm was the master bedroom and adjoining bathroom. Within months of the Sextons taking possession, Claire had finished his work. Now there would be space for the ever increasing family. Within eighteen months it would need to house 12 people. Now the upstairs became the solo realm of the children. Peg, the oldest girl got a room by herself, in the northeast bedroom. Mary and Theresa shared the room across from the bathroom, and the center bedroom was allotted to Tim and Mark.

The second story bathroom would be a continuous point of contention. The obvious disparity between genders played out in verbal confrontations which only intensified as the children grew older. Privacy was always an elusive commodity, and the eternal fight over the position of the toilet seat would never reach a conclusion. Downstairs the master bedroom was emblematic of the social structure of the family. The separation of the master bedroom from the children's bedrooms had both a physical and mental element. Joe and Marilane, though they loved the children, always put their relationship first. Joe, in a letter, would applaud the fact that Marilane always was a wife first and a mother second.

Even with a house full of children, the romance hadn't ended.(Taken in the living room shortly after the addition.)

Among all his skills, mechanical prowess was never a strong point of Joe's. He could execute minor repairs, but by and large he left most such duties to people proficient in that area. To help with the plans for the backyard, he summoned the assistance of the school's vocational education instructor, Forrest Bear (that was his name!). Forest, a stocky man, had a great sense of humor and boundless energy. Enlisted by Joe, he enthusiastically tackled the proposed backyard projects.

Joe wanted an outdoor grill, but it had to be able to service a crowd. Forest came up with a solution. Out the back door beneath this gigantic cottonwood tree, which projected skyward towering 50' over its neighboring maples, Forrest with Joe's help, hammered together 2 by 6's to make a cement base for a grill. An old cast iron cauldron a foot and a half deep and three feet across would suffice as the grill. While the poured cement was still wet, Joe and Forrest lowered the cauldron in, assuring a perfect fit. To fabricate a grilling surface, Forest cut with an acetone torch a worn steel grate (used to separate stone) in a circle which fit neatly into the kettle. This grill became Joe's pride and joy. In fact years later when the house sold, the kettle was one of the few things Joe took with him.

With the grill completed, Forrest put his talents to work again. Out of the 2" tubular steel he fashioned a swing set with three swings and a teeter-totter. The welded steel frame, unlike flimsy aluminum, proved stable and rugged, lasting for years, and years through two generations of children.

Every farm has a plethora of work to be done, and at most farms you can keep a lot of hands busy, especially in the summer. Next to the barn was a repurposed hog house that was renovated into a tool shed. Lawn mowers, bicycles, awnings for the house, and old paint cans were stored haphazardly. Joe bought oil based paint in 5-gallon buckets. The painting ritual usually started in July after the rains of May and June petered out. First it was necessary to pick a paint brush which hadn't stiffened up too severely; next it was necessary to mix the paint. Oil-base paint separates easily, the thick emollient settling to the bottom of the paint can. With a stick the laborious process of mixing the paint would take several minutes till the greasy streaks disappeared from the top of the paint and the thick, goopy paint base finally couldn't be detected on the end of the stir stick. Now it was time to paint. First came scraping the boards that had been painted a few years prior. Then came the tedious back and forth of the paint brush with fair share of the paint being applied to surrounding vegetation and the painter.

Painting was an annual event but not the only summer chore. Joe, before leaving for work in the morning left instructions with Marilane for that day's tasks. Invariably there would be grumbling from the minions, but his retort would always be the same. "If you get it right at it, it won't take but a few minutes." That never proved to be the case, however, and this always led to more grumbling. The end of summer didn't mean the end of work; Joe usually raised livestock, so chores were a continual, year-around activity.

Joe had a penchant for raising sheep. He never considered raising hogs or cattle. They were more labor intensive, and sheep were docile and could be manhandled even by teenagers, but that didn't mean there wasn't work involved. March was the most time consuming month. This is when the ewes lambed. Without fail during that month there would be a late winter snow storm. Normally it was still dark when it was necessary to trek across newly formed snow drifts to reach the barn. Climbing the wooden ladder into the hay mow, the workers would throw down a couple of bails still with the sweet alfalfa smell of last years cutting into the sheep pens below. After removal of the two twines the bails were broken apart, the compressed flakes of hay parceled out to the lambing pens. On those days when the wind outside was blowing snow down the driveway, inside the barn was a tranquility serenaded by bleating lambs. The newborn lambs appeared dark colored at first, their fleece soft with the feel of Berber carpet and with a smell that was somehow pleasing. Not restricted to lambs and human babies, newborns all seem to exude an aroma which is not disagreeable; this has to contribute somehow with the survival of the species.

Of all sheep varieties, Joe preferred Suffolk sheep. They are a large breed with black heads and legs which gave them a rather clean appearance. Docile and not the heaviest of sheep, the ewes might grow to two hundred pounds. They would lamb once a year, and twins were not uncommon. Not with Suffolk alone but true of all sheep, there was a problem with orphaned lambs, a situation that occurred more often than one would expect. Either the ewe would die, or one of the twin lambs; if the latter, the ewe sometimes rejected the surviving lamb. Either way, drastic measures were implemented to save the lamb. One method used if a ewe had one of its lambs die would be to tie the fleece of the deceased lamb to an orphaned individual. The scent of the dead lamb tricked the ewe into accepting the orphan. The other way, much more time consuming, was to bottle feed the lamb. On more than one occasion lambs could be found penned up in the corner of the kitchen being fed by one of the children. Months after lambing came the next chore; vaccinating and docking tails. All lambs are born with long tails, but for cleanliness, the tail is cut, leaving only a few inches of flesh. Even with shortened tails the wool had a tendency to collect feces, and the build-up would be referred to as "dingle berries." Though the problem still occurred with docked tails it would be much worse with a full length tail. Docking tails and shearing wool all required the sheep to be corralled in the barn. Without fail the process of herding the flock into the barn on the Sexton farm ran the same pathetic course.

One door was strategically opened on the back of the barn. One unlucky soul would remain in the barn manning the door while Joe and the other boys gradually herded the sheep toward the open door. The flock, now pushed toward the barn, would start to run in, then, usually when the last remnants of the flock were about to enter, one lone lamb would buck the trend and leap out. This started a chain reaction, and all the sheep would follow the roguish animal out of the barn. Verbally the fireworks would start. The boy positioned inside the barn normally was the first to draw the ire of his brothers, who now needed to round up the flock again. The incriminations would fly. It probably can be safely said that it normally took a couple attempts to finally secure the entire flock in the barn.

Though sheep were the predominant livestock, the Sextons did manage to have other animals on the farm. Without doubt, the number and variety of farm animals that inhabited the farm were in direct relationship to the number of children. Joe by himself would have never tolerated animals in the same numbers.

While running calls Joe occasionally came across a lame or disabled cow that the farmer had not the time to care for. Trucking the impaired animal home, Joe would allow the beast to become the ward of one of the children. Either it would die, becoming cargo for the rendering truck, or, if it survived, it would be fattened up and sent to the locker, returning in the form of two-and four-pound hamburger packages. Most meat arrived at the Sextons ground-up; the idea of having steaks for twelve people was a completely alien idea. Besides the odd beef roasts, the children grew up thinking shredded and ground was the natural state of beef.

Like sheep, chickens were continuous inhabitants of the farm. Housed in George Wescott's old gun shop, they supplied eggs daily and meat in the fall after butchering. These weren't, however, the plump white birds prevalent today; they were bantams. About three quarters the size of a 'normal' chicken, they were awash in colored plumage. Like Suffolk sheep, Joe had an eye for animals that were slightly different from the norm and bantams, in an array of colors and patterns, satisfied that warrant. One drawback was that the eggs collected from under the pecking hens were very small, just a portion of normal commercial eggs.

Most livestock raised on the farm were for the most part docile and harmless, with the exception of one bantam rooster. Pugnacious, the little bird was protective of his harem, attacking all outsiders no matter their size. Armed spurs on the back's of its legs, he would fly at any interloper, intending to impale them with his spurs. One day Tom became the belligerent fowl's target. With damage done to one of the children, the bird's fate was sealed. He would be repurposed from the chicken coop to the dinner table. Having the last laugh, the bantam, after years of running free in the yard, had developed tough lean muscles. The carcass, though cooked for a long period of time, proved to be entirely inedible.

Harkening back to the days of Daisy, the Shetland pony, Joe deemed it appropriate that his boys also have horses to ride. Mike was the first to get his own horse. Paul Springer, a rotund friend of Joe's, evidently knew something about horses, and through friends had heard of a horse for sale, a cast off circus horse named Tex. A carefully trained performer, the horse did have a limited variety of tricks. His most memorable trick was to bow down on his front knees, surely part of the finality of his act at a circus. Also noteworthy, and probably important to Mike, was that the horse was a palomino. This was the golden age of the palomino, the breed ridden by matinee stars like Roy Rogers and Gene Autry. Along with Davy Crockett coonskin hats, palominos were both the rage during this time.

The next two boys after Mike also got horses, but the quality of horseflesh dropped off abruptly. Tom's horse was Stubby, so named for one of its ears which had had a fair portion accidentally removed. A large bay colored horse, his dubious claim to fame was his advanced age. Like Daisy, Stubby was old enough to outsmart most juveniles who wished to ride him. When it was time to eat, Stubby was the first one to the feed bunk, but approach him with a bridle and his ear lay back and his neck went up. He was old, but how old no one really knew. Tom had owned Stubby for several years when one summer morning he found him dead in the pasture out past the corn crib.

Dan's horse wasn't old like Stubby but was just mean and ugly. He was named Dynamite, and the moniker fit. Calling him a horse may have been an insult to all other horses. Dynamite would fit better into a category of homely mules. With a parrot shaped mouth and a bad disposition, the beast most likely didn't cost Joe much money. Prone to bite and buck, he was more of a pest than a pet. The three boys riding together on disparate animals--a show horse, a geriatric equine, and a mutant strain of horse-- was a sight to behold.

One August afternoon the boys teamed up to incorporate their horses into their seasonal sweet corn business. On the farm a portion of the land was reserved for the sheep pasture. Forming an L shape, it extended from the barn to wrap around the yard. The remaining land was usually planted to corn. Of that field the first two or three rows nearest the pasture were reserved for the planting of sweet corn. The whole area probably comprised an acre or more. With so much sweet corn there was plenty to spare, so the boys established a brisk business selling it in town. Today the numbers sound preposterous but then a dozen ears brought twenty five cents and a bushel sold for a dollar. As petty as it may seem, the boys had one customer who would count the ears in the bushel to make sure she was getting her dollar's worth. Who determined the exact number of ears per bushel has never been settled on, but evidently this woman had the definitive answer.

The majority of the time Marilane supplied the means of delivery, driving one or more of the boys to town, but on this August afternoon the crew decided to blend corn delivery and horseback riding. They found a large black baby carriage discarded in one of the sheds, and filling it with corn they ran a rope from the buggy to the horn on Stubby's saddle. The three boys were just about to depart when their mother walked down the sidewalk from the house, Tim in hand. She wanted them to take their younger brother with them. After a few moments of loud dissension they meekly agreed, and Tom hoisted Tim up, placing him on top of the corn in the carriage. Marilane turned back toward the house as the brothers left the drive and headed north to Sumner.

Its narrow wheels and the road gravel combined to cause the buggy to rattle and jump at the end of the rope behind Stubby. Hearing the sound, the horse turned his head back to see the black wagon following closely behind. The jarring of the carriage also bothered Tim. With Tim near tears, the boys pulled their horses to a stop. Still complaining for having been forced to drag Tim along, Mike grabbed him from his perch on the sweet corn and hefted him to the back of his saddle. Rearranged, the caravan continued their trip. Vexed, Stubby again noticed the pesky black object coming up behind him. Disturbed he increased his pace, but still he couldn't lose his pursuer. Now panicked, he took off for the ditch dislodging his rider, Tom. But still he was dogged by the wagon. In desperation, Stubby turned for home, now at a full run. Turning in the driveway, his ears peeled back, his mane and tail flying, he headed straight for the gate to the pasture at the end of the drive, the baby buggy now spewing corn and flipping violently. Nothing was going to stop the beast. Through the wooden gate he plunged, throwing splintered boards into the air.

Standing at the kitchen sink with a clear view of the driveway,

Marilane saw the entire drama. Assuming Tim was still a passenger in the now destroyed baby buggy, she whirled out the house searching the carnage for her son. With her stomach in a knot she turned to see the boys riding in off the road, Tom on foot and Dan and Mike on horseback with Tim quite safely perched on Tex. After this, the Sexton boys' sweet corn business discontinued horse delivery.

There was far too much sweet corn grown every year to be strictly used by the young entrepreneurs. The bulk of the corn was for the family's consumption. During peak season corn was on the menu every day. Boiled in a huge pot, the mass of corn sat on a plate next to Joe. To cut down on the inherent mess having the children buttering their own ear of corn, Joe did the honor brushing butter on steaming ears and passing them down the line to the children. For several weeks even those with missing incisors got their fill of corn.

This didn't mean corn was off the menu the rest of the year. A nightly ritual during the season, Joe and Marilane "canned" corn. Canning is an inaccurate term. The sweet corn was frozen in quart waxed-paper milk cartons. Since the Sextons had their milk delivered in four-gallon boxes, friends would collect the quart containers for them all year. They would need over a hundred of them. The same huge pot used to cook corn for dinner was filled up again with dozens of ears of yellow corn boiling away, filling the house with its distinctive odor. The production line started at the sink. Boiled corn needed to rinse with cold water just enough to allow handling. Then Joe, working on the counter top, sliced down each ear, peeling off slabs of kernels that fell on the wooden cutting board. He then scooped the yellow kernels oozing with white starch and packed them it into the cartons. After a date was written on the carton the nights tally would be taken to the basement and placed in one of the two large chest freezers, the cartons carefully stacked next to the meat and vegetables for the coming year. Though the cartons were dated, very rarely were there any left over from the previous year. Joe and Marilane became expert at accurately predicting the exact amount needed for the coming eleven months.

Just on the other side of the white board fence that surrounded the yard, Joe installed a gate that opened to the area of the reclaimed pasture, which was tilled and fenced for the family garden. Roughly twenty paces by forty paces, this was no quaint garden plot. It was closer to a commercial sized garden. Surrounded by woven wire fencing to keep the sheep out, the area's rich black soil was carefully turned over every spring leaving a rectangle of soft, sweet smelling soil. Armed with packets of tiny seeds, the Sextons neatly laid out row upon row of vegetables. Each row ended with marked sticks indicating the variety of the vegetable planted, quite necessary until the first few leaves broke the ground. Radishes, onions, and lettuce always comprised the first rows in the front of the garden. Then bush green beans, and tomatoes commanded the center section. Beyond them vine plants like cucumbers and squash would be allowed to spread unrestricted across the earth. As labor intensive as the planting could be the maintenance was even more so. Here is where all those little hands proved useful.

During the growing season, weeding represented the daily drudgery. Schooled in the art of recognizing the early shoots of weeds, the children, after finishing their breakfast, were assigned a set number of rows to weed. First they would run a push tiller down between each row to churn up as many weeds as possible, and then they would drop to their hand and knees, their little fingers carefully pulling the emerging weeds from beside the rows. Invariably a young carrot or onion would be removed, but like breakage in any enterprise this was the price of doing business.

Once free of their gardening duties and also done with chores such as painting, mowing, laundry or housework, the children had the rest of the day to themselves. Whether baseball, golf, swimming or bicycling to see friends was their chosen diversion, there was one firm requirement: be home for dinner. Joe and Marilane gave their children freedom; even at young ages there weren't many restrictions. After the children either walked or biked to town, they were free to wander, but once 6:00 PM arrived all the rambling Sextons needed to be home.

When they were seated around the grand oval dining room table, the daily ritual commenced. Joe served the food, passing each plate down the line. In retrospect there may have been two reasons for this. First, the children understood where the food came from and second, if they already didn't know, this was a not democracy. They had no voting rights. A few more things were very evident. Joe's fraternity experience, emphasizing polite conversation and manners, as intimately woven into the act of eating, and most importantly dinner was a family event for twelve people who formed a single unit.

Conversation revolved mainly around activities. Sports, school functions, and academics comprised the bulk of the give and take. Bickering between children was not tolerated well. The dinner table wasn't the format for disputes; besides, dinner guests happened to be a common occurrence. Bill Whitmire, Becky Harms and a plethora of childhood friends were regularly squeezed in around the table, and their added numbers were hardly noticed.

Discipline at the dinner table was administered by Joe, who was the final arbitrator. Marilane would be vocal in her disciplining, but the children knew the limit had been reached when she invoked their father's name. Joe reflected on discipline years later in a letter from 1991 when he wrote: "Raising 10 kids wasn't all easy. Both mom and I realized we wished our children to grow up to be happy, independent, and strong people. I am sure at times we appeared heartless, but there are certain things that one must learn. We were raising children and not pets".

The total farm experience--the chores, the livestock, and the seeming lax concern for their children's whereabouts presents some questions concerning Joe and Marilane's aims and attitude. Joe's insistence on manners was generally connected to his upbringing and college years, which led to his impression of what constituted a complete man and woman. The freedom of movement that the children enjoyed could be directly linked to their parents' up-bringing in small towns. Both Sumner and Bancroft were closed societies where everyone knew everyone else. Both towns were safe environments, a prime illustration being two disabled individuals, John Paul Sorge and Doug Hennings, who both lived in Sumner during this time. Both men were watched over by the citizens. John Paul, an epileptic, was an adult with limited mental capabilities. He roamed freely throughout the town and was known to suffer seizures in public. Everyone knew who he was, who his parents were, and where he lived. On more than one occasion John Paul was taken home by a sympathetic neighbor. Doug was a slightly different case. He had cerebral palsy and could be seen wheeling himself around the community in a red flyer wagon. Just like Paul he was accepted and watched over. Given these examples it is easy to understand how the town's children were also watched over. The town's adults might not know a child's first name but they very likely knew who their parents were. Anonymity was a very rare commodity in Sumner.

It is worth noting that neither Joe nor Marilane grew up on a farm. The farm experience, quite possibly, had more to do with the size of their family than with any deep seated desire to be farmers. In fact the question might be raised as to how much the family's size influenced the patterns and lifestyle the couple adopted. Later in life the common reaction was to point to Joe and Marilane as the driving force within the family. This might be true but thought might also be given to how much the size of the family influenced their lives.

Partnership

After the war Earl Ritter returned to Sumner and had every intention of resurrecting his vet practice, however, he found his role reversed from when Joe took over his father's practice. In 1942 George's vet practice had all but dried up when his son assumed the reins, Earl then had the lion's share of the surrounding clientele. Now it was June 23, 1948, and when Earl reopened his office in the Munger Building on the west side of Carpenter Street he had only a small smattering of his original business. The gracious reception Earl had given George's replacement years before gave Joe the ideal opportunity to reciprocate in kind.

For three years after Earl returned, the two vet practices coexisted in Sumner. It's hard to say why in 1951 Earl closed his practice and left Joe the sole vet in town, but he had been approached by the National Laboratories, a veterinarian pharmaceutical company out of Minneapolis. Earl took their offer of employment. Working as a salesman he found himself on the road selling drugs to regional vet offices across Minnesota and Iowa. After selling his home in Sumner, he moved his family, Dori, Sue, and Jack, north to the Twin Cities.

It is almost impossible to know exactly what is in a man's mind but ten months prior to his decision to move Earl Ritter had been involved in a very emotionally damaging event. It was late February when Earl had been on a call at the Gaede farm. Lester had a cow 'off feed'. After the morning milking, Lester had left the cows, which would normally have been put to pasture, in the barn before he left for town. Arriving after Lester departed, Earl would need to have Lester's wife show him the cow in question. Earl was standing by the trunk of his car organizing his grip when Mrs. Gaede came out of the house. She'd left two children, four year old Patricia and two year old Paul, alone for a few minutes while she pointed out the ill bovine to Earl. Both Mrs. Gaede and Earl were in the barn when Patricia in a state of panic came running to the barn door and proclaimed her brother Paul was on fire. He'd been playing with matches, and a struck match had fallen on his clothing. Terrified Mrs. Gaede ran toward the house with Earl in pursuit. Flying by the horrified woman, Earl reached the child first. Smothering the flames, he realized the toddler now was in shock and needed immediate help. With only his vehicle on the farm Earl put the children in work car raced to the hospital in Sumner. Severely burned, the young Paul would survive for only two hours.

Two years would pass with Earl driving the back roads of the upper Midwest while Joe, remaining in Sumner, had his practice firmly established and expanding. Earl and Dori still stayed in contact with friends in Sumner all during this time and through them word would filter down to Joe of Earl's disenchantment with his new job. We have to imagine that Joe driven by either a sense of friendship or a true need of assistance with his growing practice reached out to Earl and proposed a partnership. There has never been a mention of any details of the union. Whether money changed hands or it was simply a gentlemen's understanding can't be known from this distant vantage point, but it is clear that in all Joe's writing and papers that there is no reference to a formal partnership agreement. The only thing evident was that an equal partnership which lasted for twenty years and a friendship which would last a lifetime sprang from that meeting.

It would be a partnership which augmented the two diverse personalities. Earl was a blunt man, someone known 'to cut right to the chase.' He'd come flying into the farmyard and bolt from his car already armed for treatment, to impatient for small talk, he'd go right to work and just as quick as his arrival would race to the next call. Joe was more diplomatic and didn't mind talking with the farmers, who were normally starved for a little conversation. Taking a few minutes to ask about the farmer's kids, his wife, or maybe to make some idle conversation about the weather, Joe preferred a little more personal approach, a little like Russ Beebe, the ice man, giving the customer just a small portion of his time. There were farmers who had preferences for one or the other demeanors. The combination proved highly successful.

Both had stories to tell, but possibly Earl's bluntness presented the most color. Once a client named Erhardt Haar called early one evening adamant that one of the vets look at his sick cow. Now Erhardt had a history of calling the office after hours because he never seemed to bother with such details until after his evening milking. Apparently unconcerned with repeatedly calling the vets after hours, Erhardt had become an annoyance to the practice. One day Earl was on call and wasn't going to tolerate this behavior any more. To Erhardt, who had just phoned the office as they were preparing to close, Earl explained that he had several calls to run and it might be around midnight before he would make it to his farm, so would Erhardt wait up for him so they could examine the cow together. Earl's bluff paid off. Erhardt, unwilling to be inconvenienced himself asked if Earl could come in the morning instead which of course the sly Dr. Ritter consented to do.

Another time Earl pulled onto Henry Thompson's farm. Henry had a bloated cow (the stomach grossly distended with gas). Prior to Earl's arrival he'd practiced a little vet medicine himself. Taking a pocket knife he had stabbed the side of the cow. Actually this was a practiced procedure to treat bloat; however, usually a vet would use a stainless steel tube with a sharpened rod extending through its center to puncture the wall of the cow's stomach (a cow has four stomachs). The removed rod would then allow the pent up gas to escape. By the time Earl arrived on the farm, Henry still proud he'd 'treated' the cow already wanted the vet to explain why the bloat wasn't decreasing. Once Earl got to see the cow the explanation was quite easy. Henry had stabbed the cow too far back and the blade had lacerated the cow's kidney. Calmly Earl told Henry to load the cow up and get her to the locker because she would be dead in a few hours. Flabbergasted Henry couldn't understand it. The cow should get better and how did he know that within a few hours the cow would die? When Earl pointed out the amazed farmer's error, Henry was astonished by Earl's near psychic prediction of the cow's demise.

Another time the vets' personalities combined to run them afoul of a client. On a Friday afternoon a local woman had brought her large shaggy dog in to have its hair clipped. Since neither vet was back from running calls, she left the dog with instructions for the vets to call her when they'd finished trimming her pet. Large animals comprised the vast majority of the practice, with the exception of vaccinations of cats and dogs for distemper and rabies. No one spent a lot of money on farm dogs and cats so trimming dogs was more of a nuisance than anything else. It happened that both men were in the office late that Friday and decided to trim the dog together. They started very innocently, cutting away the hair from the torso first then the bulk of the fleece remaining thick on the tail and legs and head. Their sense of humor getting the best of them they finished the dog, leaving it looking like a male lion. When the woman came to pick up her dog she failed entirely to see any humor in their technique. After a tongue lashing by the irate woman they sheepishly finished the job and the disgruntled woman stormed from their office.

The office she left wasn't the little office Joe had built next to Huebner's garage. Once the partnership was formed that office couldn't possibly hold both Joe and Earl, so that space was sold to Mr. Robertson, the local jeweler. On May 21, 1953, Sexton and Ritter closed on a building just recently vacated by the Nieman's Grocery. Ironically this was the family that had rented Joe and Marilane the little country house on Main Street. Sharing a wall with a tavern that at one time was Tibbets Pool Hall, the building was a remnant of the turn of the century on the same block as Dr. Whitmire's modern new medical office. On their northern wall, just before the alley, Vernon Vierth ran a modest printing business. Vernon's father Frank had published a rival newspaper to the *Gazette*, the *Sumner Herald*. Though the paper didn't survive long the family was able to make a comfortable living printing for nearly half a century.

The building Sexton and Ritter took over was more than adequate for the vet business. Unsure as to whose brain child it was, the men decided to establish a sideline selling over-the-counter medication, gum, candy, and small essentials. Lacking in flash, they named their enterprise, S & R Sundries.

Unlike unfortunate George Sexton, the partnership of Sexton and Ritter opened their doors at a very opportune time economically. Not facing calamity of the twenties and catastrophic thirties, the fifties and sixties were an economically balmy era.

After World War II, unlike after Would War I, agricultural exports increased. The Marshall Plan for the economic rebuilding of ravaged Europe, the intellectual offspring of General George Marshall, kept ships bound across the Atlantic brimming with America's agricultural products along with goods of every description. Retooled from war production the industrial machinery of the country continued to churn. Gross production increased from 3 to 5 billion dollars in 1940 and to 15.5 billion in 1947. The mechanization of the nation exploded. By 1954, for the first time in recorded history, there were more tractors than horses and mules on the farms of America. With material and production released from the demands of the war, the farm tractor began to be engineered with increased size and power. By 1953 the average tractor sold by Adolph Miller at his Farmall Dealership boasted of a capacity of fifty horsepower. Increased power meant larger plows, larger discs, and larger corn planters. All of this led to less time farming, which led to larger fields. This was the tipping point which would dramatically alter the Midwest and farming sections of the country. What appeared to be an economic boom, doubling the disposable income of rural America, was in hindsight the slow demise of the small rural town. Adding to the momentum of this rolling snowball, science

developed new stains of grain to increase production, along with an-
hydrous ammonia in the late 50's, which fertilized an accelerated production output. Inevitably, the number of farmers necessary to produce
an adequate harvest decreased. In 1950 the number of single farms in
the United States peaked and then started a slow decline which would
halve the number of existing farms by 1970. Sexton and Ritter just
happened to practice during those first halcyon days.

From the first days of their collaboration, the vets would have
hardly noticed these life-changing events unfolding. In their environment four farms still occupied every section of land which was one mile
square. The template for each farm had milk cows, and their twice-daily
milking only was recently made more efficient by mechanized milking
machines, though most farmers still had hands with large sausage like
fingers from the days of hand milking. Hogs and chickens were still the
profit portion of each farm. Farmland was then a quilt-work of fields
separated by barb wire fencing, with the obligatory pasture land, an
alfalfa field for winter hay, an oat field for straw bedding, and a corn
field. And a soy bean field that were rotated to fix nitrogen to the soil.

It was surprising but the smallest animal on the farm, the chicken,
supplied an important and steady stream of income for the vet practice.
In the moldy basement of the office, down the counter-weight-driven
freight elevator and clear in the back of the building were row upon row
of glass gallon jugs. All used and dirty, Joe would pay a few cents each
for each jug scrapped of its old label and rinsed out. He could usually
find at least one of his children to spend an hour or more in the dark,
dank cellar cleaning containers for chicken medicine. Refilled and re-
labeled the gallons of yellow "chicken medicine" would fill the top shelf
in the back storage room. With plenty of farms and chicken flocks, there
was a perpetual turnover of bottles.

Not long after taking possession of the building on Carpenter
Street, S & R Sundries must have been successful enough or possibly
enough of a distraction that the men decided to sell that portion of
their partnership. Joe had a prospective buyer in mind, his brother, Jim

and LaVonne now had two girls, Debbie and Cathy and were living in Independence, Iowa where Jim worked for the Independence Canning Company. Here was an opportunity for brothers to work side by side and also for Jim to return home. Jim appeared to be enthusiastic about the potential to run his own business. The week prior to the transfer of control he ran an advertisement in the Sumner Gazette offering a twenty-five dollar prize for a new name for his enterprise. With the sanguinity of a new endeavor, he immediately expanded the space available in the old building by cutting an opening in the center of the floor for a stairway to the basement. Once he'd remodeled the central portion of the grimy old cellar, the space had clean paneled walls and linoleum flooring giving the area a tidy look.

Even though Jim, and most likely Joe, assumed the new business had every chance of success, there was trouble brewing. The local pharmacist, Everett O'Brien sold the same array of items at his pharmacy on Main Street next to the Ritz Café. In a small town, two competing businesses less than a block from one another is like locking two bulls in the same pen; someone is going to be roughed up. When S & R Sundries started, it was merely a side light to the vet business and a mild irritant to Everett, but with Jim he now had a very aggressive competitor – one he needed to take seriously. And Everett did. The battle lasted twenty four months, and Jim Sexton, a novice to the business world, came out second. He closed down the firm and went to work with Allen Kroblin. Everett, who might have graciously accepted victory and gone about his business, still harbored resentment against Sexton and Ritter for instigating the rivalry. Eight years later pharmacist O'Brien, still carrying his grudge, made his move. For a decade Howard Senft had manned the front office of Sexton and Ritter, talking calls, keeping the books, and dispensing drugs. Surreptitiously, Everett contacted Howard with a proposition to come and work for him surely for more money. Mr. O'Brien planned to expand into the over-the-counter sale of animal pharmaceuticals. The two vets were stunned when Howard quit and moved, and the tarnished relations between the two businesses would remain frosty for years. Ironically, it wouldn't be long before Sumner Pharmacy saw its erroneous course in business judgment and closed down its animal drug section, and poor Howard was rewarded for his disloyalty by losing his job.

By the time of the O'Brien drug war, Jim Sexton was already secure in his new job with Kroblin Refrigerated Xpress. He had a dual role working for Allen. For one thing he dispatched loads for the trucker, making sure outgoing drivers also had a load coming back. This wasn't as simple as one would think, because with perishable cargo, matching loads with timing and location was a challenge. His other function was piloting the plane Allen had bought for the business. The plane Jim had flown in the war, the C-47, was actually a beefed-up version of the commercial C-3. That plane would be the dominant plane flown by commercial airlines till the advent of Boeing's first commercial jet liner. Allen's plane was a twin engine just like the C-3 but on a much smaller scale. Though small it was one of the top of the line business plane of the day, very comparable to a business jet of today. From its humble location in a little town in the middle of farm fields, Kroblin trucking had expanded to business that stretched across the country. Beside business dealings with firms, and shipping weekly loads, Allen had regular encounters with the Teamsters Union and the United States Government. The trucking business was highly regulated by the FTC, and Allen's dealings had also piqued the interest of another government agency, the IRS.

Kroblin was not the only Sumner business on the move. In October 1958 Sexton and Ritter moved, leasing their old office to the Post Office and moving right next door. The old Veirth Printing Building, now vacated, was razed to the ground, and a brand new cement block building took its place. A much smaller space than their previous office, the next building needed to be compact and efficient. The floor plan was quite simple. It was split down the middle, and the north half held the front office and reception area highlighted by a trophy of a northern pike mounted above the desk. The prize fish had been landed by Joe on a fishing trip to Canada with Adolph Miller, and its prominent exposure belied the pride in its capture. Under the pike and through the doorway was the back lab, which held most of the stock of drugs and supplies for the business. Then down the south side of the building were small animal examination rooms, a utility room and in the front half, two private offices. Initially Joe's office was just across from Howard's desk.

Two proud veterinarians, Joe and Earl Ritter, are pictured in front of their new office building.

Neat and precise, Joe's office wasn't ever cluttered. He appreciated order. The desk surface might have papers and files, but they were arranged and stacked crisply. His car trunk reflected the same desire for order, with supplies and instruments all in pre-determined spaces. In the back seat he always carried a bucket and a brush, and without fail he used them before leaving a farm, applying soapy water to scrub down his boots, assuring that bacteria and viruses would not be transmitted from one farm to another. Unlike today's vets, Earl and Joe drove cars not trucks. Just surmising the rationale, cars were probably more efficient. One of the three auto dealers in town would supply the practice's cars. One of their classic purchases were two black Chevy Corvairs, which were small cars with the engine in the rear. Now at the time, these vehicles had their own set of problems, exemplified by poor rear engine mountings, the brackets that secured the engine to the frame of the Corvair. Earl experienced the flaw first hand while driving on the rough gravel roads. Bouncing across the numerous potholes, Earl had the mounting break on his car allowing the engine to fall out on the road, leaving him marooned and no doubt out of sorts.

They may have been conservative in their choice of work vehicles, but that didn't mean the two vets weren't on the cutting edge of technology. During the war the science behind the walkie-talkie allowed transmission from one station to any receiving device. In the fifties, the offspring of Motorola's invention saw expanded commercial use as the two-way radio. Sexton and Ritter were among the first in Iowa to see the advantages of this technology. In the alley directly behind the office a latticed aluminum tower projected far above the two story buildings of downtown Sumner. Visible for miles, it proudly proclaimed their "progressive vet practice" and increased their efficiency dramatically.

Leaving the office every morning, both vets were normally armed with a list of calls they would need to be running that morning, but on completion of the calls they could, with their two way radio, be informed of any emergencies. This was especially helpful if the next farm call happened to be in the vicinity of their location. The technology was helpful in other ways as well; the two vets could confer with one another while driving between calls, and information about previously treated animals could rapidly be ascertained.

With the new technology, however, came regulation. The FCC dictated that all transmission follow a prescribed formula. Adopted from the convention used by pilots to communicate, the two-radios chatter carried words like "roger" to affirm understanding and "over" to close out conversation. Earl and Joe took the rules seriously. Names were never transmitted, references were made only to 'car one,' and 'car two' and the office was always referred to as the "base."

Facilitated by the two-way radios, the practice became more prosperous and efficient. With efficiency, the vets could take more time off than before the radio's introduction. The two vets not only got along well working together, they also played together, and this obviously revolved around golf. During the six months it is possible to play golf in Iowa, Wednesday and Saturday afternoons were set aside for golf. Several men sometimes played, but the core foursome consisted of Joe, Earl, Les Teeling, and Wayne Schutte,

Wayne Schutte is congratulating Joe while Les Teeling looks on.

The last on the list, Wayne, was a local man born and raised just two miles due east, on a farm that in the 1870's had been a stage stop. Wayne was a study in persistence. As a young man he had farmed, but when the old Overton Chemical building was demolished to make way for McAloon's Supermarket, the company went on the market.

Without a background in the chemical business or for that matter a college degree, Wayne and a partner bought the company. They built a new facility three blocks north of Railroad Street, and the firm started a steady expansion with Wayne at the helm. In time he would buy out his partner's share, and learning the business by immersion, he proved to be very adroit.

Though a successful businessman, Wayne was self-conscious about his lack of higher education. Compensating, he became a voracious reader. Invariably he would bring up books he'd either read or was reading at the time, allowing him to pursue conversation past the mundane. The second thing he deemed necessary to overcome was his lack of golfing skill. Not a natural athlete and wishing to compete with Joe, Earl and Les, who were already accomplished golfers, Wayne took to practicing every day. His house, a quintessential white colonial, was right across the road from the fifth green of Meadowbrook Country Club. With the new Overton building only a block and a half away, Wayne had the lunch hour every day to practice his short game, chipping and putting on the fifth green. Practice is the secret to improving at anything and Wayne did improve. In fact, he became very skillful and confident. He did, however, develop a curious and somewhat annoying habit. When standing over a putt, Wayne talked out loud to himself. Just before pulling the putter back he'd utter the phrase "Wayne you're a good putter." If this wasn't amusing enough for any fledgling golfing partner, he had one more quirk. Standing on the tee box, Wayne would tee his ball abnormally high. Then with his driver he would take two practice swings, gouging out large pieces of turf each time. Anyone seeing this for the first time would assume he would miss the ball, but instead he would send it straight down the fairway.

Wayne and his wife Lucille adopted two children. In some ways his children reflected the dichotomy within Wayne's life. Their daughter, Lori, was a parent's delight: smart, socially active and a breeze to raise. Their son, David, was the exact opposite: overweight and socially challenging. For years he would waft from one disaster to the next, both financial and social, until he died from a heart attack while fairly young.

Les Teeling, the fourth member of their golfing group, wasn't a Sumnerite. A native of Dubuque, he'd gone to Loras College on a basketball scholarship. After graduation in the early 50's, Les spent two years in the service. Still with a large presence in Germany, the United States Armed Forces had multiple installations spread out through their sector in the western half of that country. After boot camp, Les drew an assignment at one of the bases near Frankfurt.

Shortly after arrival he heard about an interservice basketball game to be played on base. Each base scouted their personnel for talented athletes who, if selected, would become part of the "special troops." Their only duty then was to play their assigned sport. The night he attended the scheduled basketball game, Les was spotted by a teammate from Loras. The two struck up a conversation, and his friend realized the tall crew cut blonde from Dubuque who had been a stand-out for the Duhawks would be perfect for the special troops. The encounter was reported by Les's teammate to his commanding officer. Within days surreptitious orders arrived at Les's unit, ordering him to report to the 4th Infantry, stealing him away to play basketball before his initial unit realized what they had.

Rubbing shoulders in the 4th with other special troops, Les met a man called Stan Sheriff. Within a few years of their discharge from the service, these two men would reunite in Iowa. A draftee also, Stan had played center for Cal-Poly-San Luis Obispo in California. He'd gone on to play a few years after the service in the pros before he would move on to coaching. Les would hear Stan's name again when he was named an assistant coach for the University of Northern Iowa Panthers in Cedar Falls in 1958. Within two years, Stan's talent would gain him the job as head coach. From there Stan would go on to achieve national acclaim.

Meanwhile Les had progressed on his own coaching career. Returning to Iowa after his discharge, Les sought a teaching and coaching position and he landed a job in Lawler, Iowa twenty miles north of Sumner. Teaching Latin, and English and coaching basketball, he was half way through his first year when the irrefragable M.M. Rogers showed up at Lawler High School. Someone had gotten to M.M. with intelligence about Les's basketball prowess. Sumner needed a basketball coach, and Superintendent Rogers was going to make sure they got one. Interrupting his Latin class, M.M. offered the young teacher a job. To grease the skids he offered him a sizable pay increase to $4,500 a year. More money, a larger school, and who could say no to Malcom? The next fall, Les took over as the head coach of the Sumner Aces.

A tall straight-backed man with a reserved manner, the new coach rapidly made his presence felt. In what would become a theme throughout his coaching career he laid down rules for his players and he would be rigid in their implementation. On more than one occasion he would lock horns with parents who deemed that their child shouldn't be held to such a firm set of edicts. Such behavior caused Coach Teeling to have a small set of detractors among Sumner's populace. Joe, however, fell in with that larger group that supported Les's stand. This very likely arose from the fact that Joe took the same stand with his own children.

Les moved into a home on a quiet street exactly one block north of George Sexton's original office. With his wife, Joyce, he filled the house with children, four boys and three girls. The Teelings hadn't been in Sumner long and their family hadn't grown to its full count when their home phone rang. It was late Saturday afternoon, and Joe Sexton was calling. Announcing that he had already dispensed his daughter Peg to their house with orders that when she arrived she was to baby-sit for their children, Joe said he expected Les and Joyce at his home that evening for a steak dinner. The couples hadn't ever socialized before, but this impromptu evening would lead to a life- long friendship.

Two episodes completely exemplify the bond that grew between the two men. Years later, during the depths of winter, Joe received an emergency call. The winter that year had been rough even by Iowa standards. Frequent snow storms had left enough snow to completely fill in the ditches. This situation makes driving exceedingly difficult.

With any wind at all, any dip in the road or grove of trees allowed snow which normally blows off the road to form drifts. Drifts come in several varieties. The hard- packed drift occurs when the wind has enough force to compress the snow into a surface that can support a man's weight and stop a car making extraction nearly impossible. And then there are tightly packed drifts that lull the driver into a false sense of security until the length of the drift slows the cars momentum to a stop. On this night, the wind was blowing. Secondary to the drifting was the problem of visibility. That night sheets of snow blowing in front of the Joe's car reduce the perceivable road to only a few feet past the hood of the car. On numerous nights Joe had driven in these conditions, but on this particular evening the weather caused him enough concern that he didn't wish to venture out alone. The person he called to accompany him was Les Teeling. Leaving the warmth and safety of his own home, Les agreed to go with Joe. Though the men made the trip safely, Joe appreciated the company on that lonely drive.

Another incident revealed a more personal aspect of their relation-ship. Miles west of Dubuque, Iowa, Les, behind the wheel of the family car, was alerted by Joyce that something was wrong. They had spent the week-end with relatives, and on that Sunday evening they were progressing through locked-up small towns on their way home. About half way, Joyce, several months into her pregnancy, asked Les to pull over on the road. She was miscarrying. Off on the shoulder of a two lane road, Joyce gave birth to an underdeveloped fetus. Distressed, the Teeling family finished their trip.

Unsure what to do, Les turned to his friend Joe. Driving into town after talking with Les, Joe was also at a loss as to what to do, so he de-cided to call the local priest, Joe Kleiner. There may have been a time when the parish priest was one of the more highly educated men in town. Those days had long since passed, however, and Joe Kleiner was hardly an intellectual powerhouse. In future years, Joe would find the priest to be a contemptible human being, but at that moment his advice was all they had to go on. Father Kleiner advised baptizing the fetus and placing it in a shoe box and at midnight bringing the box to the back of the Catholic Cemetery. The reason for the clandestine hour was questionable at best, but that night two silent men dug a small grave out past the rows of granite headstones and laid the child to rest.

Bonded by friendship, this divergent group of men bonded also through golf. Reconnecting with Stan Sheriff, Les brought his foursome in contact with the coaching staff at the University of Northern Iowa. What started as a golf outing with Stan and some fellow coaches grew into a regular event. Stan, Chuck Patton, the wrestling coach, and athletic director Jersey Jameier and usually another coach would meet the Sumner foursome at Gates Park Golf Course, one of three municipal courses in Waterloo. Situated on the far northern edge of town, it was within easy access of Sumner, being only thirty-five miles away and a short drive from Cedar Falls. Playing Wednesday afternoons, the eightsome enjoyed spirited competition and without question, betting.

After the round, the eight men took the short drive to Nary's 19th Hole, a squat little bar right on Highway 63, where the group had a standing order for drinks. After pulling two tables together, the bartender would immediately bring over sixteen beers. This was only the opening round. There were evenings when the post round merriment might become quite protracted. Before drinking and driving had assumed the stigma and penalty we enjoy now, no one gave a second thought to having a few beers and driving home.

As the relationship grew between the groups, the University sports department benefited. Wayne Schutte was especially generous in giving to the athletic program. He gave enough to grab the attention of the administration, and Wayne was appointed to the UNI sports board. Being the least athletic of the Sumner foursome, his appointment most likely didn't have anything to do with his intimate knowledge of sports. As far as the other members were concerned, it's very likely Les couldn't give as much with his large family to support and only teacher's salary. And Earl and Joe may have contributed, but it is highly unlikely it was a sizeable amount, as least not matching Wayne gift. One other friend from

Sumner who also got caught up in the UNI craze was Jim McAloon, who would become a ticket holder and contributor.

Jim was known to play golf with the group from time to time. A left hander, he enjoyed the game but never had the passion of the others. It wasn't that he lacked athletic talent. Jim had played first base for the Sumner Cubs, a popular adult baseball league.

Jim's father arrived in Sumner just about the same time as George Sexton. A merchant he set up business in Dr. Wilson's old building, McAloon and Beck's General Store would progress into McAloon's Dry Goods, remaining a staple in the community for the better part of half a century.

Because Jim and his wife Yvonne's four children were approximately comparable in age to some of the Sextons', the two families spent a lot of time together. Two of the children grew very close. Their oldest, Mike, was Dan's good friend and their second youngest, Ann, was Mary Sexton's compatriot.

Jim and Joe were good friends, but Jim had two personality traits that Joe chafed at. Jim never knew when to go home. He was always the last to leave any party. Invariably at two in the morning he'd still be positioned with drink in hand, locked in conversation with a barely conscious host. The inverse of this personality flaw was that Jim was always late. Joe enjoyed punctuality, and certainly on the majority of occasions Jim would arrive at the golf course (he lived only a block away) just as the foursome teed off. Joe probably needed to bite his tongue, but very likely Wayne would remind Jim of lack of promptitude.

Very much a part of this social clique but not a golfer was Bill Bradford. If this wasn't already a very diverse spread of personalities, Bill added to it! He had moxie. Originally from Waterloo, he migrated to town to run a tavern. Brash and straight-forward, he succeeded in wedging himself into typically closed circles of small- town society. His personality helped make his bar a success, but he had bigger plans than serving beer. Selling the tavern, he moved into real estate establishing an office on the western edge of Main Street. Prospering from Sumner's housing boom, Bill switched gears again and went in a completely different direction; farming. After purchasing the farm just past the new city pool on the top of the hill at the end of Pleasant Street, Bill and his family got into the cattle business. Buying and raising feeder cattle wasn't a business for the faint of heart. The cattle market suffered wide swings in prices, and when cattle were ready to go to market the seller was at the mercy of the prevailing market price. This sometimes led to a wide divergence between farm losses and large profits. Bill's hard nosed style could manage these peaks and troughs. With cattle feeding he found his true calling. Still not content, however, he expanded again. Purchasing another farm further east, he built large feeder lots with enough room to feed hundreds of head of feeder cattle.

Bill and his wife, Miriam, were a study in opposites. As brash and profane as Bill was, Miriam was reserved and refined. Their one son, Jim, was the oldest, followed by five girls, all of whom shared their parent's personalities in a fine mix, their mother being patient and understanding and their father more strict and uncompromising. The story was told of Bill's run-in with one of his grandchildren in a dispute over pilfering from his gas barrel. One evening a grandson pulled into the farm lot and filled his car's tank from Bill's barrel without asking permission. Bill, subsequently made aware of fact, was about to pursue legal charges for the theft, his rationale being that it didn't matter who "stole" from him, they would pay the price. At this point Miriam stepped in to avert a family disaster, but Bill still got his point across; family member or not, don't take him for granted.

Ironically, Bill's hard-edged view would make him one of Joe's good friends. Joe certainly appreciated the straight-forward approach Bill took to life. Although the town held several other couples who Joe and Marilane consider to be friends, these were couples at the core of their social environment. It is intriguing to consider that two people laboring to raise ten children would even have a social life, especially one as active as theirs.

Established when he was young, Joe's reputation for golf prowess continued into adulthood. An annual pick to win the tournaments at Meadowbrook, he also carried that reputation on to the wider stage. By 1952, he had won the individual state "vet" tourney three times and the local Meadowbrook tourney twelve times. In that year, by his victory at the state vet tournament, he qualified to play in the tourney at the National Veterinary Medical Convention being held in Atlantic City. The format was a two man best ball. A two man team played together scoring the best score between the two of them on each hole. Partnering with Joe was Dr. Carl Tucker of Cedar Rapids, who had been a perennial opponent for the state veterinary title.

The two would be playing the Atlantic City Country Club which had its own storied past. The club was renowned as the site where the term 'birdie' had been coined. Referring to being one under par, 'birdie' originated fifty years earlier, arising from a golf shot by a local player by the name of Abner Smith. In 1903, Abner's second shot from the fairway of the 12th hole came to rest just beside the pin. It's not that this had never happened before in golf, but on this particular occasion one of the Smith's playing partners cried out "that was shot of a bird." In the local jargon, the term "bird" referred to something incredible. Shortened to its present state the term fell into common use at the club and spread from there.

Playing the venerable course, the team of Tucker and Sexton faced and bested the two man teams from every state across the nation. The Iowans' claimed the honor of national champions by posting a score of even par.

The fifties also saw Joe bringing his boys into the game. Once the boys had reached the age when they were relatively proficient in the game, summer Sunday mornings would be when their father took them to play. At 6:30 am Sunday, Kleiner would serve his first mass of the day. Lasting only 30 minutes, it sufficed for the Catholic requirement and had the added bonus of freeing the celebrants from having to endure one of Joe Kleiner's patented rambling sermons. During this time the Mass was still said in Latin, making the entire ceremony an act of mimicry.

The three eldest and Joe, after mass and breakfast, made for Meadowbrook. At that hour of the morning they were normally the only group standing on the tee. Typically these early Sunday mornings were so still that the song of the mourning dove could clearly be heard echoing across the open green fairways. The tranquility of the moment normally did not last long. An interesting aspect of golf is that it is physical, mental, and social. To play golf the right way, all these things must be in harmony. This was the difficult lesson Joe had to impart to his sons. It can probably be said that Joe didn't view any of these golf outings as a "bonding" experience. This was a time for instruction. He may have given minor aid to the boys as far as the golf swing and short game technique, but the hard lessons were restricted to self control. Invariably, golf being a difficult and frustrating game, the young men would fall prey to anger and annoyance at their poor play. Any outburst or club throwing brought immediate rebuke by their father. On more than one occasion, the miscreant was sent off to the clubhouse, or worse-for home. Joe never felt it necessary to be chummy with his children. Not until they were adults would they be friends. They were children, raw material to be molded. Praise was a rare commodity. Doing things the right way has its own reward and thoughts about building a positive "self-image" never entered into the process and surely it wasn't a paramount concern labored over by their parents.

The same attitude extended into the children's physical well being. Going to the dentist and the doctor took on the look of an assembly line. Horace Karsten was the family dentist. A long-time friend, he'd been with the younger version of Joe when he set the course record at Meadowbrook. Playing with E. Bonovsky and Les Schicknecht, Horace witnessed the 30 on the original course. Older now, Horace practiced by himself having moved his dental office into the modern Whitmire

Medical Clinic. His waiting room was just right of the office's reception desk, which had a thick glass barricade separating the patients from Mrs. Cass, the receptionist and office despot. Speaking through a circular opening cut into the glass barricade, she'd interrogate the poor patients as to their reason for the visit. The hole was small enough that it was necessary to speak loudly, which inevitably announced to the full waiting room just what kind of embarrassing problem the poor patient was seeking help with.

Mrs. Cass was married to Dick Cass, the grandson of Stephen Cass, who was living proof of the watering down of the generations. But as unenthusiastic as Dick was toward entrepreneurship, his son took that to a new level, living his life as the complete antithesis of his great grandfather. The youngest Cass, Ted, would float from one dreamy eyed experience to the next and never was able affix any real accomplishment to his name.

Joe and Marilane, out of self preservation, maintained a steady demeanor around the children, but they still could let their hair down.

They threw were numerous parties, the most remarkable of these were Joe's birthday parties. The 6th of July, the heart of summer, boded well for a back yard party. Memorable among these festivities was the year of the pig roast. It's unsure exactly where the idea arose, but Joe and a few of his friends thought that roasting an entire pig would add spice to the annual birthday party. The small circular fountain in the backyard, unlike the front basin, which had been buried, still existed. Here was their ready-made pit in which to cook a pig. Early the morning of the party, three men stood beside the pit to discuss their culinary strategy. It is easy to picture the men shuffling around the pit their shoes wet from the dew, doing their best to avoid the smoke from the recently lit charcoal and Joe standing in his work coveralls with his arms crossed, hardly able to rein in his boyish excitement.

The main course, the pig, was the easy part. A young suckling pig had been purchased, gutted, and had its hair removed. Prepared the day before, the pig now was resting in the basement freezer, ready for the fire. After lining the bowl-shaped cement with charcoal, the men patiently waited till the coals were white hot and producing enough heat to warm the cement for slow, day-long roasting. Once deemed the fire adequate, the carcass was placed in the pit and then was carefully covered with a piece of canvas. Throughout the day, one of the three periodically checked on the cooking, adding more charcoal as he felt necessary. Early that evening after cocktails and, no doubt, some lively conversation concerning their culinary skills, the chefs brought forth their pig. With great fanfare the cooks presented the roasted pig, surely with the entire cooking process being described in embellished detail. How the actual product turned out we don't know but the fact we do know, for sure is that a suckling pig was never served again!

Socially the annual party constituted only a portion of the social schedule. Joe and Marilane loved to entertain. Putting the children to bed, adult couples would enjoy delicacies like steak and even lobster. These items never made it onto the family's daily menu, where tuna casseroles and ground beef were the staples. But during these dinner parties, Joe or Marilane would go the foot of the stairs and call down the children, at least those still awake. Treating each to just a bite of the delicacy being served, they would then send the children back to bed. The message was clear: there is a distinct set of norms and expectation separating adults from children.

Joe and Marilane can't be faulted for their moments away from the children. Most days were a perpetual struggle just to endure. Daily the washing machine ran and either the drier or the clothesline, positioned out by the cottonwood tree, was in use on the same schedule. Cleaning and cooking seemed to never stop. Picking up laundry, making beds, patching jeans; the list of daily chores proved tiring just to read.

Besides all the drudgery of the housework Marilane also had tolerate Joe's fastidious nature. One later afternoon Joe, after locating his wife by yelling up the stairs, found her in the center bedroom pressing clothes on her antiquated mangle iron. At her feet was a circle of toys where the children had played that afternoon. The clutter was more than Joe could bear, so he gathered as many toys as he could carry and stomped down the stairs, rounding the corner to the top of the basement steps. From there with great ceremony he tossed the armfull down the steps. When he returned to the second floor bedroom where Marilane still stood rolling the laundry between the steaming rollers, she said in a judicious tone, questioning Joe's wisdom, that in the morning she was going to have bring all those toys back up.

The three girls, as soon as they were old enough to help, were recruited into the crew doing the housework. The girls grumbled incessantly "The boys never help." Whether viewed as chauvinistic, that was the way it was. Harping about the situation wasn't going to bring about change. Joe and Marilane never gave a hint as to whether they actually paid attention to such comments. Among the children, grumbling was fact of life in the household. There was always someone who felt aggrieved, but their asseverations typically fell on deaf ears.

The social dynamic of the family, then, could be challenged by the progressive thinking of today, but it worked. Certain things were necessary just to maintain order. A lot of effort went into rearing that many children and Marilane, like many mothers, was ferociously protective of her children, but there was a subtle undercurrent in this complex affiliation. Joe said it best when he wrote about his "mate" that she was a wife first. Sometimes when Joe came home from work and before dinner, he'd go to take a bath downstairs. While he was languishing in the tub, Marilane, cocktails in hand, would go into the bathroom with him and shut the door. Putting the lid down on the toilet she'd sit down and for a few moments, locked away from the children, they'd share a drink and adult conversation. Surprisingly, no matter the chaos outside the bathroom, the couple would be oblivious to it, and the children knew better than to interrupt.

Like any large group of organisms in a confined space, bacteria and virus found multiple hosts on which to thrive. Chickenpox, measles and the common cold found fertile ground in the Sexton house. Tonsillectomies were a group function. Going to the dentist and the physician for vaccinations were done by the car load. A good example was when the children were carted to town for tetanus shots. They were lined-up shoulder to shoulder in the rear most examination room of the Whitmire Clinic, and squirming in anticipation of their expected discomfort as Mrs. Brocka, the nurse approached each one in turn with her hypodermic syringe.

Outside the routine medical visits, with such a large number of children there were the inevitable bumps and bruises. Even when they lived in town, there were "accidents" like Mike hitting Dan in the face with a shovel and crushing his nose. Traumatic but not life threatening there were other more dramatic moments outside the inevitable brother beating on brother.

Shortly after the twins, Matt and Pat, were born they had been home for about a week when both developed a severe respiratory infection. Fearing the worst, their parents bundled the infants up to return them to the hospital. There must have been some serious doubt whether the boys would survive, because just prior to taking the twins both back to the hospital Joe and Marilane performed a baptism. Holding the boys each over the kitchen sink their parents performed the ritual in keeping with their faith. Before the harrowing evening baptizing the twins, they had experienced other travails mostly revolving around Mark.

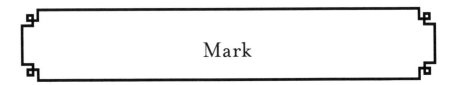

Mark

The sixth child, Mark, born weighing only four pound seven ounces, was two months premature. After delivering the diminutive baby, Marilane rested in room #4 at the Sumner hospital which was directly across from the nursery, an easy walk across the linoleum floor to the bank of windows guarding the newborns. The night of August 13, 1950 found newborn Mark confined to an incubator safely behind that window in that nursery, but he'd stay there for two months before reaching seven pounds. After reaching the weight of a normal newborn, he was finally allowed to leave and join his siblings in the house on Division Street. A short year and a half later he'd be back in the hospital.

At eighteen months of age, everything goes to the mouth and with a house full of children there was a full range of things to taste. Mark somehow got a hold of a peanut. Everything would have been fine if he had swallowed it, but instead he aspirated the nut. Lodged in his tiny esophagus, the peanut caused him to start to choke. With her toddler in obvious distress, Marilane did the only thing she knew how to do, she inserted her finger in his throat began feeling for the peanut. She was able to hook a portion of the obstruction with her finger nail and dislodge just enough of it to open an airway, but the remainder of the nut stayed in place. Whether Jim Whitmire was unavailable or unable to help, within the hour Marilane had Mark in Waterloo at Schoitz Hospital. The staff there successfully removed the last portion of the peanut from Mark's airway but a subsequent infection set in. It would be days before the infection was under control and Mark was released back into his parent's care. This may have been one of the first rigid bronchoscopies done in the area. All though the procedure had been invented in 1897 in Germany, the use of a scope to locate obstructions in the trachea and lungs had only started to have widespread use.

Almost as if it was ordained, eighteen months would pass before the next emergency. After three days of Mark's intermittent complaints of a stomach ache, Joe took Mark to Dr. Whitmire. Mark was diagnosed with an enlarged appendix, and treatment was rendered. After the appendectomy Mark would spend another week in the hospital.

Tuesday, July 5th, a day before Joe's birthday and two years after his appendectomy, Mark was complaining again of stomach pains. That afternoon he was checked into room #2 at the hospital. Dr. Whitmire's new partner, Dr. Lasiak, was put in charge of the case. Initially treated for dehydration, Mark would spend another six days in the hospital. The first day or two Mark had vomited up bile. X-rays and clinical symptoms didn't lead to any diagnosis. The daily administration of fluids seemed to correct the situation. After six days with no firm diagnosis, Mark was released.

Eleven months later Mark again saw the inside of the hospital. This time his stay was scheduled. Persistent tonsillitis mandated removal of his tonsils. At eight thirty on a Monday morning in June, Dr. Whitmire excised the offending nodes. Mark's recovery was rapid and uneventful, and within twenty four hours he would be going home. Plagued by the medical establishment during his first brief years, however, he wasn't done yet.

Mark Sexton is sharing a moment with Santa.

A month and a half later July 18 was a perfect summer day. In the low 70's and without any wind it was an ideal summer's day. The morning was wonderful, the whole day was full of promise, but by afternoon Mark's stomach ache had returned. He started vomiting. By early evening the vomiting started to subside but Joe, remembering Dr. Lasiak's treatment, suspected dehydration. He gave Mark an enema and put him to bed. Mark was restless all night and by morning Joe recognized his son was quite ill. Still vomiting fluid which now had the consistency of mucous, Mark had one other concern; there hadn't been a bowel movement for well over twenty four hours.

Once again Mark found himself in the hospital. Dr. Perrin, another associate, was the first to see him. Mark's body temperature and his pulse rate were both rising. A six year old with a 102 degree temperature and tachycardia of 160 was cause for grave concern. Dr. Perrin's diagnosis was that he had an acute small bowel obstruction. Surgical intervention was the treatment of choice. There was one problem; the surgeon Dr. Whitmire was away on vacation. So Marilane's brother Art, who was a practicing general surgeon in Waterloo, became the obvious choice to contact. At 11:00AM on August the 19th, Art had been called, and it would be only forty-five minutes before his arrival at Sumner's hospital. A tragic course of events had been put in motion.

11:00AM – Cradling his small son in his arms, Joe carried Mark into the x-ray room.

12:00AM – Art Devine by then had arrived at the hospital. He'd brought with him a colleague, Dr. Cooper, and together they examined their diminutive patient.

1:40 PM—Mark was on the operating table. Drs. Cooper and Devine had opened his abdomen and located the section of small bowel housing the obstruction. Slicing away tissue surrounding the adhesion, the surgeons reattached the healthy tissue, but gangrene had already set in. Mark's temperature and heart rate indicated he was in septic shock.

3:30 PM—Mark, now out of surgery was resting in the hospital bed. Art noted in his chart that Mark's "color" was good

5:00 PM – A nurse checking on Mark noted in the chart that he appeared restless.

6:30 PM – Dr. Perrin, on rounds, prescribed sodium Phenobarbital to hopefully calm Mark, but he still remained "restless." His temperature had also increased to over 103 degrees.

9:00 PM – Dr. Perrin made the diagnosis that Mark was again going into shock.

11:40 PM—Dr. Devine having returned to the hospital and after reading Dr. Perrin's note Art decided to perform a "cutdown." As Mark went into shock, blood flow decreased and the small subcutaneous blood vessels in his hands and arms became imperceptible. Art, looking for a blood vessel, made a small incision through Mark's skin. It was vital they start an intravenous line for fluids and medication.

12:20AM—That Friday morning Mark's temperature continued to increase. It was now at 106 degrees, the nurse started alcohol sponge baths and ice packs, frantically attempting to bring down his fever.

3:50 AM—His temperature had dropped to 101, but now his pulse was weakening. Art Devine, now hovering over his patient, noted in the record that Mark's color was poor and respiration was becoming more labored. While nurses were watching over him, Mark's temperature began to rise again, and for the next two hours nurses toiled with alcohol sponges and ice packs to reverse his temperature. When they checked his pulse, it was barely perceivable.

9:00 AM —Mark seemed to rally. His color improved and he rested more comfortably.

1:00 PM --His pulse felt stronger.

1:45 PM – The nurse on duty thought he looked better and that he was sleeping peaceably.

5:45 PM—Dr. Cooper returned to Sumner with another colleague Dr. Zager. Along with Dr. Devine the three physicians discussed Mark's case.

10:30 PM – Art examined Mark. He detected a decrease in circulation. His little hands had gone cold. Art now maintained a constant vigil over his nephew. He had to have had a terribly lonely feeling as the minutes passed slowly in that quiet hospital room. The day before, he had responded to the pleas for help; now, with Mark's life ebbing away, the burden he had assumed weighed heavily upon him. Seated in the dim-lit room with the only perceptible sound the infrequent passing of a nurse in the hallway, he felt the minutes pass at an agonizing pace.

2:30 AM—Mark's breathing became more labored and periodically his small body would become rigid. With his patient lying quietly, Art felt his thin arms and leg. Mark's limbs felt cool. Reluctantly Dr. Devine got up from his chair and walked down the hall to the nurse's station. The time had come to call his sister and brother-in-law.

4:35 AM—Mark's parents arrived minutes after the call. There couldn't have been much sleep that night. For nearly two hours their vigil was timed by movements of Mark's chest, discernibly slowing. Now the respiration ceased. It was Saturday morning July 21st,1953.

Back at the Sexton house in the center bed room abutting the "dorm," two beds remained unused. Since Mark's departure for the hospital, Tim had been moved into the big boy's room, bunking above Dan. The faint light from the rising sun gave just enough light to illuminate the bedroom. The paneled glass door leading to the dorm squeaked on its old hinges as Joe opened it. Joe now standing just inside the doorway awakened the boys with a muffled, "Boys." A moment passed before he said another word either he wanted to wait until everyone was awake or he needed to summon enough courage for his next utterance. His statement was short; Mark had died. After his few words he turned and left to wake his daughters with the painful news.

Samuel Johnson, the 18th century Englishman of letters, wrote that grief is the suspension of life till living is imposed again upon it. So it was in the Sexton household. That day and the next few days to follow had an unreal quality, a detour from the known world into a place of continuous sorrow with seemingly no exit. Never given to any outward signs of affection, the family now paid the price. Their grief wasn't something to be shared. Each individual dealt with it alone.

Mark's small body was waked twice. The first night, the casket sat in Berg's funeral home, a flat-roofed building situated just past the old Cass mansion on Railroad Street. Friends and neighbors formed a line from Mark's plush covered five foot wooden casket out the visitation room through the reception hallway, out the door, down the steps and back down the block. Only Mark's parents accompanied him that evening. He'd have one more evening with his family.

Just off the foot of the stairway on the north end of the living room stood the front door. On it someone had placed a black wreath. Seldom if ever used by the Sextons, the door needed to be forcibly opened due to repeated layers of paint which had never been cracked loose. Through this door Mark in his diminutive peach-colored bier would reenter his home. Positioned at the front of the staircase, he would reside there throughout the next twenty four hours. That afternoon, he would be waked again with just the family present. Gathered in the living room, the family punctuated the service by kneeling on the carpet, reciting the rosary.

That long evening, those who could sleep did, but to a person they were still acutely aware of the silent inhabitant in the living room. Early the next morning Walter Berg arrived to collect Mark, who would take one last ride up the gravel road to town. The funeral mass was performed before a crowded church: the loss of a child touches a primal nerve in the human psyche. Later that morning he would be moved up the road to the Catholic Cemetery only a quarter mile from his home.

Life Intervenes

The next morning, life would intervene. Joe needed to run calls, the laundry had built up, hay needed to be carried to the bunks for the sheep, and the grass certainly would need be mowed. Life looked normal but it had changed forever. A bed now sat vacant. Small personal items, Mark's toy guns and some of his other toys, were boxed up and carefully tucked away in the back of the downstairs coat closet. One less chair was needed at the dinner table. Not visible were the emotional scars. There were no "grief counselors." Time was the only balm for these wounds.

Joe expressed a parent's lament best years later. Thirty years after Mark died, a local dentist, Dave Hennessy, had a daughter die from cancer. Stopping to give his condolences, Joe said, "You'll never get over it, you'll only get used to it."

Back within the walls of the Sexton house, routines again directed the course of the days, but there were certain signs of the lingering injury. Among family members, Tim and Joe presented the most visible signs of emotional damage.

Within days of the funeral, Tim presented symptoms of psychological change; insomnia. Insomnia usually wasn't an affliction of a seven-year-old. Closest in age, Tim and Mark had been buddies. They played together and slept together in the same room. After his brief stay in the dorm, Tim moved back into the center bedroom, but even with his twin brothers sharing the room, there was a void. Tucked into bed,

Tim would wait at night till the house grew quiet; then, in pajamas and barefoot, he'd go downstairs and knock on his parents' door. Either Joe or Marilane would get up and usually go to the kitchen and heat a cup of milk. When he'd finished his warmed drink, they'd take him back to his bed and tuck him in again.

This became almost a nightly occurrence. For the first month, his parents thought this odd behavior would gradually abate as time lengthened from Mark's death. As the night visitations continued into the second month, however, their concern grew that Tim had some serious mental issues. Maybe it was time to take Tim for some psychological help. Joe and Marilane had just about reached the tipping point when their nightly caller stopped coming.

Joe's psychological manifestation took a more subtle form. During the previous twelve months, Mark had attracted special focus from his father. First, after the family moved to the farm, Mark was the next child to enter school. With the older five already attending school in Sumner, they would continue attending "town" school being grandfathered in. But Mark, since moving to the country, would be required to attend country school at the one room facility across the road from their neighbor Olive Wescott. Joe appealed to the school board to allow Mark to join his brothers and sister now attending Durant School. But open enrollment wasn't even a concept at the time, his petition was denied. Events would then take a bizarre turn.

Joe had been quite verbal in his condemnation of the school board's decision, and it wasn't but a few weeks later that the one room school house in question caught on fire and burned to the ground. The only recognizable thing left were piles of pennies collected for the half pint milk boxes. Immediately gossip filtered through the small town suspecting arson, and Joe's name was bandied about. The state fire marshal after his investigation ruled out arson and, luckily for Joe, the issue soon died out.

More disquieting for Joe, however, were the events a week prior to his son's death. The chicken house south wall held nearly a hundred

6" x 12" glass panes, for whatever reason, Tim and Mark had thrown rocks through several of the windows. This transgression could not go unpunished. Joe had always been the disciplinarian, and for years physical punishment was dealt out to the boys, with some punishments being very severe. Mike, the oldest, had probably received more than his share, but all the boys at one time or another felt Joe's wrath. With Mark's passing all this would change. Joe suffered great remorse after Mark's death over the beating he had applied to the youngster. To know a man's heart exactly is nearly impossible, but Joe's heart did change. From that moment he would never raise his hand to any of his children again. This didn't mean he couldn't be stern, but the raging physical terror that was Joe Sexton left, never to be seen again.

In fact it might be argued that he viewed his role as a father in a whole new light. One incident in particular exemplified this change. Not so many years later, Dan and Tom were on the same junior high basketball team. Coaching the team was a pugnacious little man named Dick Hogan. Short and stocky and prematurely balding, Coach Hogan for whatever reason took a dislike to Dan. One day during practice Dan ran afoul of Coach Hogan, who instituted his own perverse form of discipline. He forced Dan to "run the gauntlet" between his team mates. Coach Hogan's only possible reason was to humiliate the boy. That night at home, Joe overheard Tom and Dan talking about the incident, with Dan still livid over his treatment.

The next afternoon the team as usual held their practice in the old gymnasium, a compact brick building where the school played their games. The compact basketball floor was encased on two sides by double deck bleachers, and the baskets were abnormally close to a stage on the north end and a set of double doors on the south end. Just beyond the doors sat the ticket office and the stairs to the balcony.

Midway through the practice that afternoon, Coach Hogan had the team running plays in the half court on the south end of the floor. Partway through his discussion on the next play to be run, the doors below the basket opened. Standing now below the basket was Joe Sexton in his work coveralls. As everyone turned toward Joe, the room became quiet. Staring directly at Coach Hogan with his face expressionless, Joe relayed what he'd heard from his boys the night before. His last sentence was a question for Coach Hogan, "Was that correct?" Dick, on the spot, had no choice but to confirm the incident as true. Joe, in a voice that left no doubt as to his sincerity, told Coach Hogan that what transpired would never happen again. It was never stated in so many words, but Joe's tone conveyed the implication that their next encounter might involve physical violence. Joe then turned and left. For a few seconds there was only stunned silence, not only on Coach Hogan's part, but also on the part of the team and especially Dan and Tom. The boys had never seen that side of their father. This was a different man from the one they had known.

Mending the Wounds

In retrospect, it seems that one of the most memorable trip that occurred the summer following Mark's death could have been some form of healing. The possible evidence for this assessment is that since the trip to Cleveland there hadn't been a "family" vacation. Maybe this also couldn't be called a family vacation, since only the five oldest would go, but then there wouldn't ever really be a vacation with the entire family.

It's not known who hatched the idea, but the initial plan incorporated the Mangans. Tom and Vera Mangan had lived for a short time in Sumner while Tom, a physician, had worked with Jim Whitmire. After leaving Sumner, he set up his own practice in Forest City, Iowa. Oddly enough where Tom and Vera lived in Forest City was at the top of a hill overlooking the town. At the end of their long driveway and across the street was nascent mom and pop business that built small pull-behind trailers called Winnebagos.

The Mangans and the Sextons had planned to go to a dude ranch out West, a ranch in Montana called the Nine-Quarter Circle Ranch. Traveling together the two families planned to drive the over 1000 miles after teaming up in Forest City, but their plans fell apart. When the Joe and his family arrived at the Mangans', they backed out at the last minute, but Joe decided to go anyway. His decision proved the right one.

Much earlier that morning parked in the farm driveway, the Sexton station wagon had the back end stuffed with luggage. The sun wouldn't rise for more than an hour, but already seven people had wedged themselves into the two bench seats. Though the hour was very early, everyone was far too excited to sleep. The four boys lined the back seat, the squabbling hadn't started yet. There would be plenty of time for that in the following days. In front, Peg sat between Joe and Marilane. Restricted to two lane roads it would take them two hours to reach Forest City, and over three hours after that would pass before they reached the Missouri River. Crossing the river would be like crossing over into an alien land. Just prior to leaving Iowa, however, Joe needed to find a pharmacy. Contacting Jim Whitmire by phone back in Sumner, Jim called in a prescription for Peg, who was prone to car sickness. The next few days would be more pleasant without a vomiting child.

Turning north once they had crossed the river, they got on route 85 in South Dakota and headed due west, straight toward the Black Hills. It seemed like a magical road. Signs began to appear for Burma Shave and Wall Drug. Both signs were everywhere. Comprised of multiple small signs, Burma Shave carried a slogan in groups of six signs. A typical phrase would be: " A shave/that's real/no cuts to heal/a soothing velvet after feel/Burma Shave." Wall Drug signs were just as prolific. Counting down the miles, each sign reinforced the sales pitch till stopping at the store almost became an obsession.

With only a few miles left to Wall, South Dakota, the hook had been set. After viewing signs for hundreds of miles there was no way one could drive by without stopping. Enticing the Iowans, the bill boards sold the store as the "cowboy" drug store. Master pitchmen, the parking lot was full when the Sextons arrived. Bounding from the station wagon, the five children couldn't get enough of this exotic cowboy culture. Once inside they weren't disappointed. Knotty pine boards covered the walls festooned with stuffed animal heads, and carved statues of horses and riders were stationed beneath the heads. Aisle after aisle of amazing trinkets lured the children. Like looking at a catalog at Christmas time, there were too many things that the children wanted. Practicality won out over the visual overload; they were forced to settle on just hats. Surely going to a ranch demanded cowboy hats. Their shopping finished, five proud kids plowed back into the car, all sporting new cowboy hats.

About done with the day's drive, they had only thirty five miles left. By late afternoon they found themselves in Rapid City, looking for a motel. What they came across was a hotel, but not as someone now would know it. Built into a ravine, individual cabins were situated half way up the side of the hill, and together they formed the hotel. In a single day, the Sexton children had a lot of firsts; the first time checking into a hotel, the first time eating in a restaurant, and before the day was over, their first exposure to snakes and alligators in South Dakota. Entering the outskirts of Rapid City huge billboards had advertised the local reptile garden not far up the road. Why should the Sextons pass up this tourist trap?

An oval pit confined a slithering floor of serpents. Raised up on a platform in the center of the pit, a man holding a long rod reached into the boiling mass of snakes plucking one after another onto his platform. Describing in detail the dangerous nature of the snakes, he mesmerized the Sextons, now interspersed with the crowd surrounding the pit. The snakes were the main attraction of exhibit but beyond the snake pit alligators sat half submerged in pools but they did prompt the same instinctual repulsion as the serpents. Once the family was back at the motel's cabin, sleep came easily. Though the wonders of the first day were enough to excite anyone's imagination, it had been a long day, and fatigue overcame excitement.

Bright and early the Sextons walked down the hill from their cabin to the car and loaded up again. There were new adventures to be had. Leaving Rapid City, the west- bound road headed straight for the Black Hills. Covered with pine forests, the mountains of the Black Hills cradled towns like Deadwood and stories of gold fields and Indians. Once on the road, the station wagon traveled upward until it terminated in a small parking lot. Climbing wooden stairs at the northern edge of the lot the Sextons emerged from the pine trees at an observation platform. Leaning against the platform's wooden railing, they looked across the canyon. There to the west a solid granite mountain faced them with four heads carved into its side: Mount Rushmore.

They didn't linger long. The station wagon soon took to the road, which wound beyond Rushmore and curved through the Black Hills skirting the Badlands. There was so much to see – mountains, pine forests and graveled canyons; it was all an alien and spellbinding landscape. Leaving the Black Hills the road headed northwest into Wyoming. Now they were really into cowboy country.

Hours after they left Mount Rushmore, another set of mountains appeared on the western horizon, growing closer in the windshield of the car as the next few hours passed. After what seemed like an eternity, they started their climb into the Little Bighorn Mountains, weaving back and forth as the cars on the road in the valley got smaller and smaller and the overloaded station wagon labored to the summit. Once through the mountains, they spilled out onto the high plateau of southern Montana.

They were miles out of their way, but Joe had a particular locale in mind. Turning off the highway 212 after passing through the Crow Indian Reservation, Joe pulled into a parking lot overlooking what appeared to be a brown, grass-covered field. A park ranger's shack sat next to a trampled path leading toward a grassy knoll. On top of the hill sloping gently down to a cottonwood-covered river valley stood a monument surrounded by white stone slabs randomly poking from the dried grass. This was the Little Bighorn Battle site, Custer's last stand. As the ranger started to explain the site's history, the seemingly barren landscape came to life. The vivid description of George Armstrong Customer and the 210 men riding with him being methodically killed by their Indian adversaries on June 25th, 1876 fueled the imagination. Joe certainly had to have had a knowing interest in the battle to drag his family to this deserted part of Montana.

With everyone's minds filled with visions of flying arrows and smoke drifting from the barrels of the carbines, the Sextons turned back south. Reentering Wyoming, they weren't far from the city of Cody. Immersing themselves now in the "west" they sought out the Buffalo Bill Museum in the town. A stuffed buffalo and rows of rifles were housed in a log cabin built in the 1920's further stimulating the mental picture they had of the 'wild west.' So far the day had just offered up appetizers. After staying the night in Cody, they'd head west the next morning towards Yellowstone National Park.

When Joe pulled into the parking lot there were only a few cars there. In fact, in spite of it being summer there didn't seem to be much activity at all as he parked the car across the road from the main lodge of Yellowstone Park. The massive lodge built during Teddy Roosevelt's presidency was a wonder to behold. The central foyer opened up skyward, towering four stories with its main supports being single gigantic pine logs. Its sloped gabled roof would give the building a look very much like a lodge from the Black Forest of Germany. But the lodge wasn't why they stopped. They had come to see Old Faithful, a geyser shooting super heated water five stories into the air every hour. One of the major attractions of the park, it had a ranger assigned to it.

Gathering a small group from the parking lot that included the Sextons, the park ranger walked the anticipating party across the street, stopping a safe distance from an alkali circle around the geyser. While waiting for the eruption, he described the volcanic nature of the park and its history. This was only the first course in the menu of attractions.

Leaving the lodge and winding northward through the park they passed the Yellowstone River which dropped 132 feel down a granite face, the Tower Falls, then past bubbling mud with the pungent smell of sulfur, the Porcelain Basin, and finally past giant layer cakes of travertine limestone, the Mammoth Hot Springs. All these natural wonders were the products of a huge dome of lava not far underfoot.

As intriguing as these spectacles were, the family's time was limited, and they soon found themselves heading north out of the park. As they followed the road, an impressive mountain range sprang up in front of them. The road led directly over the snow-capped Beartooth Mountains, which guarded the park's northern border.

Chugging up and over the Beartooths, the Sextons finally reached its western slopes, which drained into the watershed of the Gallatin River. A north-flowing river, it joined the Madison River on its way to the Missouri. Across the river and up in the Madison Mountains at 7000 feet sat the Nine Quarter Circle Ranch, their destination. Patches of meadow were interspersed with pine forest on the drive up from highway 191. The winding two lane road followed beside a branch of the Gallatin River. The Sextons, gawking out the car windows as they drove along the ravine, were excitingly close to the ranch.

As they turned through the weathered gate, the ranch came into view and it was everything they had expected. Neat rows of cabins lined the road. Off to the right a barn, bunk house, and corral filled with horses lined pointed up a gentle slope to the main lodge of the ranch, which was framed in the distance by the 12,000 foot peaks of the Madison Range. For miles in every direction not a fence was to be seen, only meadows with wild flowers and grasses broken only by the islands of pine trees. Nothing could have been further from Sumner, Iowa.

After checking in at the lodge they drove down to their cabins. They would not need the car again till they left. They split up into two cabins. Joe, Marilane, and Peg shared one and the boys bunked right next door. The cabins were rustic, with wooden floors and a pot bellied stove in the center of the room. Though it was the height of summer, the stove proved very useful on the cold mountain mornings. At 7000 feet, cold was a fact of life, exemplified by the following Sunday when their plans to attend church in the little hamlet of Taylors Falls were shelved by a snow storm.

All their meals were served at the lodge, which was separated from their cabins by a small stream that flowed down out of the foothills through the center of the ranch. Just west of the cabins, a small arched bridge sat on a dirt path that wound its way up the hill. The back of the main lodge held the kitchen and dining hall. To gain access to the dining room it was necessary to go through the Trophy Room, a greeting space with a small bar. The captivating part of the room was an immense fireplace, large enough for a man to stand in, and it could easily hold a five-foot log. Probably the most memorable aspect of the room was the stuffed mountain lion adorning the mantle, preserve in a gaited stride with its head turned toward the visitors as if it were looking for its next meal.

Spread out like a little village, afforded the children freedom to roam the ranch at will with the exception of the bunk house that housed the ranch hands. The men understandably didn't wish to have children hanging around their living quarters. Of the Sextons, the only one who took exception to this prohibition was Mike. Completely captivated by cowboys, he couldn't understand why he could not see first hand where real cowboys lived.

Though they were free to wander, there were certain organized activities. Scavenger hunts and horse back riding comprised some of the planned events. Joe and Marilane also had daily duties like the daily inspection just before dinner of everyone for ticks. Inhabiting the tall grass on the ranch the little bloodsuckers were a chronic plague.

Waiting by the horse corral, the Sextons are anticipating the trail ride. Mike and Peg are seated next to Joe, and Tom, Tim, and Dan flank Marilane.

The week's stay culminated in a trail ride for all guests. When everyone had arrived at the start of the week, one of the first stops was to report to the corral. There the cowhands would assess the rider and assign each person a horse for their stay. A prime example of their work was Tim, the youngest of the Sextons who drew Jawbones, a squat black horse who was certainly not a danger to any of his passengers but had the annoying habit of biting the other horses. On the morning of the trail ride, all guests met down by the corral. All the horses were already saddled and everyone, now quite familiar with their own horses, made the process of getting under way fairly smooth. Once the head trail guide took off, the horses, which had probably gone through the same drill untold times, fell into line and a fastidious single file assemblage started up the path into the mountains. Higher up the mountain, the narrow path wound across the slopes with one side being a fairly steep drop off. The horses knew the way and all the riders had to do was to stay in the saddle, but Marilane couldn't help but feel anxious. She could only imagine that at any moment a horse carrying one of the children would stumble off the trail and topple down into the valley. Obviously nothing like that happened.

Miles above the ranch the horse parade came to a stop. Prior to their pause a chuck wagon had come up the valley by a less scenic route, and a crew was already preparing lunch. A wood fire billowed smoke into the dark blue sky while the ranch hands busied themselves preparing to move large black skillets on to its embers. With lunch completed, the saddle weary group made its way back to the ranch by the shorter route. This probably was a relief for Marilane.

In the east the first rays of light peeked through the distant mountains casting long shadows as Joe closed the rear gate on the station wagon. Loaded again, they would need to retrace their steps back to Iowa. Like any trip home, it was longer without the exhilaration of the anticipation. What before had been exciting sights on the trip out now were just milestones to be counted down on the increasingly laborious drive back home.

A Taste for Travel

The Volkswagon Bus sat in the driveway with five of the Sexton children already squirming in the back seats, and Marilane in the driver's seat with window rolled down was saying good-bye to Joe. They were leaving for the annual summer pilgrimage to Bancroft. Joe never went. He hadn't returned to Bancroft since the Christmas the family spent there in the late 40's. Whether that particular week had soured him on visiting Bancroft or he simply needed to stay home and watch over the rest of the family is debatable. The truth was probably he saw no need to visit his mother-in-law since she was already a frequent guest in their home. No matter, Marilane would still dutifully make the four hour journey every summer. For the younger children the week in Bancroft was very exciting, but once they were old enough to have a summer job most of the children declined the week long stay with Grandma Devine. This wasn't true, however, of Peg. She enjoyed the time in Bancroft. Part of this may have been due to her friendship with one of the Clark girls. In fact, Peg was known to stay nearly a month at her grandmother's.

Joe's avoidance of Bancroft didn't necessarily mean he shunned the Devines. There were several he took a liking to, one being Margaret's husband Ray Goodenow. Ray was a job analyst for the government, but as a civilian like Mardy, he worked for the armed services. And like Mardy, his job had him relocating on a regular basis around the Midwest. Luckily with a master's degree in medical technology, Margaret was able to move from place to place and find employment.

Their five children, John, Tom, Jim, Dan and Helen, outwardly seemed to adjust to the moves.

At least once a summer, the Sextons and the Goodenows got together, either when Ray came back to Colo, Iowa to see his relatives, or when the Sextons drove to their home. Margaret and Marilane enjoyed seeing one another, and the children meshed well. Their ages overlapped, and the Goodenow children were witty, intelligent, and inventive. Though Ray and Joe were political opposites, they also got along well. Pointedly, Ray held politically liberal viewpoints and Joe was entrenched in more conservative sentiments.

Evenings together after the children went down were lively times for the adults. All four held strong opinions, even Margaret and Marilane who as Devines had "argumentation" as part of their genetic make up. None of these late night discussions, however, flared into open conflict.

The last time the Sextons would see Ray was in June 1962. He was dying by the time the Sextons arrived in Columbus, Ohio. Now in renal failure, Ray had a form of genetically transmitted kidney disease. He was already in the terminal stages, when either Ray or Margaret must have requested the Sextons to come for one last visit. Sadly, only days after their arrival in Columbus, Ray died. For Joe to travel to Ohio there had to have been a special bond between these men. And between the wives too.

For the Sextons and the nation the late 50's and early 60's were a watershed moment in the new nuclear age. The cold war had been slowly brewing throughout the decade, and there were now signs it was heating up. With Von Braun's help, the US had intercontinental missiles capable of carrying nuclear war heads halfway around the globe, and the Soviet Union shared the same capability. As a deterrent to a Soviet nuclear attack, the US had placed missiles on the USSR's southern border in Turkey, a NATO member, allowed the US to establish bases for their nuclear tipped, medium ranged Jupiter missiles on its northern border within the short distance across the Black Sea to the USSR. Supervising the installation of the missiles was Colonel Emmett Devine.

Possibly without a full comprehension of the geo-political implication of the missile bases, Joe and Marilane accepted an invitation to visit Turkey from Emmett and Nan. While the Iowans were enjoying their visit the Jupiter missiles that Emmett oversaw might not have been fully operational, yet only a thousand miles north, in the Kremlin, plans were being hatched for a showdown with the west and in particular with the United States.

After their return to Iowa, Joe and Marilane read about Moscow's provocative opening act of war. In August 1961, almost overnight, a cement wall went up in Berlin between the east and west sectors of the city. The East Germans, puppets of the Soviet Union, controlled the area surrounding the sectors of Berlin under governance of the US, Britain and France. Besides building the wall, the East Germans blockaded the roads in and out of the city. It was unsure what the Soviet had as their objective, quite possibly the forced withdrawal of the Allies from Berlin, but refusing to withdraw, the western powers enlisted an armada of C-47's for daily flights to land supplies for the isolated city. For over a year, day after day, no matter the weather, food supplies poured in until out of frustration the east lifted the blockade.

In the spring of that year President John Kennedy had sanctioned a covert invasion of communist Cuba, a constant thorn in the side of the US only ninety miles from its shore. The operation run by the CIA was called the Bay of Pigs. Ineptly handled, the invasion was crushed by the Cuban army. Though the Cubans easily subdued the operation, it still raised alarms for Fidel Castro, Cuba's dictator. In response, the Soviet Premier Khrushchev ordered soviet fighter jets and bombers to be stationed in Cuba.

On October 22nd 1962, a U-2 spy plane captured the first pictures of something troubling for the US. The photos showed bombers of a long-range variety parked on airstrips. These planes were fully capable of carrying nuclear bombs in to the heart of the US. Within days, further reconnaissance by the high-flying planes produced pictures of missile installations. Median and intermediate ballistic missiles were disseminated across Cuba. The next thirteen days would have the U.S. and the world holding its breath. With the world's two great nuclear powers nose to nose, nuclear annihilation became a viable and terrifying option.

Going to Defense Readiness Condition 2,DEFCON 2, the United States Strategic Air Command had B52 bombers armed and in the air in preparation for nuclear war. Besides the giant B-52 bombers, hardened ground silos housing missiles which were spread across the central part of the country were on alert to launch, and the submarine George Washington carrying the first, ocean-launched Polaris I missiles, prowled the sea, ready to release its cargo.

After a chilling speech to the American people, President Kennedy initiated a naval blockade of Cuba. Now the world waited to see who would blink first.

The impasse ended in a surreal manner. Over dinner in New Your City a reporter for the NBC news, John Scali, was passed a letter by a low-level Soviet agent. The note was from the Premier himself, Nikita Khrushchev. It was an opening for both nations to save face, Kennedy seized the opportunity, and the next day he met with Ambassador Anatoly Dobryurn. Both sides took a step back from the ledge. After the Soviets dismantled their missiles in Cuba and loaded them back on ships, the US quietly did the same with the Jupiter missiles Emmett had supervised in Turkey.

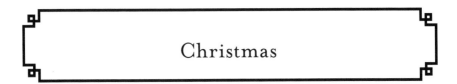

Christmas

Christmas is a time of family and ritual. For Joe the ritual actually started in mid-November when Jim Sexton, given his artistic bent, was recruited to be the family's photographer. Scrubbed and neatly dressed, the tribe would be aligned either around the sofa or on the stairs in the living room for the annual Christmas picture. Invariably there always proved to be some form of disruption. An abiding image from these episodes was Joe shouting, "put the crying one in the back." Regardless of the trauma, the resulting picture gave no hint of the tumult, but there is no way to know how many pictures were required before everyone looked reasonable happy. Once a picture was chosen from the selection Jim had taken, the suitable negative was sent to the printer, along with Joe's Christmas poem. A box of finished cards then arrived weeks later and phase two would start.

After dishes had been cleared from the dining room table, the Christmas cards would come out. Spreading them across the table, Joe labored to write personal notes on each card to the multitude of friends whose addresses he'd carefully catalogued over the years. For all the time it took, the whole enterprise must have been an act of great pride for Joe. Compiled over the years the pictures would annually document the steady aging of the family. One poignant note was the obvious inclusion of Mark's picture on the wall in all Christmas cards after his death.

Strings of colored lights circled the tree with every fourth bulb out or threatening to burn out, and long stands of aluminum tinsel were draped over the limbs, with a fair share ending up on the floor and clogging the vacuum cleaner. Vinyl albums of Christmas music rested on the turn table to be run periodically, and there were stacks of presents forming a circular mound at the base of the tree. Most of these, though useless, and their quantity was enormous, as everyone would purchase gifts for all the other family members. Fake foam snow adorned the windows in the living room, and was restricted to that room alone since it made too big a mess. And the smell of white square anise cookie being emitted from the kitchen would fill the whole downstairs. All of these smells, sights, and sounds were just a prelude to the twenty-four hours of Christmas.

The night of Christmas Eve all those presents would be opened. Every family member staked a claim to a seat in the living room, and beside their space would form a neat pile of presents. After every present had been ripped open and all the shreds of carefully taped wrapping paper cleaned from the floor, the family waited for midnight mass.

Father Kleiner put extra effort into this late night extravaganza. Outside the church paper bags with a small amount of sand at the bottom held single candles. These bags were uniformly spaced along the sidewalk in front of the Catholic Church with their dim light reflecting the snow. In the balcony, the choir, after weeks of practice, was already in full throat as the crowd sought out space in the pews. Six altar boys in black and white cassocks held lanterns forming a processional line to usher Kleiner to the altar from the back of the church. Even at this late hour, it was hard to find a sleepy eye in the congregation during the service, but it wasn't long after mass and after the adults had exchanged greetings with those who passed their way that the children started showing signs of drowsiness. Why the air felt colder on the way home after mass is hard to explain, but it always did. Everyone was much less conversational on the drive home, with youngest ones starting to nod off. Within thirty minutes of arriving back at the farm, almost everyone was in bed except Joe and Marilane. When the children were younger, the toys left by Santa needed to be unwrapped, assembled and placed near the tree.

The chaos had ended by the time this picture was taken. Donna and Marilane, each holding one of the twins, appear to have the same sober expression as Joe.

Early the next morning, after Santa had left dolls, toy guns, farm sets with a hundred pieces, and clothes for everyone in the living room, the children filtered down from their beds. The presents were as pristine as they would ever be, but not surprisingly some wouldn't make it through the day. There was also the familiar smell of Christmas morning. A turkey large enough to feed the family would go into the oven early in the morning and the aroma drifting from the kitchen, tantalizing even for that early hour, promised a feast later that day.

Invariably at midmorning the awaited call came in. As much a part of Christmas as the tree and the presents, the few hours spent at the Millers' unfailingly completed the annual ritual. Adolph and Helen Miller had moved off Division Street years before and now resided in a neat red home beside the hospital on Main Street.

Helen, who was always impeccably dressed with large heavy earrings pulling down her ear lobes, met everyone at the kitchen door as they filed in from the driveway. Like the Sexton house, the Millers' home embraced everyone with the smells arising from the Christmas dinner. Noise filled the small house, as grandchildren played in the living room and from the basement loud voices could be heard. The adults were down there.

Once into their teens the Sexton children were allowed admittance to the basement sanctum. Progressing down the narrow basement stairway, dipping their heads to clear the low ceiling on the lower landing, the guests would gaze upon a rather plain linoleum covered room. At the far end was the bar, manned by the three sons-in-laws: Tom Masterpole, who was short balding and gregarious; Vic Gallow, a totally bald man with a distinctively large nose; and Jack Swisher, who was tall and more reserved than his other two relatives. They mixed drinks, or more actually "the 'drink," whiskey and 7-up. As the years passed a right of passage was performed on Christmas mornings. As the children reached a suitable age of 14 or 15, they were allowed to enter the adult realm, and it was then that they got their first whiskey and seven. More than once the Sextons would go home with a couple of individuals partially impaired.

As the Sextons left the Millers, Helen would give Marilane a Christmas present. Helen was a woman of exquisite taste, with an eye for antiques that would lead to her own antique store years later. Her presents normally were figures of Madonna with child, some stunningly exquisite in their details. Hopelessly over matched, Marilane would attempt to come up with something for Helen, but would always fall short of her friend's generosity.

Upon arriving back at the farm, one final scene remained of the holiday. After Joe or the boys collected Grandmother Inez from town, everyone would gather for the meal. All that food prepared in the morning would be spread across the dining table. Appetites whetted by the lingering aromas could not help but lead to overeating. With the table cleared and Grandma taken home, Christmas officially ended. A subdued atmosphere settled over the house, as the youngest members played with their toys and the older ones napped.

The Sixties

Each decade seems to have its own personality; the 30's with the poverty of the depression, the forties consumed by the war, the fifties a go-go period of growth and expansion, and finally the sixties, a period of change and social upheaval. Nationally the populace had seen the age of Camelot abruptly end in an assassination, and a war in the jungles of Southeast Asia split the nation along generational lines. Closer to Sumner, the demise of the family farm continued its slow and barely perceivable progress, and the very first vestiges of large farming operations started to appear. Within the Sexton household the children were aging, preparing to leave for college, and a few would be getting married before the end of the decade.

Like the forties, this time revolved around a war-- not only a military war overseas but a cultural war at home. Secretary of State, Dean Rush's domino theory of communist control over Asia influenced President Kennedy to slowly draw the US into the conflict between the two halves of Vietnam. This backwater of the world would attract the nation's attention for the next twelve years.

In 1963, with John Kennedy's televised assassination, a brazen political animal from Texas would assume the presidency, Lyndon Johnson. He would, in the following years, attempt to change the social face of America and see his presidency be destroyed by the war he inherited. Lyndon had followed his general's advice and expanded the scope of the Vietnam War. The Gulf of Tonkin Resolution based on false reports of an attack on an American destroyer, enlarged the war; for the first time US planes would flying over North Vietnam, bombing that small country. Believing in US military might, the President and his generals thought the war could be won with a larger army. In response, the local draft boards were asked to feed more young men in to meet the demands for more troops in Southeast Asia.

A rift soon developed which was to split the country mostly along generational lines – those in favor of the war and those who doubted its worth. The era of the "hippy" was born, protest music, drug use, long hair and campus riots. Though Vietnam captured most of the attention of America, it wasn't the lone hot spot in the world. In the Middle East, the Six-Day War erupted and was the initial salvo into decades of Arab- Israeli hatred. In Northern Ireland 'the troubles' erupted and the centuries-old hatred between the Irish and the imported Scottish overlords boiled into conflict. In China, the Cultural Revolution caused death and destruction in the most populated communist nation on the planet.

Within the United States the pace of change seemed to be on steroids. It only took a decade to go from Uri Gazarin being the first man into space to Neil Armstrong walking on the moon. In medicine, birth control pills forever altered women's role in society and for the first time a physician in South Africa, Christian Barnard, transplanted organs from one human to another, opening a whole new wave of replacement body parts.

With the introduction of semi conductors and microchips the technology boom was off and running. Microwave ovens, lasers, satellites, automated teller machines, and computers appeared during the decade. The shift from a manufacturing to a service economy had begun.

Socially, television brought its own change. People now stayed home for their entertainment. Televised sports enhanced such events as professional golf and would propel the NFL and AFL into joining forces. The first of the super bowls would be broadcast late in the decade.

Back in Sumner, TV would claim one victim, the Sumner Cubs. At one time the Cubs were the biggest sporting event in town. The players were young men from town augmented by recruits from the surrounding communities. To prove how big a draw the team was, just behind the municipal light plant the city built Cub Park. A baseball diamond flanked by wooden bleachers down first and third base lines. Behind home plate were covered bleachers. When filled to capacity the stands could hold two thousand people.

Joe never played for the Cubs but his friends Jim McAloon and Les Teeling did. None of the boys played but Dan, a baseball fanatic, along with his buddy Mike McAloon served as bat boys for two seasons.

In the thirties the team only played on Sundays, drawing large crowds to watch the game against neighboring towns. With the installation of lighting during the fifties, evening games became the rage. The Sumner Cubs reached their zenith during the mid 50's. During that time they won the Amateur Baseball World Series. After their victory in Battle Creek, Michigan, their return was feted by a parade down Main Street with the town turning out to cheer home their heroes.

The team was good enough to host exhibition games with semi-pro teams. Teams like the Philadephia Zulo Jungle Giants, the Legions Colored All Stars, and the Carolina Hobos played with the Cubs, with probably the most famous among these players being Satchell Paige who pitched one night in Cub Park in 1959. The local players were celebrities in town. They were players like Chuck Morgan, a turkey farmer, Chuck Anderson, who worked for Wayne Schutte, and Cal Harms, who worked as insurance agent.

TV played a big part in the diminishing interest in the Cubs, and better roads and more dependable cars allowed people to travel further for their entertainment. By 1958 attendance showed the first signs of decrease. Soon, with interest waning even attracting players started to become a problem. The club would continue to struggle till 1965, when both players and fans were hard to come by and the team finally folded.

Cub Park survived, and for years the high school and little league used the field. But finally the wooden bleachers fell into such disrepair that for safety's sake Cub Park was demolished. Today not a shred of evidence remains of the glorious Cubs, and soon all those able to remember nights with 2000 cheering fans will be gone.

Though the Cubs were fading, the enthusiasm for baseball hadn't. In the summer of 1961, Joe and Jim McAloon wanted to take their boys to Chicago to watch the Yankees play the White Soxs. For the boys it was going to be just a baseball game, but for their fathers the entire trip had a lot to do with a passing of an era.

They had booked seats on the Land O' Corn train. Since 1941 the train had carried passengers from Iowa into Chicago, but like other passenger car trains, its days were numbered. After picking up the train in Dubuque, the Sumner party rode it to its terminus in the Union Station in downtown Chicago. Once one of the most bustling railroad hubs in the country, its days were also waning. The atrium for the station consisted of a massive space covered by a barrel vaulted ceiling filled with sky lights towering 110 feet tall. To leave the station, marble staircases brought passengers up to street level. (The Canal Street entrance would be featured in the movie the *Untouchables*.) The space, though past its prime, still captivated the imagination of travelers like the Sextons and McAloons in the sixties, as it had done in the forties.

Following the theme of the trip, their hotel was also scheduled for termination. The Edgewater Beach Hotel would serve as their lodgings. Once a premier hotel, the 400 room building on Lake Michigan from its beginning in 1916 had been the place to see and the place to be seen. Movie stars and presidents graced its rooms. One of the memorable stories about the hotel occurred in 1949. A Philadelphia Phillies first basemen by the name of Eddie Waithus was shot in one of the rooms by a deranged fan, Ruth Steinhager. The incident became the basis of a book and subsequent movie by Bernard Malamud called "The Natural." Until the late 50's the hotel had direct access to the shore of Lake Michigan. At the end of that decade the city of Chicago through eminent domain gained ownership of the land directly in front of the hotel. Lake Shore Drive would now separate the hotel from the lake. The road construction started the demise of the once great hotel.

Even though the hotel only had a few years left, on the week-end the two families stayed there it still retained much of its panache. Adding to the experience that week-end, the hotel also hosted some famous guests. The New York Yankees who were in town to play the White Sox had booked rooms there and a famous movie and TV star, Groucho Marx was there for the week-end. Though almost 70 he still was the host of the TV show "You Bet Your Life". He was readily recognizable to the Sextons as he passed them with his ever present cigar and the boys stood gaping at him in the hotel lobby.

In the mid 60's Joe and Earl recognized the minor changes occurring in the farm community. Their vet practice was riding the top of the curve, but little by little people were leaving farming. Parents who as they grew older and wanted to leave the farm would find their children showed no desire to continue the farming operation. The process began whereby land would be sold off and the buildings would be sold as an acreage. The blueprint was in place. Starting slowly at first, with just a farm here and there; the trend was obvious, the era of family farm was over.

The changes to the vet practice were almost unperceivable, but Joe seized the opportunity presented by the available farm land. He started buying land parcel by parcel. Always impressed by the success achieved by the Bowling Brothers, he adopted their theory of buying land, since they had accumulated numerous farms. The Bowlings held that they would never buy another farm till they paid for the first one they had bought, never willing to gamble on leverage. They did, however, famously gamble once.

On most of their farms, the Bowling boys ran cattle, and during the Second World War cattle prices were strictly controlled. With the end of the war, price controls were scheduled to come off on one set day. Prices could go up or go down, but the Bowlings were willing to bet on the former. Loading every available steer they had onto a fleet of trucks, they drove overnight into Chicago. At the start of business the next morning at the Chicago Stock yards, the Bowlings had their trucks lined up at the gate. They won the bet. Beef prices spiked that day, making the boys a tidy fortune.

Renting out the farmland he purchased, Joe would soon need the extra income. With Mike's graduation and enrollment at the University of Iowa, every subsequent year would see another Sexton go off to college. For the next fourteen years tuition would be fact of life.

Prior to his graduation and unknown to him at the time, Mike had followed in his father's footsteps. In the dark long before sunrise Mike left for his job at the bakery. Without a car, he somehow managed to get himself to work. (None of the children would ever have a car of their own in high school.) In Hizzie's old bakery the Volker Brothers, Dan and Eddie, had built a thriving business, daily shipping bread and pastries out to neighboring grocery stores. Mike might have been the first off to work every day, but he was by no means the only one who worked. Without allowances, work outside the farm proved to be the only access to spending cash for the children.

Tom worked at the municipal swimming pool, following his older brother who had worked there the first year after its construction in 1960. The hours were better at the pool but boredom certainly was a drawback. In an effort to compensate for the tedium, Tom and fellow life guard Barry Zborinik peroxided their hair white. The new look hardly impressed his parents. Peg would succeed Tom, working for a time at the pool, but she never considered any change in her personal appearance.

Dan and Tim took a different route. They worked for Jim McAloon at his supermarket, stacking shelves, cleaning floors, and bagging groceries for the princely sum of 60 cents per hour; this was the true definition of minimum wage. Meager salary wasn't the jobs only disadvantage. An anguished and lonely woman by the name of Leota Delahunt supervised the check outline at the store. The bane of every bag boy she relished censuring the young men on a continual basis. The poor woman who lived next to Max Hill at the end of the neighborhood block on Division Street would eventually die all alone in her house, achieving a sad ending to a sad life.

During this time, with a busy vet practice, and nine children on the go it wouldn't seem possible that there would be time for vacations, but Joe and Marilane had a knack for finding time. They alway found time for themselves. In 1959, accompanied by the Mangans, they flew to the Rose Bowl. Since Joe and Marilane were graduates of Iowa State, it might be safe to assume the Mangans were the inspiration for the trip. It was a rare Hawkeye win, Iowa trouncing California, quarterbacked by Joe Cap, 38 to 12. Enthralled by the Rose Parade and the massive Rose Bowl, Joe regaled everyone with his vivid descriptions upon returning home. Every trip he took, no matter his age, seemed to excite Joe. He could always find something novel in every excursion.

That same year they traveled to South America. Part of the reason was accompanying Lillian Devine on her visit to see her youngest son, John, then living in Rio de Janeiro, Brazil. John and his wife Mirga, both foreigners in Brazil, had taken curious routes to arrive at such an exotic location.

While still in college John had been drafted. It was the height of the Korean War, and draft boards again were asked to increase their output. John would fall victim to their monthly quota. Enlisted but never leaving the US, John's military service coincided with the last vestiges of the police action. With the signing of the truce, John's military career was cut short. He ended up enlisted for only 21 months. Now eligible for the GI bill, he enrolled in the University of Arizona for a two-year course in the Foreign Service. Just before graduation, the Bank of Boston offered him a job which he accepted. His first assignment would be in Rio de Janeiro. The position came with some strings attached. Once transferred there the posting required three years of service without any possibility of a return state side. Once on site in Rio, John realized, whether due to this restriction or not, most of the American employers were from the MidWest. It is hard to say exactly why Midwesterners were more suited to that particular posting. Falling into a clique of young professionals, he was introduced to Mirga Jergutes, a beautiful Lithuanian immigrant. Mirga had taken her own twisted route to Rio.

While living in Lithuania, Mirga's father had served as a colonel in the army. It was 1940 and the Molotov-Ribbentrop pact had just been signed. The Nazis and the Bolsheviks had carved up the nations between themselves, the Baltic nations and Poland. As an officer in the army, this meant almost certain death for Colonel Jergutes and most likely a trip to Siberia for his family once the Soviets crossed the border. With the annexation of the Baltic Republics, Estonia, Latvia, and Lithuania, the Colonel decided to take his chances with the Germans. Covertly smuggling his wife and two daughters across the East Prussian border he was welcomed by the German forces. Migrating through German territory the Jergutes finally settled in Berlin. The family remained there content enough until the British Air Force started aerial bombing in Berlin. Once again fearing for his family's safety he was forced to move. Working their way southward through Vichy France, they then crossed the Spanish border. Settling in Barcelona, the Jergutes applied for American visas, but fascist Spain wasn't considered to have favorable nation status, and it soon became apparent that America wasn't a viable option. Determined to flee Europe, they finally succeeded in booking passage to Brazil.

By the time Joe, Marilane, and Lillian arrived in Rio, John, now married, had established roots in the city. Besides working with the bank John had pursued other investments in and around the city. He had already purchased 10 acres of beach front property as a home site or a speculative investment; John had an eye for real estate. He even had ventured into farming. His purchase of 11,000 acre banana plantation outside the city would have impressed his father and Uncle Art. But dabbling in banana farming wasn't without its problems. Squatters started taking advantage of the immense space of John's plantation. Troubled by the situation he sought the advice of his neighboring plantation owner. That man, experienced at dealing with squatters, advised John to hire the crew that had worked for him to solve a similar problem. Totally unembarrassed he described how the men fell upon the squatters raping their wives and burning their huts. He assured John their methods were quite effective. Taken a back, John deemed it more effective to sell the land than venture into rape and pillage.

Within months of their South American trip, Joe and Marilane took another "family" vacation. The younger half had the honor of journeying this time. A world's fair was being held in Flushing Meadows, New York just outside New York City in Queens. Tom Devine would host them. He had also taken a curious road from the tail section of a bomber to New Jersey.

After his discharge from the air force, Tom reentered Iowa State, completing his degree. A devoted Catholic he pictured himself going into the priesthood, but his mother, Lillian, who should have been proud of a son for committing his life to the church, was skeptical of Tom's choice. She proved to be correct. Tom Devine did enter the seminary, but before taking his final vows he abruptly left. The entire episode is shrouded in murky facts. Tom never talked about it. In fact, years later when his daughter brought up the seminary, her father curtly refused to discuss anything about it.

Once more back among lay people, Tom took a job selling pharmaceuticals on the road. Playing in a little semi-pro baseball league on the side, he kicked around for a year or two. It was obvious to those people who knew him that he wasn't cut out for a life in sales. One day his cousin, Juanta Clark called. She'd heard that the FBI was hiring. They'd dropped their long standing requirement for applicants to be either accountants or lawyers. Applying, Tom was readily accepted into the FBI.

After his training, he was stationed in New York City. This was in the fifties and at the height of McCarthyism and the red scare. Assigned to follow known Communists, he found his days consumed by tracking suspected members and monitoring their movements and contacts. Probably his most famous subject was Angela Davis, an active member of the Communist Party. Today, the politically correct term for her would be an activist or organizer.

A secretary in the New York office, Mary Elizabeth Dougherty caught Tom's eye. The fourth oldest of a family of 12, she still lived at home with her widowed mother. Liz and Tom started dating. Completely smitten, Tom proposed marriage. The prospect of marriage placed Liz in a bind. Her income, which she shared with her mother, helped to sustain the family, which still had eight children at home. Forced to choose between Tom and her family, Liz couldn't abandon her mother. Heartbroken, Tom decided to move on and started dating other women.

A few weeks passed, and Tom received a letter from Mrs. Dougherty, Liz's mother. As a true gentleman, Tom Devine never divulged the confidential contents of the letter and Mrs. Dougherty also remained silent on its subject. It probably can be inferred that Mrs. Dougherty placed Liz's future ahead of the family's needs. Conjecture aside, Tom and Liz were married shortly thereafter.

By 1964, the year of the fair, Tom and Liz were settled comfortably across the Hudson River in New Jersey. Ever the great host, he would usher the Iowans around the big city. John and Tom might have had unconventional career paths but the other relatives of Joe and Marilane had their own stories to tell.

Donna and Mardy had left Cleveland and moved to Elmhurst, a suburb of Chicago, Mardy finally leaving a job he didn't want in the first place. It was in Chicago that Donna finally had the permanence she'd wanted for so many years. She would fall in love with Chicago, reading both of the city's major newspapers daily. Even in her final years when she was confined to a nursing home she still insisted having those newspapers delivered.

Emmett relocated state side, being stationed at Wright Patterson Air Force Base in Ohio. His work, however, didn't have the same international repercussions.

Within the family Kenneth Devine, without a doubt the most

reserved of any of his siblings, normally shunned the lime light, but ironically in October 1965 he would find his face plastered all across the national news. The serving president at the time, Lyndon Johnson, needed his gall bladder removed. With all the fine doctors at Bethesda Naval Hospital who were able to perform this minor surgery the question would arise why he needed physicians flown in? For whatever reason, Johnson requested five surgeons from the Mayo Clinic to perform the surgery. Kenneth happened to be one of those chosen. Once the surgery was completed in the congested operating room and LBJ recovered adequately to greet the waiting press, the iconic picture of the president pulling up his shirt to expose the surgical incision was fed out to newspapers and TV. Prominent behind the narcissistic commander in chief were his five physicians looking uncomfortable, and probably none more so than Kenneth.

Sending Them Off to College

Never overly sentimental with their children, when their eldest son left for college, Joe and Marlane implied that maybe Mike could get a ride with a friend, so when Mike moved his Smith Corona typewriter, desk lamp, and clothing up the flight of stairs to his dorm room, there wasn't a doting parent there to help or tearfully wish him well. Enrolled at the University of Iowa in engineering, Mike discovered that first year that he wasn't cut out to be an engineer. His grade point for his freshman year was less than adequate. When he broke the news to his father, Joe remained composed. It's natural for all of us, when pressed with a new problem, to hearken back to things we know and are comfortable with. This was the case that day. Mike's father compassionately encouraged him to consider transferring to Loras College. Maybe a smaller school might afford Mike a more suitable environment. His advice would be the tonic Mike needed.

The next year when Mike settled into his dorm room in Keane Hall, Tom took off to Iowa State. Emulating his father that fall he rushed the SAE fraternity. All seemed well. Mike adjusted well to life at Loras, and Joe and Tom would share a bond as fraternity brothers. During Tom's second year, however, on a week-end in Des Moines this tranquility would be disrupted. Teaming up with a fraternity brother and out on the town, Tom would achieve unsought notoriety. A caustic combination of alcohol, poor judgment and a Des Moines policeman congealed in Tom's arrest and a front page article in the statewide paper, the Des

Moines Register. Distributed throughout the state, more than a few copies prominently featuring the opprobrious story were being read over morning coffee in Sumner, one of them by Joe Sexton. In this case, Joe's compassion must have been sorely pressed. Whatever the tone of the conversation between father and son, Tom enrolled at Loras College the following fall.

Both boys were at the school when Dan's turn came up in the rotation. Leaving high school after one semester of his senior year, he'd go directly to Loras. By the time the third child was ready for college Joe was further along on the learning curve.

With three boys in school, Joe had already worked out pragmatic financial considerations. To be fair Joe and Earl had a lucrative practice. Each brought home about $40,000 a year (about $220,000 in today's dollars), but Joe limited his allotment to tuition to $1000 a year for each boy. At, Loras room and board ran about $3000, the difference was up to each man to make up on his own.

By mid May 1964, finals' week was coming to an end and the three boys would be heading home for the summer. Surprisingly with a modest enrollment of only 1400 students, you would think the three boys would cross paths on campus frequently, but that wasn't the case. They saw more of each other off campus at a small neighborhood bar three blocks away from Keane Hall, the Avenue Tap. The corner saloon wasn't much to look at. As you entered you saw a narrow beer-soaked wooden bar running down the right side of the tavern. Impregnated wood floor and old stools added to the aroma and atmosphere. Cheap 15-cent draws and a lackadaisical attitude toward crudely made fake ID's made it one of the premier hangouts for Loras' men.

Finding their way home for the summer break with bags of evil smelling laundry, they all had work lined up for the summer months. Unknown to them at the time, the summer of 1964 would be the last summer the entire family would be together at home. Mike, though, would only be there on the week ends. He had taken a job out of New Hampton working on a road construction crew.

Dan landed a life guarding job while Tom managed an interesting job with his uncle Jim. Still with Kroblin Trucking, Jim, besides dispatching loads across the nation, was in charge of securing what the industry called the "authority." The trucking industry was regulated by the Interstate Commerce Commission (ICC), and part of their mandate was issuance of "authority" for routes and the corresponding cargo from point A to point B. True to the bureaucratic form of the ICC the authority was accompanied by a tariff. The government surely intended to make money off this deal. Every authority needed to be published and then filed in a log. Jim dispensed this tedious task to his nephew, Tom.

A hot topic in the office at Kroblin's that summer was the pending negotiations with the Teamsters Union. Jimmy Hoffa and the unions had their tentacles extending into even off-the-beaten-track little towns in Iowa. Allen Kroblin later that year did come to terms with the Teamsters. Whether it was braggadocio or fact, Allen claimed that "once you have a deal with Jimmy (ie: pay him off) he would deliver."

September saw the three oldest boys, their clothing clean and folded, heading back to school. Two months later, the presidential election put Johnson back in the White House defeating Barry Goldwater in a landslide election. This was significant because the US was still deeply embroiled in the Vietnam War, and Johnson's victory would bring no relief to the nation. Ramping up the military, the war would within a few years have its creeping tentacles enter the Sexton family.

Resurrecting his grade point average after his dismal freshman year, Mike, now a senior at Loras, applied to law schools. Tom, a junior studying economics, had more non academic pursuits in mind. For years he had been captivated by a red haired beauty from Sumner. Now he pressed his case every free week-end, traveling to Cedar Falls where the woman in question, Bea Callahan, attended school. Within a year he would secure victory and be engaged and Mike would be accepted to law school, settling on Washington University in St. Louis.

Near Disaster

Wednesday evening, Mike's white Corvair sat in the farm driveway. He and his brothers were all home from college. That night Marilane surveyed the children looking for anyone who might want to go with her the next morning to visit their grandmother now in a nursing home in Rochester, Minnesota. It was a hard sell, who wanted to make that boring drive two days before Christmas? The older children certainly didn't want to go. The twins found watching TV vastly more appealing. Theresa was staying the over night with her friend Becky Harms who lived in town, and she had no desire to get up that early. Mary agreed to go but she had an alternative motive. Marilane had promised her that they would go, shopping once they had finished visiting Grandma. Mary had a keen interest in buying some high heeled shoes. At 13, the shoes were important as a means of peer acceptance. All her Protestant friends owned high heels because the shoes were a mark of passage worn during their confirmation ceremony. One of her Protestant friends, Ann McAloon, had agreed to ride along with Mary and her mother, surely just for the shopping experience.

Early Thursday morning, Marilane busied herself going back and forth to the car carrying Christmas gifts for her mother and a green leather footstool. The footstool had always been a prominent part of Lillian's living room back in Bancroft. Marilane thought it would add a homey touch to her room in the nursing home. Bundled up against the cold morning air she came back into the house. She wanted to get going. Mary was on the phone with Ann McAloon. Ann couldn't go. It was just going to be Mary and her mother.

It was eight o'clock, December 23, 1965 when the pair left the driveway in Lillian's big blue Chevy BelAir. Marilane had had it since her mother left Bancroft for the nursing home. Joe wasn't the type to see them off; he had been at work for more than an hour already. The two left Sumner taking all two lane roads north to Minnesota, where the last eight miles to Rochester would be a four lane road. The trip was a tedious progress from one small town to the next. Halfway on their route was a familiar site, the massive Catholic Church on the hill beside Lourdes, Iowa. North of Lourdes, Highway 63 crossed the Iowa-Minnesota border then meandered on to Spring Valley, Minnesota. After passing through the little town of Racine, which was only a huge grain elevator surrounded by a handful of houses, the road made an S curve toward Stewartville, just 15 miles from Rochester.

As Marilane and Mary passed by the Racine elevator their journey was just about over, Marilane anticipated seeing her mother and Mary grew more excited about the prospect of shopping. As they emerged from the gentle S curve north of Racine, two cars were stopped in the southbound lane with their turning signals flashing.

In the first car sat Carl Schroeder, a local man, waiting for the blue Chevy and the following car to pass to make a left turn onto a gravel road. Stopped right behind him was Ann Chaffee, also from Stewartville. While waiting for the traffic to pass, Ann happened to look in her rear view mirror. Coming over the gentle slope behind her she a truck was bearing down on her in her lane, and she perceived that the truck was moving too fast. At the wheel of the grain truck was twenty-five year old Lowell Statudaln. Heading for the Racine elevator, he was in a hurry to finish his route before the Christmas break. Loaded and moving too fast, he recognized the stopped vehicles far too late. Lowell applied the brakes, but the cogs of fate were already in motion.

Ann had the feeling the truck was coming down on her too fast, and in a desperate last second move, she pulled the steering wheel of the car to the right in an effort to move her car off the road. Angled now toward the shoulder, Lowell veered toward the left but still caught her rear bumper shoving her further toward the ditch.

Now Carl had seen what was going on behind him, and he also instinctively tried to pull to the right and get out of the truck's way. Now the grain truck straddling the center line smashed into the back left side of Carl's car.

These events were all playing out in Marilane's windshield. She also attempted to move the BelAir to the right, out of the truck's path. A head on collision was averted by Marilane's split second maneuver, but the left corner of the truck still smashed into the driver's door of Lillian's car, shattering glass and crushing steel. The heavy blue car veered toward the ditch and sped down the grassy depression between the road and the railroad tracks to the right of Highway 63. Following closely behind Marilane was a car carrying four family members from Illinois, which hit the truck square head on. The explosive sound of the collision took only seconds to die down, and then there was only silence. The whole episode had taken mere seconds but lives were forever altered. Ann and Carl were shocked but unhurt. Lowell was mentally stunned but physically fine. In the car from Illinois compressed into half its original size, none of the occupants survived. In Lillian's Chevy, one passenger was fine, but the driver had suffered life threatening injuries.

When Lowell's truck hit the Buick, the steel pillar and door frame were blasted inward, lacerating Marilane's face and crushing the bones of her skull in the area of her temple. Mary, unhurt, quickly recognized her mother's condition was serious. She was semi-conscious, and the facial laceration was already bleeding profusely. The cut ran down Marilane's left jaw line to her chin, deep enough that the underlying muscle and connective tissue were clearly visible. Disoriented and feeling helpless, the teenager crawled out of the crumpled blue car and walked back up the tire tracks in grass toward the crash site. The only person standing there was Lowell. Imploring his help for her mother, Mary waited for his reply.

Clearly dazed Lowell agreed to try and help and the two of them walked down into the ditch to where the car was resting. Lowell leaned down and peered through the shattered remains of the driver's window. It's hard to comprehend exactly what passed through his mind when he saw Marilane, but he clearly wasn't in any condition to help. Lowell was futilely sympathetic to the young girl's terror when he said, "I can't help you. Just try to keep your mother warm." With that he turned and walked back to his truck.

In the back seat, Marilane had carefully folded her winter coat, intending to wear it once they reached Rochester. Her "good" coat, it was cloth with supposedly a mink fur collar. Mary took the coat from the seat and shook off the broken glass. After draping it over her mother, the blood still flowing from her face ran down and onto the coat. Mary remembered thinking how upset her mother was going to be if her coat was ruined by the blood.

By now the road, blocked by the crash, had traffic backed up in both directions. Out of their cars, sightseers started milling around the crashed vehicles. Mary sat next to her mother as innumerable individuals walked by and leaned down to gawk at her and Marilane. Never saying a word, they moved on to the next car as if they were viewing exhibits in a museum.

Finally one man bending over to see Mary asked, "Are you a Christian?" After Mary answered in the affirmative, he said he'd say a prayer and remain with her until help arrived. The accident had been a blur, flashing by in a manner of seconds, too fast to allow a reflection, but the moments after were excruciatingly drawn out. Each minute cruelly played out second by painstakingly long second. Time required for the ambulance to arrive was impossible to calculate. It was hard to locate a point of reference but the ambulance did come and the 'good Samaritan' took his leave, never leaving his name.

Marilane was carefully removed from her mother's car and carried to the waiting ambulance, still unconscious. Behind the fragments of her crushed skull hemorrhaging was already putting pressure on the brain. Mary, without anyone to take care of her was asked to ride along with her mother in the ambulance. Crowded into the ambulance which was little more than an oversized station wagon, mother and daughter rode to Rochester, the siren squealing.

The ambulance was bound straight for St. Mary's Hospital, an eight-story brick building that towered over the Minnesota town. Associated with the Mayo Clinic it had grown quite expansive, far larger than the townspeople would require. The fact that the clinic attracted nationally known medical talent would play a critical role in Marilane's fate. As a small crowd of hospital staff attended to her mother in the emergency room, Mary was left with a young nurse in the waiting room. Making small talk with the anxious teenager, the nurse hoped to distract her in those anguished moments. In a moment of clarity, Mary remembered her Aunt Evelyn. Interrupting her nurse companion she asked, "I'm all alone. Would you call my Aunt? She knows we were coming today." The nurse readily said yes but asked who was her Aunt.

"Evelyn Devine, Dr Kenneth Devine's wife" Mary replied. Although she was young and the Mayo Clinic was large, the nurse recognized the name. With a look of affinity, she told Mary she would call her Aunt right away, and with that she headed for the reception desk.

The Devines had just finished lunch in their home. Just blocks south of St. Mary's in a spacious wooded neighborhood, Evelyn and Kenneth had been watching the noon news over lunch. Breaking news had been the story of a horrible accident south on Highway 63. Evelyn had commented how tragic to have something like that happen just before Christmas. Within minutes of that statement their phone rang. It was the nurse from the hospital. Time now became of the essence, and Kenneth, when he arrived assumed command of his sister's treatment.

Marilane had suffered multiple injuries. Beside her facial laceration, she had a fractured pelvis and broken ribs, but the most immediate concern was the sub dural hematoma. When the steel frame of the car crushed her skull, the underlying cranial blood vessels ruptured. The blood pooling under dura mater now was pushing against the tissues of the skull and brain. The softer of the two, the brain, received most of the pressure. Unless lessened, the damage could be permanent or fatal.

Realizing the moment's gravity, Kenneth started calling his medical colleagues. One of the first men he called was Dr. Uline, the head neurosurgeon at St. Mary's. Heir to the Schultz Brewing fortune, Dr. Uline had, fortunately for Marilane, never proceeded into the beer business. Kenneth also contacted a fellow plastic surgeon and other friends to assist Dr. Uline.

While her husband organized the medical treatment, Evelyn located Mary and took it upon herself to alert the Sexton family.

With lunch over, Peg was cleaning up the kitchen when the phone rang. The news from Evelyn threw the remaining children at home into a commotion. Joe hadn't come home for lunch; he still had calls to run. At that time Mrs. Gaede ran the office for the practice, but she had gone home for lunch. Earl was also home for lunch, but with his two-way radio he could call Joe. For whatever reason, the three oldest boys thought it imperative to talk to Earl in person.

The kitchen door leading to the drive way was at the end of a poorly light hallway. The southern sun shining through the door illuminated the three boys standing on the porch as Earl walked toward it. He must have suspected something seeing all three boys huddled there. After the boys informed him of the situation, Earl hustled to his car and started hailing Joe, hoping to catch Joe between calls.

Sitting in his car writing a "ticket" for the call he had just finished, Joe heard Earl's voice coming over the radio. There was urgency in the tone of his voice. Getting right to the point, he brought his partner up to speed on the accident and Marilane's perilous condition.

Joe at the time had been parked in the yard of a farm just south of Hawkeye, Iowa, about 10 miles from Sumner. The road back to Sumner led right past Doug Grahlman's farm. Doug was out walking beside the barn when he heard the sound of the car even before he saw it. When it finally came into view he recognized it as one of the vet's cars, and the car was flying. Literally it had four wheels off the ground as it came over the hill north of the farm. Though it was almost a blur, Doug could make out Joe at the wheel with a grave expression on his face.

Theresa had come back home from Becky Harms', and when she saw Joe she was frightened by her father's appearance as he came into the house. She would remember him as a "wild man." Almost oblivious to his children, Joe dashed into the downstairs bedroom. After a very quick bath and emerging in one of his suits, Joe gave orders for his children. He would drive to Rochester and the three oldest boys, also now attired in suits, would follow in the family car. Peg would remain home and be in charge of the younger children. There was no debating the plan, Joe was grimly serious.

Joe and the boys teamed up once they reached St. Mary's. By now Evelyn and Mary were in the hospital chapel accompanied by two nuns. Not long after the family members were united, they heard footsteps echoing on the marble floor of the chapel. Dr. Uline was out of surgery and had news for the anguished family. Marilane would survive but her recovery would be lengthy. Relieved from their worst fears, Joe told the boys to take Mary home, and he would stay with their mother. To this day we don't know if he remained in Marilane's hospital room that night or went to the Devine's. Due to the chaos and trauma of that evening no one ever thought to ask Joe exactly what he had done the night. But either way, he would return to Sumner the next day. It would be a Christmas none would forget.

While the older Sextons waited in the ornate chapel, the home portion of the family had a much different experience. In a small town gossip spreads faster than a brush fire on a windy day. By mid afternoon, friends were showing up at the farm, bringing food in every conceivable form. The kitchen countertop soon overflowed with cake pans, oven dishes, Tupperware, and bread.

Christmas Eve morning found Mary and the three boys all in their beds, having arrived home late the previous night. Some of the younger Sextons were up early, and rummaging in the kitchen, looking for breakfast. With thick grey clouds guarding the eastern sky, the sunrise was subdued. The impending chance of snow and the cold temperature were enough to dampen any mood, but especially in combination with the previous day's events. The entire day would have a disjointed feel about it. The lights were on the Christmas tree, the presents were arranged beneath it, and fake snow adorned the windows, but the emotional trauma of the preceding twenty-four hours understandably infringed upon any festive ideas.

The parade of concerned friends continued that day until the counter top had very little room left, and the refrigerator was filled to capacity. The day culminated with the arrival of Miriam Bradford. She had cooked an entire Christmas dinner the preceding night, and now she and two of her daughters ferried back and forth between their car and the house, carrying all the food. She had thought of everything: a cooked turkey, mashed potatoes, and salad. The overflow from the refrigerator was now relegated to the back porch.

Looking haggard, Joe arrived home late that afternoon. Christmas would proceed, even in its numbed form. On Christmas Eve, the gifts were opened per ritual. Shredded wrapping paper, torn boxes, and orphaned bows still littered the floor, but neatly stacked in the corner were unopened gifts. They would need to wait for their recipient. Though everyone was tired, mid-night mass found the Sextons, plus Tom's betrothed, Bea, crowded into a pew at the Catholic Church. The music and the message of Christmas rebirth and hope may have had added significance for those awake enough to grasp it. For Joe, there had to have been an emotional relief. He had come within a breath of losing the love of his life and being left to care for that pew full of children on his own. It's hard to say how he slept that night. Was it a deep sleep from exhaustion, a sleep of relief, or a fitful sleep of lingering anxiety?

Two days after New Year's, Marilane was released from St. Mary's Hospital. Though home, her convalescence would take another nine months of gradual recovery. Her lacerated jaw had been expertly sutured and in time only a faint hint of a scar remained. The broken bones would mend. Marilane would be confined to the sofa for weeks, nursing the pelvis back to health. Her brain compressed by the hematoma would demand more time.

Our brain is unique in that certain sides of the brain control certain functions. Marilane was right handed, so some cognitive functions were only restricted to the left of the brain, the side of the injury. One such function had to do with speech. Controlled by the lobes in the temporal region of the brain, these neural areas luckily weren't destroyed but only bruised. Still, nerve tissue, one of the slowest healing cell tissues, would take months to regenerate. Finding appropriate words and arranging logical sentences proved confusing and frustrating for Marilane. In conversation she would misplace or substitute words. While still hospitalized, Marilane sent a note to Mary. She felt sorry Mary never had a chance to go shopping. Reassuring her daughter that she had not forgotten about the shoes, she wrote that once able she "will buy you high hells."

At first her speech problems caused everyone concerns, but soon it became a source of entertainment for the children. If Joe also found it amusing he never let on, and Marilane never took offense at their laughter. Maybe she viewed their amusement as a small price to pay for still being with them.

Christmas break was over. School had started in Sumner, and the three older boys were packing up to return to college. Mike was going to drive the two still at Loras back to school on his way to St. Louis. All their clothes were packed in Mike's car, and the three came back in to say goodbye to their mother, still confined to the couch. Normally a stoically composed woman, Marilane couldn't restrain her emotions and broke down crying. The moment left a strong enough impact on the three boys that they would vividly remember it years later.

For months Marilane restricted her activities, driving a car being one she wouldn't attempt. But the day finally arrived when she decided it was time for her to get behind the wheel again. It was a spring morning when she sought out Mary. "Well, you were with me in the accident, you may as well be with me now." If either of them had trepidations, they did not voice them.

Marilane had one more hurdle that coming summer to overcome: Tom and Bea's wedding. Her issue had to do with her hair. It was gone. She had had her head shaved before the surgery and it would be months before her own hair would grow back in. At first Yvonne McAloon came to her rescue. She gave her friend an old wig she owned. Yvonne's wig and the first couple wigs Marilane bought weren't entirely satisfactory. The portion of her skull crushed in the accident never returned to its natural curvature but instead always appeared caved in. This left any wig looking like it was suspended in air on the left side of her head, appearing more like a helmet more than anything natural. With the eminent wedding and reception, she had no choice. This was how she would present herself to the world.

Start to Move Them out of the House

Mid summer 1966 and after months of planning, the happy week-end arrived. For Marilane an ill fitting wig was not going to hamper the first wedding of one of their children. Unlike their parent's wedding, Tom and Bea's and those to follow would be held on week-ends. The festivities commenced with the rehearsal dinner held at the Ritz Cafe, run by Loyal Pierce and his sister Bulah Finch. (Bulah's husband Molely would plow Joe's farm drive every winter. He worked for the city and the new sewer treatment plant had been built on land across the road. The road to the plant needed to be cleaned, and Molely used the Sexton driveway to turn around his grader, clearing the driveway in the process.) The wedding held the next afternoon in the Catholic Church showcased Bea's musical prowess. As a music major at UNI, she'd been able to attract some of the best talent from the music department for her wedding. Sherri Greenwald, who later became a famous opera singer, sang Mozart's Exultate Jubilate during the wedding. Even Father Kleiner, a self described music expert, was highly impressed. As with any wedding, some last minute problems arose. Margaret Murphy, recruited much earlier to be the pianist, found that she was too pregnant to reach the piano keyboard. Scrambling, Bea had to bring in a Methodist, Pat O'Brien, to substitute for her.

The wedding mass was over, and the wedding party moved to the reception, which was being held in the Sextons' back yard. Years of birthday celebrations left Joe practiced for this wedding reception. A wooden dance floor was laid over the lawn beyond the back porch, surrounded by tables and chairs and a carefully positioned bar. Ideal weather, good food, and fine music led to a great evening. It was so successful that Joe finally had to politely ask friends of Tom and Bea to please go home. After honeymooning for one night at Jim Whitmire's "cabin" out past Wilson Grove Cemetery, the newlyweds burdened with their earthly belongings headed east.

Tom had been accepted to Boston College Law School, and the two planned to drive there in Tom's Ford Falcon. To make enough room for their possessions Earl Ritter had given them his wooden cargo carrier, a square plywood box. With the carrier strapped to the roof of their car, two products of an Iowa farm community waved good bye and started off on their new life in Boston.

Mike married shortly thereafter. His bride, Jana Cleary, lived in Decatur, Illinois. With one wedding at home and one away, Joe and Marilane were getting their schooling. They would become quite practiced. And just as with Tom's, every wedding has an issue. Mike's occurred just after the wedding. Leaving after the ceremony, they headed for Ames, Iowa where both of them had jobs waiting. Mike was employed by a law firm, Gilcrest, Reynolds, Neetly and Smith, and Jana, a nurse, would be working at Mary Greeley Hospital. Part way across Illinois they stopped at a motel for the evening. The next morning they discovered the car had been broken into and robbed of several of their wedding presents. Evidently sentimentality was not a hindrance to thievery.

Marilane and Joe's house was slowly thinning out. The next three in line had moved out. Dan attended medical school at Northwestern University in Chicago. Peg, after attending Iowa State, had transferred to Clark College, Loras's sister school in Dubuque. Tim, like Dan, would be leaving mid semester his senior year for college, and now the only logical choice for a school was Loras. While in college no one ever had a car except for Peg, who had Marilane's Mustang Ford. In graduate school it was a different story. Mike had the Corvair, Tom the Falcon, and Dan had a Hudson Rambler. Depending on your perspective, Dan's pink Hudson was the most unique car. One of the few cars to have an ignition button stuck under the hood next to the engine, it allowed someone to start the car on cold days after removing the air cleaner and manually holding open the choke. (If someone was born after 1970, they would not have the slightest idea what chokes are!)

Peg's Mustang had been Marilane's. The sporty Ford was a marked change from the line of cars Marilane had been subjected to. She had had a VW microbus with a fifty horsepower engine, a red Valiant station wagon which was functional but not very plush and a car Joe had spotted one day in a car lot in Sumner. The odd looking vehicle Joe pick up for Marilane was almost a cross between a Willis Jeep and a station wagon. The hideous looking car was more than Marilane could bear. After only two days she made Joe return it, as it was totally unsatisfactory.

Aside from cars, it was during this time in October of 1967, that Joe gave up writing individual letters to his absent children, theorizing that, "When the number (of letters) was only two or three, it was a snap, but now with five, it does tax the 'old boy' to come through, and I'll be damned if I'll give up now-SO-I have decided to publish a weekly letter which will give the uncolorful happenings of the homesick folks and incorporate the news gleaned from your letters home. This way everyone can keep in contact with each other, and as everyone leaves home it will be something to hold the clan together. So all you out there I in college land, keep those cards and letters pouring in!"

The Practice Goes on the Auction Block

In the fall of 1968, the corn standing in the fields had turned brown. The corn leaves were wrinkling up, and the black birds were already gathering in flocks. Mother Nature was preparing for a change, and so were Joe and Earl.

Earl, having turned 60, had raised his children, Jack and Sue, and both were out on their own. For Earl the idea of another winter running calls over snow-covered roads in temperatures so low that syringes would freeze up was a wearying prospect. The mere mental image of standing in barns with frost clinging to the beams and exhaled clouds of vapor rising from stanchioned cattle had lost its appeal. Joe felt the same, and he also had had enough. He would comment, "I've seen it all and done it all." And being an asthmatic, Joe could barely tolerate working in dust choked hog buildings any more.

Both men could financially afford to stop. Their practice had been very successful. The last two decades had been very advantageous for the veterinary profession, and it is always better to exit while the wave is still cresting. The decision to sell the practice was like the decision to form their partnership in that we don't really know who first presented the idea. But it was evident both men were in agreement.

Resigned now to sell, they set January 1, 1969 as the official date to place their practice on the market. They had anticipated in all likelihood it would take six months to a year before any deal would be done, but the practice sold on January 7th. Fate again was on their side.

On the west of Des Moines, highway 169 runs north and south. Situated on that road just miles apart were two small towns, Adel and Minburn. Residing in those towns were two young vets who had passing knowledge of one another and were both primed to own their own vet practice. Their connection was through a college friendship between a wife and a sister. The two men had never spent much time together but now they hurriedly formed a business partnership, a union as difficult as a marriage. Dr. Ron Sietsinger, a round-faced, stout man, concocted the idea. In the most need of an opportunity, he for the three previous years had worked with a vet in Minburn. He was only an associate when he was faced with a work slow-down, and his employer released him. He had been without work for months when he heard about the opportunity in Sumner. The practice was large enough that Ron would need a partner. That is when he thought of Joe Troutman. Dr. Joe Troutman was slightly older than Ron but professionally they were both on the same glide path. For the last five years Joe had been an associate vet in a practice in Adel, and the prospects of ownership were slim. He was also was primed for the move. The two men met, and in the span of forty-eight hours had taken the measure of one another and formed a partnership, together making an offer to Joe and Earl. The offer must have been very close to their asking price since no counter offer was made, and the deal was struck. It is unclear whether Ron and Joe had seen the practice, reviewed the books, or even met Joe and Earl. It appears they were going on the practice's reputation, which was known as one of the better ones in the state. We know for a fact that their wives had never seen the town. It must have been a shock for their families to find out in the span of three or four days that they would be uprooted and moved across the state. Joe and Earl were also shocked with the rapidity of the sale. Now both men would need to move up their plans. Their future plans which had been ethereal now needed to be firmed up and given a time table.

Earl had set his sights on moving south, Florida to be exact. An old friend had a small animal practice just north of Miami, and he'd made overtures toward accepting Earl into the practice. Obviously it was not as simple as showing up on the door step one day. Earl would need to get a license, sell a home, buy a home, and move their belongings. Everything would take time.

Joe's situation was quite different. Of the four youngest children at home, Mary and Theresa were still in high school. The potential of being uprooted and deposited in a new school did not thrill them. More than likely they would be going to Ames High School. Before placing the practice up for sale, Joe had toyed with the idea of working for the state extension service after the practice sold, but a long time friend and fellow vet, Arlo Ledet, had convinced him to contact Dr. Wally Wass at the vet school. (For a short period Arlo had worked in the practice before returning to teach at Iowa State.) After a conversation with Wally, Joe was assured there would be a teaching position available if he secured a master's degree.

As part of the sale agreement, both Joe and Earl had agreed to work a short time with the new vets to smooth over the transition. Earl after only a few months left first. Once the deal was struck and the ownership passed to new hands, both Joe and Earl must have felt as though they'd sold a house and were living with the new owner; they couldn't wait to move out. Joe stayed slightly longer, working for several months out of a sense of duty, and he would fill in for the two vets when needed for years after that.

That summer, as Joe started his master's degree at Ames, Peg would be joining him. Then in the dietetic program, she was shy of a needed chemistry class, and ISU was one of the few schools offering it that summer. Father and daughter would room together in Pammel Court. Built after the Second World War, acres of quonset huts were thrown up to house the flood of GI's going back to school. Now aging, these corrugated steel shells resting on cement slabs were hardly plush living quarters. During that summer 600 huts were left, only a portion of the original number constructed. As they were populated basically by young married couples, an older man and a young girl living together had to have tongues wagging. Peg tells the story of the two of them walking to class together and reaching their point departure, where Joe kissed Peg good bye and wished her a pleasant day. Passers-by had to have had their eyes opened wide by the exchange. To further confuse the gossip mill in Pammel Court, on some weekends Peg would go home and Marilane would drive down to stay. The lechery in their midst had to confuse the uninformed in the neighborhood.

In October, Joe received a teaching position and continued his classes toward his masters. Renting a home on 3012 Woodlawn Avenue in Ames, what was left of the family moved from Sumner. Thirty-seven years after leaving, Joe and Marilane were back in Ames. This time their experience would be entirely different. First, Joe was returning to the classroom. Within those three decades the science he'd studied earlier had made dramatic new discoveries. The Kreb Cycle, DNA, and advances in the understanding of chemical interactions at the cellular level were ideas Joe had read about but never studied. It was like his freshman year all over again.

Settling into the red house on Woodlawn, the twins seemed to have no problem adjusting to the new surroundings, but Joe's daughters would test his patience. Prior to leaving Sumner, Mary and Theresa had already thrown down the gauntlet. Vowing that their new life in a big school would only lead to drugs and sex, they totally misread their parents. Joe and Marilane had already completed advanced classes in child rearing. At the heart of the girls' attitude were their boyfriends. The first two week-ends both girls drove back to Sumner to be with the boys. But that proved to be as much as Joe would tolerate. The girls would not be driving back anymore. Joe, with a clear understanding of teenagers, dictated that if their boyfriends wanted to see them they would have to drive to Ames. That was the end of it. Not long after, Joe put his foot down, and Mary and Theresa begrudgingly assimilated into the Ames High School society.

The War Comes Calling

While the younger family members were fixated on school events, world wide events forced themselves on to some of the older children. Vietnam had captured the conscience of the nation. Every one of the older Sextons knew someone who was directly or indirectly involved in the conflict. Though student deferments kept the draft board at bay, the continuing need for fresh bodies to feed into the conflict would sooner or later reach all of them. Mike, because of his age and an old knee injury, was an unlikely candidate for the draft. But Tom, once he graduated from law school, hit the top of the draft board's list. Laboring under the false assumption that if he got back into academics his deferral would be extended, Tom secured a teaching position at Loras College in the Department of Economics. That fall semester in 1969, Tom and Bea felt good about his chances to avoid the draft. It was a comfortable job placement since other family members were near, notably Tim and Peg who were both seniors in their respective colleges in Dubuque.

Returning after Christmas break, however, Tom received the unwelcome notice in the mail. His draft board deemed his service to the military much more pressing than his teaching assignment. On January 10th, he was drafted into the US army. He was to report immediately to Fort Lewis Washington for basic training. Bea, caring for infant Mark, would not be making the journey. She would return to Sumner and stay with her parents, Gar and Bessie. All through boot camp, Tom, with a law degree, was given the option to transfer to the JAG Corp, but the hook was that he would have to enlist for two more years. Tom was not about to do that; he would take his chances with the grunts.

After weeks of basic training, the GI's lined up for one final time. Standing at attention and counting off 1 and 2, the soldiers were broken into two groups, one for stateside duty and the other group to be shipping off to Southeast Asia. By sheer luck, Tom fell into the former. A trained lawyer, Tom would remain at Fort Lewis and be assigned to work in its JAG shop. With thousands of men passing through the base every month, court marshals were an ever present fact of life. Certifying all these records became Tom's full time job. Just when he thought he would ride out his time stateside orders came through for his transfer to Da Nang Airbase, where he would be an air traffic controller working within miles of North Vietnam.

He appealed to his commander Colonel Culpepper to halt the orders, but his request was curtly denied. So back sitting at his desk Tom, who by now was schooled in the mechanics of the army's complex organization, looked up the phone number for the Department of Army Personnel Affairs. Staffed by civilians, the office did not have the rigidity of the army. Moments after dialing the number he was in contact with someone in Washington DC. Explaining that he was Spec 4 with a law degree, he inquired about being reassigned anywhere except Vietnam.

"Well where to?" came the response from his contact in Washington.

Obviously wishing to play along, Tom replied "Brussels".

Once his contact stopped laughing, he realized the man on the other end was serious, and he consented to look into the transfer. Against all odds the man called Tom back the next day. He had an assignment for him at Fort Monmouth, New Jersey investigating cost overruns on government contracts. Evidently, the army never figured out how to halt supply contracts in a timely manner, leading to surpluses and overpayments, which the people at Fort Monmouth vainly attempted to correct. Tom took the offer and was assured orders would be sent out.

When Tom's new orders for reassignment reached Colonel

Culpepper's desk the colonel could smell something fishy. Calling the Corporal into his office, the Colonel pushed the orders he had just received across the desk in front of Tom and asked "Do you know anything about these order?"

"No sir," snapped Tom.

Colonel Culpepper was not fool, but he was army, and an order is an order. Tom was off to New Jersey.

A board laid across the back seat of the Volkswagon beetle became Mark's playpen for the trip clear across the county. Chugging along in the little bubble-shaped car, Tom and Bea slowly made their way to the Jersey shore, where they rented a cramped apartment two blocks from the Atlantic Ocean. They would not be the only Sextons on the east coast.

Peg was already in Boston. She had landed a plum dietetic internship at Massachusetts General Hospital in the heart of Boston. Though she was farm girl from Iowa, from that point on, Peg would never leave the east coast. Dan was also bound for the east coast. He had just graduated from medical school at Northwestern in Chicago and had been accepted for his internship in New York City. As the only gentile among the incoming interns at Mount Sinai Hospital in the heart of Manhattan, he would be drifting far afield from his cultural roots.

Joe and Marilane experienced their own life style change. Arguably it was not as exotic as Boston, New York, or New Jersey, but it was still a dramatic change in the environment for them. The new work and a group of new friends were all an enticing change. The entire experience they found invigorating, and they embraced it whole heartedly.

Marilane took a job as a dietician in one of the dorms. Though she had worked briefly as Sumner Hospital's dietician, this was different. No longer tied to the daily routine of cleaning, laundry, and cooking, she relished the change. And teaching suited Joe. With years of hands-on experience, he reveled in connecting the academic with the practical, showing his students how the dry and lifeless class study would have relevance in the real world. In the back of his mind he remembered the haughty freshmen professors and never took personal satisfaction in lording over his students. His students returned the respect by voting him "Professor of the Year" in only his first year. This award aroused resentment in some of the less secure faculty members, but Joe did also have his supporters: his friends from Sumner the Ledets, Arlo and JoAnna, and Wally Wass the man who had hired him.

Still taking classes for his master's degree, Joe had struggled with biochemistry and coming to his rescue were two fellow grad students. On Yaiyo Niyo, a veterinarian on sabbatical from vet school in Nigeria, soon became one of Joe's favorites. He was an odd mix of cultures, with skin a deep black color but with a British accent and mannerisms. Joe found it amusing when every morning Yasiyo was dropped off by his wife at the school. Leaving the car he would turn and always tip his cap to her. Joe and Yasiyo would team up to teach the post mortem clinic together.

Also helping Joe in biochemistry was a South American, Alfonso Ruiz. Long before "diversity" was demanded as part of the political religion of academics, here was a threesome with distinctive multiplicity. Joining Joe's circle of friends was another 'foreigner,' Ed Moss, a Canadian. Destined to be one of Joe's closest friends, Ed had a very different background. Educated in Calgary, Alberta, Ed with his wife Berna and their two sons had come to Ames for graduate school. A very large man at 6'4," it was hard to imagine that at one time he had been a fighter pilot in the Canadian Air Force. Ed had a ready smile and a good sense of humor, so in spite of their age difference, the two made quite a pair.

The social circle Joe and Marilane fell into contained a large number of 'younger' couples, like the Mosses, whose infectious desire to entertain themselves found the two Sumner transplants as willing participants. Joe and Marilane, with frequent parties, had their social calendar full. Ironically their social outings even drove Joe to try new things. In their circle was one Irishman who threw regular parties entertaining his guests by playing the piano. So impressed with the man's skill was Joe that he started taking piano lessons. He pursued it vigorously, but alas the theory of old dogs proved true, Joe would never become a prolific pianist.

Seemingly set free from the Sumner lifestyle, Joe and Marilane let their hair down. One night Mary and Theresa were at home when they heard a commotion in the back yard of their rental house. Their parents after returning from a party and had forgotten their house keys and were also oblivious to the fact that anyone was at home. Attempting to scale the six-foot fence in the backyard, both were giddy with laughter. This is where Theresa found her parents, very possibly a little tipsy, with Joe attempting to shove Marilane over the fence.

In more sober moments, Joe started sending out weekly newsletters to all the children who were away. A thousand of these letters would be sent in the subsequent years. Before e-mails and text messaging, this kept the entire family up to date. After describing the week's events, Joe wrote separate messages to each of the children. News, as disseminated through Joe's central clearing house, served to keep the family bound together.

As the school year ended, Joe was antsy to return to Sumner and the farm. Maintenance and care of the property demanded constant vigilance. They had moved out of their rental home, leaving some things at Mike's and Jana's house for the summer. The previous fall Mike had dabbled in politics, running for the position of district attorney for Story County against Ruth Harken. He would lose that political race, but Marilane, ever the protective mother would curse the name Harken the rest of her life. (Ruth's husband was Tom, who would be a long standing senator from Iowa.)

That summer would reunite the family. Dan was getting married and according to Marilane, none to soon. In Dan's junior year in medical school he took a semester in London studying at Astor College near Charring Cross in the heart of the city. Once the term ended he planned to travel to Europe but not alone. While in Chicago he had met a nurse named Maureen Griffin, who would be accompanying him. For the next three months they traveled Europe, starting in Spain, then hitch hiking through Italy and finally hopping about the Greek Islands. When it was time to go home they took the train which ran from Athens to Brussels. They shared a sleeper compartment on the train with a man from India, and as the train made regular stops in what was then Yugoslavia and Austria, more people crowded onto the train, more than the available seats available. With people hovering over them looking for any available seats, Dan and Maureen were forced to eat and go to the rest room in shifts with someone always there to protect their seats.

In Brussels they disembarked from the train. Short on money they sought a cheaper means of travel but were subsequently arrested for hitch hiking on the Autoban. Released from jail after a small fine, they sought clean sheets and hot showers with the little money they had left.

All during this European odyssey, this 'free' lifestyle Dan was living did not go unnoticed back home in Iowa. Joe and Marilane may both have been unhappy with Dan's behavior, but his mother was the only one to verbally comment expressing "now he has to marry her!"

Unknown to Dan, he made his mother happy when he proposed marriage during the end of his internship. Maureen, visiting from Chicago, attended a dinner with Dan at Uncle Tom and Aunt Liz's home in New Jersey. At the completion of the dinner, Dan popped the question. When Maureen accepted, Dan broke it to her that the wedding would need to be in June so his buddies could attend, and also that he had been drafted. With these caveats Maureen still accepted his offer.

Somewhat like Tom's situation Dan, now drafted, would need to finagle a better assignment. Already having taken his draft physical in lower Manhattan, Dan felt reasonably assured he would be going to Vietnam. When word spread that Dan had received his draft notice, however, the chief of interns called him into his office. Dr. Saul Burson sympathetic to Dan's plight, thought he might be able to get Dan into the Institute of Health. Saul, like Dr. Strader, was connected and the adage, "It's not what you know it's who you know" rang true. Dr. Burson confirmed he could get Dan an appointment at the Institute but he cautioned that he was running a huge risk, Dan declined the offer as if to say "What else you got?" Luckily for Dan, Saul did have something else. What about the CDC (Central Disease Control)? The CDC then wasn't the agency it is today. Then, it was part of the State Department and run by the military, concerned mostly with biological warfare. Dan wisely took the offer.

The Era of the Weddings

Working on such a short notice, Maureen and her mother could only manage a Sunday wedding, since Saturday was already spoken for. It was a minor issue in the scheme of things, and the ladies still were able to arrange for a dignified ceremony. With the date set and the invitations sent, it was a given the Sextons would be there, but by now the family had grown and there were grandchildren to throw into the mix. Mike and Jana had Sarah, and Tom and Bea now had two, Mark and Andy.

Oddly enough, when Andy was due to be born, rational thought was stood on its head; now Tom wanted to stay in the military. Bea's pregnancy was well advanced when Richard Nixon put a wrench in Tom's plans. Nixon had already initiated his "Vietnamination" program. In response to the cacophony of objections to the war Nixon wanted to cut back on any future deployments and instead rely more on Vietnam's army to shoulder the war effort. This was the same period when, in an effort to limit infiltration from North Vietnam, Nixon had authorized the invasion of Cambodia. This sparked nation wide protests, which culminated tragically in the death of four Kent State students when they confronted National Guardsmen at a demonstration on campus. While this was headline news across the country, another protest of sort played out at Fort Monmouth.

Tom, who'd won an early discharge, now wanted to stay in the service. The same man who'd spent months avoiding the army now wanted a few more months in the army. Patriotism had nothing to do with it. He wanted the government to pick up the tab for Andrew's delivery. For those who think the government has a heart, there is a lesson here. Tom had to go. Bea would fly home with Mark and deliver Andy in Sumner, while Tom drove to St. Paul and started his new law career after detouring to Illinois just long enough for Dan's wedding.

June 24 was a pleasant Saturday evening, and the Oswego County Club was hosting the rehearsal dinner for Dan and Maureen's wedding. True to form, for every wedding something was bound to go awry. The bride's identical twin sister, Kathleen, after a beer and wine soaked evening, invited the rehearsal's guests to the Griffin home the next morning for Bloody Marys before the wedding. It is very likely Joe and Marilane, knowing their children, saw the flawed thinking in the kind gesture, but they never let on.

Sunday morning, the compact little Griffin home saw people compressed from the front porch all the way through the house to the kitchen. The wedding party was interspersed with guests milling about the house, women in the wedding party in brown formal dresses and men in their grey morning suits with cut away tails. Meanwhile, Maureen sat alone in her bedroom upstairs, dressed in her wedding gown and smoking cigarettes, deeming it bad luck for the bride to be seen before the wedding.

After the wedding mass, the troop moved to the Hilton for the reception. It was an abated affair without a band, not for financial reasons but because Dan thought that without a band's presence he wouldn't have to dance, which may have been just as well, saving the guests from that noxious sight. It was also just as well since without oppressive music the guests could carry on normal conversations without the need to shout. Milling about the reception was a relatively new face in the family. Peg had brought her recently wedded husband from Boston.

They had married the prior January. She had met him at Mass General where he headed the bacteriology department. A large man with a pronounced Boston accent, Ed Tateosian had been exposed to life past the Alleghenies when Peg brought him to Ames the preceding summer, and Ed had quite an introduction.

A product of the East Coast, Ed already had a preconceived idea about the MidWest, surely the populace there as years behind the fashionable Bostonians. Ed's visit to Iowa had been quite uneventful till near the end of their stay in Ames, he and Peg attended a dinner party at Mike and Jana's home. The splendid evening was cut short by a phone call. Mike answered the phone. On the other end of the line was his excited brother Pat. It seems Pat's twin Matt was in jail, charged with under-aged drinking and driving while intoxicated. Matt had been apprehended after running his car into a light pole, shearing it off.

Mike relayed the information to his parents who were also present at the dinner party. Marilane immediately wanted her boy out of jail, but Joe stoically took a harder line. The battle of wills had commenced when Mary arrived with her boy friend, Rod Wells. The young couple entered Mike and Janna's small home through the cramped TV room, a renovated breezeway, and walked directly into the undersized kitchen, which was now crowded with the excited dinner quests. Mary intended just to meet Ed that evening, but, inadvertently, exposed Rod to crash course in family crisis management. Rod would have a lasting impression of Joe, angrily pacing the floor back and forth between the kitchen and the emptied dinning room.

"Maybe we should leave him there for the night?" was Joe solution. But Marilane refused to accept any dissenting opinion. She wanted Matt home, and her opinion prevailed. She implored Mike to go immediately to the police station, believing that as assistant district attorney he could surely secure Matt's release.

There was no question who was dominating that discussion, so Mike dutifully obeyed his mother and went down to the jail. There he found his brother drunk and vomiting. On further assessment of the current situation Mike thought maybe his father was right. Prudently, Mike left Matt to enjoy the hospitality of the city for the night. Joe, to his credit, would never bring up the episode again to Matt, assured that embarrassment was punishment enough. And Ed to his credit looked past the humiliating evening and still married Peg.

Not all the family gathered that January in Boston for the wedding. Tom and Bea had a newly arrived infant, Andy, and remained at home, and Tim was on the "outs" with his father. Joe had earlier informed Tim that for 'financial' considerations he would not be going to the wedding. There were some very sound reasons for Joe's attitude. After graduating from Loras College, Tim had drifted into a lifestyle of long hair and rudderless wandering. Joe had all but given up on him, willing to write him off as a lost cause, but Marilane would temper Joe's disgust with Tim and instead preached patience.

Joe and Marilane arrived in Boston that January having taken an overnight train from Moline, Illinois with the four youngest, Mary, Theresa, Matt, and Pat. They arrived as scheduled in Boston and joined up with the rest of the attending family. Everything appeared to be flowing as planned, but again a Sexton wedding and some form of disaster would go hand in hand.

Peg's fiancée, Ed Tatiosian, was Armenian which played a role in the impending drama. The rehearsal dinner was held just south of the city in Brookline. Mike and Jana arrived late for the dinner. They had been lost for the better part of the evening, driving around Brookline in search of the rehearsal site. While on their rambling quest Mike lost his good humor and never found it again for the rest of the evening.

Next, calamity occurred later that evening when Ed and his best man's wife, sufficiently charged with alcohol, started opening the wedding presents. This alone would bring Peg's ire but they had also disposed of all the name tags. Now the mood was set for the wedding the next day in the Catholic Church in Cambridge.

More than a hundred wedding guests talking in hushed conversations sat patiently the next morning waiting for the ceremony to commence. Something was holding it up, and that something was

Ed's mother. Here is where the Armenian culture came into play. She could not get past the idea that Ed could not find a nice Armenian girl to marry. Now he was about to wed an Irish girl from Iowa, of all places. She could not bring herself to sit through the wedding. Now, to save the day, the very same woman who the night before had incurred Peg's wrath over the wedding present debacle leaped to Peg's rescue. Somehow she cajoled Ed's elderly mother into walking up the aisle and taking her assigned seat in the front pew. After a communal sigh of relief from the assembled guests and the wedding party, the wedding proceeded.

Back to Ames and Work

The fall after the wedding season, Joe returned to his teaching assignment in the bovine department at the vet school. Mainly his department dealt with dairy and beef cattle and their related health problems. Every once in a while something unique and intellectually stimulating would pop-up, in this case it was rodeo bulls. One Saturday morning, Tim now in dental school and thankfully back in his father's good graces, was invited to accompany his father to the clinics. A man had scheduled a hoof trimming for two bulls that were rodeo bucking bulls, both highly prized animals. Most of these bulls were Brahman-crossbreeds, weighing from 1500-2000 pounds. With assets worth thousands of dollars the owner had sought out the school to perform the task at hand since it was equipped to handle such large animals. The event had drawn a fair crowd of spectators due to the exotic nature of the patients.

The plan was to unload one bull at a time, the hulking animal was then to be ushered down a blocked alleyway to a waiting chute with a special rotating table forming one of its sides. Positioned initially upright, the animal was supposed to be run into the chute and then, after straps were positioned snugly over the animal, the table could be rotated flat, securing the bull on its side.

The first bull came out of the stock trailer and trotted right into the steel barred chute. The strap went on and the table was rotated onto its side. The first bull, which was held firmly by the thick straps, remained surprisingly compliant and within twenty minutes its curled and split hooves were trimmed and flat. As confident as the men were upon completing the first bull you would think they had done this a thousand times.

Now as the men assumed almost an air of complacency, the second bull came off the trailer. A large black bull with blunted horns, its eyes had a heartless stare. Turning its head from side to side almost as though it was choosing a victim, it trotted toward the chute. As the bull stood nervously in the chute, the first strap was pulled up against its belly. Before the loose end of the strap could be secured in place, the bull reared up, its front legs lunging over the bars of the chute as the black giant started to pull itself over the gate. Within a split second the six men in attendance leapt to safety behind the red block walls. While seconds before there had been eager speculation, now there were only heads cautiously peering over the barricades. The bull's owners, with casualness born of years of handling these animals finally stepped forward and helped strap down the animal. The trimming finished and the beasts safely secured back in the trailer the only thing left were six people with a tale to tell and thick steel bars of the chute which were permanently bent.

Time passed quickly, with most of the year being was taken up with teaching in Ames. By now Joe had earned his masters and was embedded in the world of academia. He enjoyed teaching, and he and Marilane fit comfortably into the social scene. However, there was a "university" mind set Joe could never quite agree with. A prime example occurred over a fracas between the school's football coach and a political science professor. The professor had pompously made remarks to a local newspaper which were highly insulting to the coach and the newspaper felt compelled to print them. In response the coach, Johnny Majors, challenged the professor to say to his face what he'd said to the reporter and threatened to punch him. Fanning the flames, the newspaper also reported Coach Major's comments.

A faculty council of the vet school called a meeting to discuss the matter. What possible ramifications a dispute between a coach and a political science teacher could have for vet medicine is anyone's guess, but that did not seem to matter. The crux of the meeting, as spelled out by the self-proclaimed chairman, was to analyze Johnny's barbaric physical threats and not the inane and boorish remarks of the professor. Joe at first quietly listened, but after several hand-wringing comments he couldn't stand it anymore. Rising to his feet he said he could not bring himself to understand what the faculty of the vet school had to do with the personal disagreement of these two men. He said if there was a problem they should work it out between the two of them.

That day an element within the faculty realized Joe was not "one of them." This revelation would play itself out a few years later. Some faculty members might have time to sit around discussing a petty argument, but Joe and Marilane were far too busy. Joe still had piano lessons, their social calendar was full, and they had the family to tend to.

Mary and Theresa had graduated by now and were both attending Iowa State. Only Matt and Pat remained at home, and they were already planning their exit. Although all their brothers had gone to Loras College, the twins were looking for something more exotic. From a neighbor, a fraternity brother of Tom's, they first heard about Baylor University. Tom Goodale evidently thought it a fine university and, far away in Waco, Texas, it would have a foreign quality to an eighteen-year-old's mind. It so happened that a classmate at Ames High, Nick Classic, was being recruited by the Baylor basketball coach. The 6'6" senior had scheduled a campus visit during spring break so along with a friend, Kyle Williams, the twins thought they would all drive together to Waco: four young men on a road trip.

At eighteen and on their own, they expectantly packed up the car with everything they thought they would need for the week-end but left their common sense at home. Arriving in Waco they checked into a motel. It's hard to say how much time they spent touring the campus, but being that it was a Methodist school they very likely missed the tour of the chapel. They did, however, manage to buy beer. After a whirlwind two days, the foursome started for home, the last of the beer still in the trunk of the car.

After they left Waco and were on Interstate 35 heading north, a Texas Ranger pulled up behind them with his lights flashing. They had not been speeding, but the boys were still nervous, knowing they had a trunk full of beer. Pulling them over, the square-jawed ranger immediately asked the boys if they had just come from Waco. It appears the motel owner had called the police after the boys left. The call had to do with the condition of the rooms they had occupied. Evidently neatness wasn't in fashion for eighteen year old boys. The ranger soon determined these were in fact the culprits he was looking for; four young men in a car with Iowa plates were not all that common a sight on the Texas interstate. There were to be a few anxious moments for the boys staring out the car window at this no-nonsense lawman. A day or two in the Dallas County jail would not have been very appealing. Instead of arresting them, officer gave them a firm tongue lashing. "Leave Texas and don't ever come back!" were his parting words.

Relieved when they finally crossed the Texas border, Matt and Pat within five months would be coming back. Both ended up enrolled at Baylor for the next fall.

After almost thirty years, Joe and Marilane were only months away from an empty house. Finally they would have an opportunity to consider that luxury. Before that event they would take two weeks which could give them a taste of true retirement.

Wally Wass owned and flew his own plane, and Joe had traveled with him on several flights to vet meetings around the Midwest, so when Wally hinted he would be going to Atlanta on business, the seed was planted in Joe's brain for a winter get away.

Wayne Schutte was at the time wintering in Georgia, and Earl was still working in Florida outside Miami. Why not fly to Atlanta and from there travel on to spend two weeks visiting friends? We don't know what flying conditions were like when they left Ames that March. Joe had been with Wally flying through some very dubious weather during winter travels around the upper MidWest. It is not likely Marilane would have appreciated a bumpy flight to Atlanta. No mention was ever made of the flight condition so it must be assumed it was clear and smooth.

Landing in Atlanta, Joe and Marilane bid Wally good bye and rented a car for the drive across Georgia. Wayne and Lucille had rented a home on Jekyle Island, once the private playground of the rich and famous. This island in 1913 that the Federal Reserve was first envisioned when the island still was restricted to the upper crust. Gone when Joe arrived were the Pulitzers, Rockefellers, Vanderbilts and Goulds, but the magnolia trees, squat palms, spreading live oaks draped with grey moss, and the cooling sea breeze, which had attracted that group of people who at the time controlled a sixth of the world's wealth, were still there. Recently adding to the charm of the coastal island were golf courses which Wayne and Joe eagerly indulged in. After an invigorating stay, Joe and Marilane left the Schuttes, and drove down the coast toward Miami and Earl's home. The warm Florida weather and leisurely pace had to have acted like a narcotic for the Iowans. After their stay with Earl and Dori, they were forever sold on Florida and they would annually return for ever increasing lengths of time.

Refreshed by the warm weather, the couple returned to Ames to ride out Iowa's unpredictable spring weather. By June, Joe for the first time contemplated leaving the vet school. Lillian Devine had died the previous October and the management of her farms had fallen to Joe and Art Devine. Along with care of his own property, he felt he had enough to do, but when fall came and the twins left for Baylor, Joe was back at the vet school once again. That fall in Ames life had a relaxed and comfortable feel. Joe and Marilane were healthy and happy. They had an active social life, an adequate living, and for the first time since their honeymoon they were alone.

Complacency in life never lasts, however. Shortly after Christmas that year, Joe got a disturbing phone call. His brother Jim had been diagnosed with a brain tumor. Jim had left Kroblin Trucking when the firm relocated their operations to Tulsa, Oklahoma. Working now for Overland Express in New Brighton, Minnesota, he had passed out at work. Once he was diagnosed, a surgical team attempted to remove the neoplasm from his brain. Believing the surgery to be successful, the family was relieved, but the surgery had left Jim with a disturbing side effect. Walking, driving a car, and writing were noticeably affected. Even eating was a laborious task with Jim annoyingly fumbling with his silverware. But awkward as everyday duties became he still was alive.

With Jim's prognosis guarded but hopeful, Joe and Marilane switched their attention back to the family. Marilane had quit her job at the dorm. It was probably just as well, as there was another wedding to plan. Theresa was marrying her high school sweetheart, Steve Sampson, in April. Mike also quit his job at the local law firm. After a tense month of looking for another position, he took a job in Sioux City, Iowa as legal council for Postal Finance. Tom remained in St. Paul with the Oppenheimer Law Firm, and Dan still had time to give to public health service, so he and Maureen lived in Jackson, Mississippi where he studied Rocky Mountain spotted fever. It was an ideal place to study the disease. There were hundreds of small towns consisting of hundreds of seemingly identical rectangular houses with wooden front porches and every house had coonhounds chained out back. And on every dog were multiple fattened ticks clinging to their ears some of which were carriers for spotted fever.

Half a continent away Peg was expecting her first child and filling her days arguing with the contractor who was building their new house in Norwell, Massachusetts. Tim, his wandering days over, was safely enrolled in dental school. Mary had transferred to Mt. Mercy in Cedar Rapids to finish her nursing degree. And Pat, finishing his first year at

Baylor, considered transferring to Iowa City. That would be a major break from his twin brother, who remained for the time being in Texas. They had been in school together their entire lives and this would be the first year they ever spent apart.

Dispersed across the country, the family filtered back to Ames that spring for Theresa's wedding. Saturday April 14, 1973, started off rather cool and lightly overcast, but the mood was not dampened by the weather. Father Schaeffer was beaming as Joe walked the bride up the aisle. As the proud father he probably at that moment didn't have time to reflect on the history this spot on earth held for him. The recently built Catholic Church where the wedding was held was right across from the Memorial Union, right on the same ground Joe had walked everyday on his way to the vet school thirty years before. The mind wishes to condense time into comfortable periods. How many times have we said, "It seems like only yesterday"? If Joe had given it much thought, surely he would have seen how long a journey it had been back to the same place.

The next morning the newlyweds packed up for their drive to Washington, D.C., Steve, a tall slim young man, still owed the army three years of service. In compensation for not having to wade in rice patties, he had to give the military one extra year of his life. But his deployment was anything but harsh; a part of his duties was to stand at attention in front of the White House. Surely Steve's tall erect stature helped him secure a position in the honor guard of the army. Emblematic as the face of America's power and prestige, the honor guard wasn't looking for short, overweight men to fill its ranks. Splitting his time between standing-guard at the tomb of the Unknown Soldier, attending funerals at Arlington National Cemetery, and presenting a stiff starched figure which hopefully proved impressive to foreign dignitaries visiting the White House, Steve filled his days. While Steve held the door for world leaders, Theresa was taking nursing classes at Georgetown just across the Potomac from their little apartment which they shared with a psychotic dog. For two years they would remain there; the time coordinated exactly so that Theresa could graduate from the Jesuit university just about the time Steve drew his discharge papers. Armed with a nursing degree and an honorable discharge, the couple would migrate back west to Iowa where Steve looked to complete his degree at Iowa State and Theresa, like Mike's wife, Jana, would start her job at Mary Greeley Hospital.

Passing the Crest

Returning to Sumner in the September following the Theresa's wedding, Joe had a grim errand to perform. A thick grey sky greeted him that morning as he asked Tim, who was home for the weekend, to ride with him to St. Paul. No doubt Joe wished to have company on this tedious and sober trip. They would be stopping briefly to see Tom and Bea, but the true purpose of their trip was one of those things that can only be explained as an act of love. Jim Sexton's cancer had returned. The disease now was progressing rapidly, and Jim, no longer able to stay at home, had been moved to St. Joe's Hospital in St. Paul. Here was the reason for the drive. Joe knew that this would be the last few minutes the brothers would share in this life.

The red button for the third floor lit up the elevator, the door slid back, and as Joe and Tim stepped out, Joe's normal exuberance turned to sullenness. Conversation all the way to St. Paul had been pleasant, but Joe hadn't been entirely engaged. With the hospital in sight, not much had been said as Joe looked for a parking space. Now in the hospital's hallway even the volume of their speech was more hushed.

Jim's room wasn't far from the elevator, just a few doors down to the right. Walking through the door the scene before them matched Joe's mood. Tim's uncle was lying on his back staring blankly into space. There was no TV to turn on nor any distractions at all, and the stark room had only a view of the windowless brick wall to the north. Jim didn't recognize his visitors at first, but Joe drew close to him and finally Jim uttered a few words of acknowledgment, but his speech was slow and almost inaudible. After only 15-20 minutes, which felt much longer, Jim fell back asleep. Joe and his son stood in silence for several minutes more. Tim, who had come to see his uncle, now became witness to one brother saying good-bye to another. Without a word Joe turned and pulled open the door and Tim followed him into the hall.

The two men took the elevator down and wove through the labyrinth of hallways out of the hospital. Joe still had not spoken since leaving Jim's room. He had not even looked at his son, maintaining his focus forward. As they walked side by side, Tim turned to ask a question, when he noticed a tear on Joe's cheek. He had never seen his father cry. Tim was old enough to understand, but there was still something uncomfortable about the moment when Tim had seen something he was not meant to see. The conversation between the two men during the drive back to Iowa was not very animated, with Joe obviously splitting his time between the past and the present. Jim would die within a few days.

It was a balmy summer's evening, and Joe and Marilane were back on the farm. This time they thought it was for good, but that proved to be an idle threat. Once the school year ended, almost ritualistically, Joe would walk into Dr. Wass's office and proclaim that he was retiring. Wally Wass would then convince Joe to return for "one more year." It was a dance the two men may have secretly enjoyed, Joe receiving affirmation that he was still needed and Wally that his good friend would be returning to work with him one more year. On this particular evening Joe was still ruminating over Wally's latest proposal.

They had finished dinner when the phone rang interrupting their evening. The caller, a nurse from the Hillcrest Home, advised Joe to come immediately, as his mother had become unresponsive. Inez had been living at the Hillcrest Home for several years now. Over time she had experienced a slow disintegration of health both physically and mentally. Her path had been much like that of Lillian Devine's. Widowed young, she'd spent almost thirty years alone. Inez, now a petite octogenarian, gave not a hint of the alert, beautiful school teacher who had occupied that body when George Sexton first saw her. Only the pictures in her room informed the nursing home staff of the woman she had been.

Joe arrived that Tuesday in time to spend a few last hours at his mother's side. At 1:20AM on July 9, 1974, Inez passed from this realm. After a few solemn moments and dutifully making arrangements with the night nurse, Joe walked out into the stillness of the late night. It had been in the 90's that day, and even at that hour the air was still warm. We don't know what thoughts Joe had that night. Were they sorrow, reflection, loss, relief, or a confused mixture? Whatever raced through his mind, Joe had one of those rare moments in life when in the blackness of night he was entirely alone.

Days after the funeral, Joe had reconsidered the "for good" statement he had given Wally before he left Ames. He wrote in a family newsletter, "Mom and I are going down tomorrow to look for housing for the 'ten visiting professorships.' I am looking forward to it with pleasure …. will give it hell for ten months and then hang up the boxing gloves for good."

After caving in one more time to Dr. Wass, the couple found housing in Ames and returned to Sumner for the remainder of the summer. Most of that time was filled by taking care of the farm and golfing with his "buddies," but later that month they took a little get away and traveled to Colorado.

Earl and Dori Ritter would meet them there. Their excuse for the trip was a vet convention, but golf was their true objective. Memorable was the day they played at Wisan Country Club outside Denver. Only Earl, Joe and Dori played, and Marilane rode along. According to Joe she said after the round was finished, "I wish I played golf." No doubt

Joe encouraged her, because once back in Iowa she started taking golf lessons. It was a case of 'beware of what you wish for.' Marilane was never faint of heart, and once she started something there was no stopping her.

With September, Joe returned to Ames for his 'last' ten months of teaching. Shortly after he settled into his work, the vet school needed to fill an opening on the admission board. Nominated for the opening, Joe accepted but would need to deal with the fact that his son Matt had made an application to the vet school. Every applicant for the vet school needed to address the admissions board in person, so when Matt's time arrived to be interviewed by the Academics Standards board, Joe refrained from doing any questioning but decided not to leave the room. He commented later that his reason for staying in the room was "just in case I thought I should be there." This may have been just a rationalization. He just might not have been able to help himself; he had to see for himself how his son was going to do. His decision that afternoon may have left an impression on some fellow board members, because the following year after Joe's term had expired at least some members who remained on the board that make a fateful decision which would awaken Joe's fury.

With his outstanding academic record, Matt in all likelihood would have been accepted with or without his father on the board. Once he was accepted into school, Joe surely felt great pride. Finally, one of his sons would be following in his father's footsteps.

This would make a chain of Sexton vets going back three quarters of a century. The same year Joe also took pride in being elected President of the Iowa Veterinary Alumni Association. The small town country vet had become a player on the state level, like his father earning the respect of his peers.

Their time in Ames that winter did not revolve entirely around just vet affairs. Joe also tenaciously pursued his piano lessons. It may have seemed out of character, but Joe actually had a musical bent. He loved to sing and he was a whistler. Emblematic of Joe, whistling often announced his presence, the sound preceding him as he entered the house or the office. Whistling is a unique trait in the sense that it is hard to find many depressed people who whistle.

That same winter Marilane completely out of character, took up belly dancing. JoAnna Ledet who was already taking lessons had encouraged her to at least try it and Marilane found she loved it. To see a mother of ten from a strict and proper family shimmering in a gaudy costume must have amused Joe at first, but once he saw how much she enjoyed it, he changed his tune. Writing to everyone in the weekly newsletter he commented, "I think it's great. How many belly dancers do you know?"

The previous winter had sold the couple on the idea of winter vacations. Though their schedules were tight, they found a week to hurry back to Florida. By now many of their friends from Sumner were already enjoying wintering in the sunshine state. Earl, of course, still worked and lived by Miami, but now the Schuttes and McAloons had ensconced themselves in Naples directly across the peninsula. After visiting their friends, Joe and Marilane left convinced their time in Florida had been much too short. The next year Joe would remedy that.

Back home Joe sent the weekly newsletters to the far-flung family. Mike and Tom were practicing their professions respectively in Sioux City and St. Paul. Dan, after leaving Durham, was continuing his residency in Columbia, Missouri at the University of Missouri. Peg now had her house finished in Massachusetts and had stopped brawling with the contractors. Tim had one more year left of dental school. Mary had earned a nursing decree and found work ironically at St. Mary's Hospital in Rochester. Theresa was finishing her degree, and the twins remained separated, Matt in vet school at Iowa State and Pat at the University of Iowa. Interestingly, both twins, unknowingly, had both taken the med-cat test, an exam necessary for application for medical school. During Matt's application to vet school there was little notice of disparate interests between vet and med school, but the following year when Pat went through the same process, the outcome was quite different.

June 14th, finals were completed at the vet school. The halls were empty except for some lingering faculty. Joe boxed up his belongings. He was again leaving. This time he was "retiring." That summer he threw his full attention to the farm. Joe had for a long time admired cupolas adorning the crests of barns. Originally designed to allow ventilation through their louvered sides to cool down the hay in the lofts, the cupolas were functioning parts of the building. Designed in a time when loose hay packed in the loft could be prone to spontaneous combustion, they had a purpose. Joe had heard of their function but merely thought that they were classy looking. After some effort he located a cupola for sale and at great expense had it moved to his farm and hoisted to the top of the barn. In the newsletter from August 8, 1975 he wrote, "Today was a red letter day --- the long awaited day. We had the cupola and eagle weather vane installed on the barn today. It is a beauty! It took carpenters, one derrick and the twins but it was worth it!"

That same summer Joe had a flash back to his youth. He purchased a horse for himself, a POA. (ponies of America) These ponies were a relatively new breed of horse. They were a cross between an Arabian/Appaloosas mix and a Shetland pony, like Daisy his childhood horse. Spotted rumps and a body three quarters the size of a normal horse were the hallmarks of the breed. The pony was delivered to the farm and turned loose in the pasture, but a few days later the horse took advantage of an ill repaired section of fence and left the pasture. As the horse roamed the neighborhood, it took Joe two days to finally capture it. He was convinced that it if there were two horses to keep each other company, he wouldn't have that problem again, so he purchased a second POA. Joe envisioned that he and Marilane might go riding together. Athough Joe was not prone to making many foolish mistakes, this was insane. Marilane had no desire to go horseback riding or subject herself to the "trail riding" set. It wasn't long before the ponies found new owners.

Like the ponies, retirement was an idea that didn't pan out either. After further begging from Wally Wass, Joe relented to one more year of work. Weeks before returning to Ames, Joe and Marilane accepted an invitation from their good friends the Moss's to visit them in Canada. Ed and Berna lived outside Calgary at the base of the Canadian Rockies. Ever the gracious hosts, the Mosses scheduled day trips to the surrounding attractions. Of all the sites on their itinerary, one seemed to capture Joe's interest more than the others. Mentioned prominently in letters upon his return was a site on an open plain due south of Calgary which, at first glance, could be easily ignored. It was merely a jagged limestone cliff breaking up the flat expanse of the plain, but the true interest of the vista was revealed upon closer inspection. The visible cliff rose 35-40 feet above its base, but the areas anthropological history was what caught Joe's attention. This nondescript looking place was really a killing field. Six thousand years ago a nomadic tribe had used these isolated cliffs to harvest buffalo. If they managed to drive a herd of bison toward the cliff, the stampeding animals would hurtle to their death off the escarpment. For days after the stampede the cavalcade of dead beasts lay at the base being butchered by the tribe. When Joe observed the area, centuries worth of bones were still piled at the base, fueling his interest in the historic wonder. Whether it was the plains of Canada, the back roads of Ireland, or the mountains of Peru, Joe seemed to have desire to see the exotic, no doubt a residue from the time when he was forced to give up his dreams of Panama for a struggling vet practice in Sumner, Iowa

The Family Again Takes Center Stage

Across the top of the February newsletter the banner read "Mary and Rod officially engaged." The word 'officially' was the most telling part of the announcement. Rod Wells, a quiet young man from Connecticut, had attended Iowa State because of his interest in agriculture. Dating Mary for several years he had been by the house multiple times and everyone assumed they'd probably marry, even though the two had gone separate ways – Mary to Rochester and St. Mary's Hospital and Rod back home to Connecticut to work for an Ag company. In Joe's mind there may have been relief also since this was the last of his daughters to marry and this time he would be more practiced. No matter what one does, repetition is at heart of learning. When the planning stage commenced, Joe approached Mary with an offer. He would give her a check for $1,000 to plan the wedding. An adequate amount he thought, and Joe wouldn't be dealing with months of bills coming across his desk.

It was one of those few perfect summer days in Iowa as Joe stood in the back of the church waiting to escort Mary up the aisle. At the altar Father Kleiner waited, facing them in his ceremonial robes with his phony gap-toothed smile. Aligned in front of the communion rail were the bridesmaids to the left and Rod and the groomsmen to the right. All the men were dressed in white tuxedos with white shoes. They all stood erect and comfortably facing the congregation except for Pat. Mary had ordered the tuxedos through Meyer Clothing in downtown Sumner. Phil Kuepker took all the measurements for the men weeks before the wedding, but the day before the rehearsal when the men were given the tuxedos it was discovered that Rod's pants were several inches too short, so in desperation someone decided that Pat should switch pants with Rod. Pat's demeanor would indicate that this was not his idea. At this late hour all the anger and accusations weren't going to lengthen the pants, so Pat would just have to wear them, but he would not do it without grumbling.

With the processional music echoing from the loft of the church, Joe and Mary proceeded up the aisle. The church was full and off to the right in the front pews stood the burgeoning Sexton family. Everyone was there except Peg, who was at home expecting her third child. Mike was there with Jana, and their daughter Sarah, and they were now only a week away from adopting a son, Tommy, a little blonde haired boy. Tom and Bea had their three children, and Dan and Maureen brought their adopted daughter Emily.

Emily was Guatemalan and her adoption wasn't anything like that of Tommy who came through Catholic charities in Sioux City. Dan and Maureen had flown to Guatemala to pick up the baby anticipating some red tape, but they were unprepared for what awaited them. Emily was only five days old, but that had no bearing on the bureaucratic nightmare facing the couple. Dan was forced to leave for the US before Maureen and Emily in order to fulfill paperwork on the US side before they could think about leaving Guatemala. For ten days Maureen waited for enough forms to be completed to satisfy the appetite of the regulatory beast. Finally she made it onto her plane bound for Miami with little Emily and one hundred pages of documents. The entire weight of the legal documents signed and sent between the countries was probably greater than the weight of the child. This was their education in how bureaucrats function; it's not so much the contents of the pages but the volume.

Standing prominently in front of a full church in high water pants,

Pat wasn't concerned with any government dysfunction. Despite his discomfort, the wedding proceeded. With the last blessing and the wedding party retreating back out of the church, the festive throng reassembled in Joe and Marilane's backyard. The scene was reminiscent of Tom and Bea's reception, except now all the children were of legal age.

The next morning just like Tom, Peg, Dan and Theresa and their spouses, Mary and Rod headed east, this time for Connecticut. Months after moving his bride back east, Rod received a promotion but his new position would take them to Rhode Island which is the only county in the nation be called a state. For someone like Mary, the move was like crossing county lines.

The tuxedo debacle was past history by the time Pat received the letter from the vet school. In those first moments as he read the letter he doubtlessly shared Joe's feeling when open letter from Iowa State the day Paul Wilharm came to his rescue. As Pat read down the through the first paragraph he realized he was being denied admittance to Iowa State Veterinary College. His grades were more than adequate and his brother with an almost an identical application had breezed into school. Unknown to Pat at the time there was more at work here than academic ability.

Joe had returned to teach one more year after his stint on the admissions board. He hadn't hung up his "boxing gloves" after all. He was still very much embedded in the faculty society of the school when he heard of Pat's denial. Joe could smell a rat. He had left the admission board and the next year's board had added a couple of gentlemen, one of whom Joe wasn't very fond of, a man named John Grieves. They weren't openly hostile to one another, but Joe, even before this episode, thought of him as a small, petty man.

Like Matt, Pat had had to interview in person before the board. During that session Pat candidly admitted had had sent an application also to medical school. At the time, Pat thought nothing of that, but

Joe's detractor on the board seized on the statement and pushed the board to accept his theory that Pat lacked "earnestness" in his application. Most boards, no matter their size, generally have one or two strong individuals who control the agenda, and this case was no different.

Joe was fully aware of the personalities that made up the board and was not about to take this 'blackballing' lying down. He had two sons practicing law, and the board was in for a fight.

Part of a large law firm in Minneapolis, Tom was the likely candidate to pursue the matter. Armed with the facts and fed the whisperings Joe had gleaned from the faculty members at the school, Tom confronted the board with accusations of bias. Since the board regularly didn't take minutes, they knew there was no hard record of their mendacious behavior, so they dug in their heels and challenged Tom to prove his case. At an impasse, Tom decided to go around the board.

On the last day of May, Tom arrived at Joe's house. After calling Dean Pearson days before at the vet school, Tom had arranged a meeting with him the next morning. Now he needed to gather all the ammunition he could from Joe, who for weeks had carefully written down every scrap of information he could glean from other faculty members. The school is a small place, and Pat's dispute was common knowledge; tidbits of gossip and hearsay were always flying around. When all the information was pieced together like a jigsaw puzzle, a plausible pattern emerged. Everything pointed to the board subjectively deciding who they deemed preferable as vet students. Shades of Joe's freshman anatomy came to light. A few self-appointed guardians became gate keepers for the school, arbitrarily, deciding who would be veterinarians, and their personal bias now was affecting the very futures of young men and women.

The next morning Tom sat across the desk from Dean Pearson, a small quiet man probably, like most academic deans, more interested in maintaining tranquility than imposing order. Tom started by laying out the facts as he knew them and spelling out a possible scenario whereby a law suit could be brought against the school and the board. Maybe the most saleable point concerned the unfavorable publicity the school would receive from any suit, and if the school should lose the case, the ramifications were enormous. They went far beyond Pat Sexton. If the case could be proved that the board acted in an inequitable manner in their selection process, then every candidate denied admittance by the board would have a potential suit against the school. Very likely Dean Pearson understood the gravity of the matter. In the subsequent days after his meeting with Tom, he did entice the board members to reconsider the decision, but they flatly refused. Left no option, Dean Pearson unilaterally made a decision, leaving within the small confines of the college the board with egg on their face. Pat would be admitted. On June 15th 1976, the letter welcoming Pat the fall freshman class was in his hands.

In the next few years, John Grieves and Joe Sexton retained their mutual dislike, but John as a faculty member never took out his frustration on Pat. Whether he was being a man about the situation or he did not want to cross Joe Sexton again we will never know.

Bitterly cold air settled in the northern continent that next January, setting records all across the upper Midwest and the same air mass pushed toward the eastern states. Joe's newsletter devoted an entire paragraph to the frigid air mass and the hardship endured, especially their car's reluctance to run. Sharing his hardship, his daughters out east, Mary and Peg related similar stories, but Tom and Tim in Minnesota suffered the worst of it. For over a week the temperature hovered near -40 degrees in Minnesota, the air so cold that ice crystals hung in the atmosphere like fog.

When Joe wrote the letter he and Marilane were living in a house just off the fairway of the Ames County Club. There were still a few of their children near by. Mike had moved to Sioux City but Theresa and Steve were living a few blocks away. Once Steve finished school, however, they would be moving, and the twins living together while they attended vet school would graduate some day. With these changes Joe gave serious thought to buying a permanent home in Ames. So why would Joe and Marilane consider buying a house in Ames now? The answer can only be surmised, but Joe and Marilane had always put their relationship first. They cared about their children but really didn't need to live next to them.

With the warmth of spring and the impending end of the semester Joe, true to form, contemplated retiring. In April he approached Dr. Wass once more about leaving. By now Wally must have found the ritual amusing, but there was always the chance that this time Joe might be truly serious. This time Wally thought he would put an end to the yearly ritual, offering Joe a bid for tenure in exchange for one more year of employment. Joe evidently took a dim view of the offer, writing "they can stick the tenure where the sun never shines....the good don't need it and the incompetent should not be protected." Luckily the statement was only for the ears of family members. His academic colleagues might not have shared his assessment of the system.

A weekday in March 1977, Marilane had busied herself making beds and tidying up. Their guests the Mosses had just left. Ed and Berna had come to Ames for an interview at the school. Ed was entertaining returning to teach there again, and they wanted to stay a few days with their friends the Sextons and scout out possible housing opportunities. The Mosses were well on their way back north when the phone rang in Marilane's kitchen. Answering, she must have been taken a back. Someone from the *Des Moines Register* wished to come to Ames to interview Joe and herself. The idea had to have occurred to her that this was some kind of hoax. When she pressed the gentleman caller further the entire story unfolded.

Joe had gone to Columbia College with a young man from West

Union, a city twenty five miles from Sumner. That same man after graduating earned a medical degree and returned to his home town, and over the years the doctor, Bill Wolf, and Joe had maintained their friendship. They had a lot in common. Both enjoyed playing the piano, although Bill was clearly superior in skill, and they both knew how to have a good time. Bill had recently written a letter to the newspaper categorizing the accomplishments of Joe and Marilane and their children, thinking the story would make a good newspaper article. At the paper's headquarters in Des Moines, Nick Lamberto, a staff writer, was handed the letter and asked to investigate the possibilities of an article. Nick was the caller on the line with Marilane. He conceivably thought there was little harm in making the thirty minute drive to Ames just to check it out.

Thursday morning the following week Nick arrived as Joe and Marilane were preparing to have lunch. Graciously declining their offer of something to eat, he pulled up a chair beside the small table in their kitchen. Jotting notes as they talked, Nick was still assessing if there was a story here to be told. Joe was also making an assessment of the reporter. Writing that he thought Nick looked like "an old booze fighter," he also commented how much they had in common with Mr. Lamberto. Nick was a Catholic with eight children of his own, which may explain his sympathy for the effort necessary to raise a large family.

With lunch finished, Marilane cleared the table, but Nick, now sensing something newsworthy, continued his questions at a quick pace, causing Joe to comment that Nick had "diarrhea of the mouth." Initially he'd been flattered by the interest the paper had shown, but that enthusiasm would subside when there was no word from anyone at the newspaper for the next thirty days. Just when Joe and Marilane thought nothing was going to come of this, they received another call. This time David Finch, a photographer, wished to schedule time for a visit.

Days later, snapping pictures first at their home, David requested to follow Joe back to the vet clinics that afternoon and also inquired whether the twins would be available for pictures. Just like Nick, David left late that afternoon, and it would be another month before the Sextons would hear from the paper again.

On May 29, 1977 the *Parade* section of the *Sunday Des Moines Register* ran a three-page story entitled "The Sextons An Iowa Family." Complete with pictures of the entire family and Joe working at the clinic, the article went on to document Joe's move from Sumner to Ames and the extensive education of the children. Innocuous in its reporting, for the average reader it was brief detour before turning to the sports section of the paper. For Joe and Marilane it was flattering but not something they would voluntarily interject into any conversations.

Days after the publication, Joe and Marilane started receiving calls and letters from friends across the state. Besides receiving adulations from people they knew a small group of readers took the time and effort to send the Sextons hate mail. Taking the couple by surprise, the venomous nature of the letters made no sense. How could educating their children cause anyone offense? What possible harm had they done to those people? Joe would pass it off, but it was a sobering lesson into the ugly side of mankind. One letter in particular must have caught his ire because, later, an envelope was discovered on which Joe had inscribed a note to himself, "directed to the gutless person who sent you that disgusting letter."

Heading back to Sumner, Joe wrote "I am completely convinced that now is the time to hang it up as far teaching is concerned." By now it was hard to discern if anyone really believed that statement; you can only cry wolf so many times. Beside mowing grass and playing golf, that summer had the added attraction of having Tim move home. He had left his dental associateship in St. Cloud and had returned to Sumner to start his own practice. Setting up his fledgling practice in Horace Karsten's old office in the Whitmire building, Tim was occupying the same ground on which his great grandparents, the Wests, had managed the Charles Hotel. He would also be the third generation of Sexton doctor on that block.

Vicariously, Joe and Marilane seemed to enjoy the flurry of activity surrounding the practice and the home Tim was planning to build. After purchasing a portion of a farm Joe owned near Randalia, Tim started construction on the house. Working off plans of an architect friend of the twins, Kyle Williams, Tim hoped the house would be completed by the time of his wedding in December.

Though the family had not shared Christmas together for over a decade that December they would all be together again, as is documented by a picture taken in the basement of the United Methodist Church in Muscatine, Iowa. The commotion over the newspaper article back in May had subsided, but Pat Hahn, Tim's future mother-in-law, had resurrected it. With great pride she had framed the article about her impending son-in-law's family and hung it on the wall of their cabin. Joe may have been mildly amused by all the attention and secretly enjoyed being treated as a celebrity.

It is normally brutally cold at the end of December, but the day of Mary's arrival in 1978, fortunately was mild, reaching almost 40 degrees. That afternoon in the Cedar Rapids airport Joe, normally not a patient man, was more than likely pacing and fumbling loose change in his pocket as he awaited his daughter Mary and her infant daughter, Courtney. This was no visit. She was coming to stay. For years now over the winter a parade of individuals had house sat for the Sextons while they were away in Ames. For years they had left their home in the care of people they knew from bachelors to school teachers. Now Joe and Marilane owned a home in Ames, so some long-term plan needed to be implemented. They had decided to sell the farm. Their first choice of course was to have the farm remain in the family, and luckily Mary and Rod accepted the proposal to return to Iowa and farm the land.

Rod, after working for five years for an ag business, decided to accept Joe's offer to farm on his own. For the young couple there were some obstacles to be hurdled. Moving their belongings was an issue, so following a month after Mary, Rod and his father would make the long drive to Iowa bringing most of their possessions and the family dog. Because the crop land around the home place had already been rented to David O'Brien for the next growing season, Rod would have to find work for the next twelve months. At first their arrangement was rather awkward, with Rod working for David as his hired man and the young couple sharing the house with Joe and Marilane till June when Joe would return to Ames for another six months. There was a respite from this arrangement in March, however, as Joe and Marilane returned once more to Florida.

Part Three

Now is Their Time

Joe and Marilane had rented an apartment in Naples, Florida for the month of March. Bringing relief from the abysmal Iowa winter weather and the usual program of golf and socializing, this trip would appear to be predictably the same as before, but this time there was a new twist. Marilane, since threatening to play golf during that trip to Colorado with the Ritters, had started to take lessons from Les Teeling. Now completely engrossed in the game, she looked forward to this winter get-a-way as much as Joe. The social dynamic between the couple would forever be altered. Joe, to his credit, seemed to freely accept the new relationship.

Socially they'd see many of their friends there, like the Schuttes and McAloons who were also wintering in the south. During their month in Naples, they took the short drive across to Miami on the Everglade Parkway to visit Earl, and Joe spent a few days with his old partner golfing and fishing. Earl, an avid fisherman, exposed Joe to snook fishing in the inlets along the coast. Not really a fishing enthusiast, Joe, however, would later rave about the taste of the snook they had caught that day.

Returning to Naples, by now totally convinced they wanted to winter from now on in the South, the couple moved the quest for a vacation home front and center. They must have considered their options even before journeying to Florida. Spur-of-the-moment decisions like this were not part of Joe's character. At the time when they were looking for a home, the west coast of Florida was experiencing a building boom. In the 1970's the population of Naples pushed toward 85,000, but within twenty years it would triple that number. New housing developments fanned from old Naples as fast as contractors could bull doze down the palmetto and scrub brush.

After looking at multiple sites, they finally settled on an empty lot in Rivera Golf Estates. The entire area had been nothing but ugly Florida scrub land only a few years before. Intending to build there, just off Calais Court, they envisioned their back porch would have a clear view of the eleventh tee and the green that was nestled between a sand bunker and water hazard. Beyond the green, which was only one hundred yards away, they could easily see the more palatial homes on Estelle Court, which gave Joe a reassuring sense of the stability of the property values.

By selling their Sumner home and purchasing a winter home, Joe and Marilane had clearly crossed the Rubicon. After 36 years they were cutting their ties with their old life. No longer front and center in the lives of their children they had become just observers. Jealously guarding that life, Marilane would make it clear she was not about to become a babysitter for her grandchildren. She and Joe would love to see them but they would not be surrogate parents. After closing on the lot and tidying the legal considerations they started for home. That year after their winter junket they didn't take a direct route home but a circuitous route up the eastern sea board to Vermont and then looping past the Great Lakes to Fond du Lac, Wisconsin before making it to Iowa.

Peg and Ed had recently moved to Manchester, Vermont from Massachusetts, not only moving but also changing vocations. They had purchased a motel which was odd, since at first glance a bacteriologist and a dietician would be unlikely candidates for inn keepers. They did, however, have some passing knowledge of the hotel business. For years Ed's family had owned property on the tip of Cape Cod. With his father's passing a portion of the property that contained their cottages was sold off. There remained a seaside acreage which, to Ed's eye, could hold a motel. When he passed the idea by his two sisters the vision failed to win their approval but Ed still considered a hotel as a viable objective.

Not willing to give up on the idea, Ed pursued purchasing an existing establishment. Their first attempt to purchase a motel in New Hampshire fell through. Peg and Ed, unknowingly, were lucky. Within twelve months that motel was in bankruptcy. The second attempt was more fruitful. Cutting a deal for the Weathervane Motel, the Tateosians would be moving to Manchester, Vermont. Cradled in a valley near the Green Mountains, the town of 4000 was right out of a Norman Rockwell picture. Flowing through town, the Batten River for centuries had been famous for trout fishing. Feeding off the lure of the fishermen, a company called Orvis had established itself in 1856 making split bamboo fishing fly rods. Up the road from the noteworthy company, the Weathervane Motel sat on the south side of town just off Highway 7. Separated from the road by a split rail fence, the red motel was comfortably set back from the heavy traffic. The inn was located in a rather upscale area, sharing the neighborhood with a grand estate named Hildene, which had been the home of Abraham Lincoln's eldest son, Robert Todd. He had been an accomplished man in his own right serving as Secretary of War and as the president of the Pullman Car Company. Robert had fallen in love with Vermont and had chosen that serene valley in which to build his mansion. Like Robert Todd, the Tateosians found the area to their liking. They would remain there, raising their children and expanding the motel for the next twenty years.

After leaving Peg and Ed's that spring, Joe and Marilane continued their odyssey stopping briefly in Wisconsin to see Matt. Between his junior and senior year in vet school, Matt had married Ginny Mauer. Ginny's mother, Sally, was Virginia Whitmire's daughter by a previous marriage. Sally had married a farmer from Readlyn, Iowa, Vince Mauer, but with Sally's encouraged approval he abandoned farming for banking. Moving his family to Iowa City he settled into a position as a trust officer for a large bank. The Mauers and Sextons had known each other for years and had socialized on several occasions. Everyone seemed delighted when Matt and Ginny married, and it appeared to be a perfect match, but time would prove otherwise.

Right after graduation, Matt took a job as an associate in a large vet practice that served the area around Fond du Lac, which was at the tip of Lake Winnebago and sitting in the heart of dairy country. When Joe and Marilane arrived from Vermont they found a happy couple, but the seeds of discontent were already in the ground. To blunt the growing domestic schism, Matt would take a job in Oelwein, Iowa with a vet named Mike Puff the following year. Now closer to both families everything would seem to be rectified and especially so after the birth of their son Timothy Vincent.

1983 was a bitter sweet year. First there was much happening that year to make Joe and Marilane feel proud. Mike had bounced back after the firm he was working at, Postal Finance, had been sold and in the process his job was terminated. Landing in Pennsylvania, he found a position as general council for TSO, Teachers Service Organization. For the next seventeen years he would live comfortably in Lansdale.

Mike wasn't the only one moving. Tom had left Oppenheimer Law Firm starting his own firm with two other lawyers. During the previous year the law firm of Winthrop, Weinstein and Sexton had opened their doors and by all accounts was thriving. In fact, among their clients were Tim and Deb Sexton. Tom's younger brother had become embroiled in a lawsuit over his house then under construction on the Randalia farm. Modifying Kyle Williams house plans, the local construction firm endangered the structural integrity of the octagon house by taking some short cuts in construction. Like most lawsuits this one entailed a lot of paper, effort, and time expended to reach the settlement, that everyone had known would be the conclusion from the outset.

Dan had also settled into gainful employment. After leaving Columbia, Missouri and taking boards in Kansas City, he had joined a medical practice in Edmond, Oklahoma. Now with the birth of two other children after adopting Emily, Dan and Maureen's home would become a popular site for Joe and Marilane to drive to from Florida for Christmas.

Joe could take some solace in the knowledge that all his children were productive citizens. Peg remained in Vermont with the hotel's daily grind and Tim continued to vigorously expand his dental practice. Mary and Rod were fully engaged in farming with Mary also working as a nurse at the hospital. Theresa and Steve had relocated to Iowa City, where Steve worked in the same grey stone bank building in the heart of the city as Vince Mauer. He had started as a teller but he would work his way up to a loan officer.

Nothing brought Joe more joy than when Matt decided to set up his own vet practice in Readlyn, Iowa. Months before he made the move out on his own, he had been talking to his twin brother about joining him in Readlyn. Due to get his master's degree that spring, Pat had been for three years in Saskatoon, Saskatchewan. After he graduated from Iowa State, Ed Moss encouraged Pat to pursue a master's degree, and during his search for a school he settled on the Western College of Veterinary Medicine which sat in the heart of Saskatoon only a block off the South Saskatchewan River. An island in the middle of the prairie, Saskatoon was quite modern and surprisingly comparable to Iowa with moderate weather unlikely for a city that far north.

Enrolling first in the Department of Medicine and Surgery, Pat transferred to theriogenology after his rotation in the implant department. Classically defined as the study of mammal reproduction including both males and females, Pat narrowed his focus in his chosen field to embryo implants. At the time theriogenology was an especially hot curriculum in the dairy business. The thesis behind the implant practice was that as a rule dairy cows vary in their productive output of milk per day, and the higher the daily production the more valuable the cow became. With the gestation of 283 days for a cow, to rapidly increase the total production of a dairy herd a highly productive milk cow would have multiple eggs flushed from her ovaries. Fertilized exvitro, the eggs would then be implanted into a stock cow, who would carry the fetus to delivery, thereby increasing milk production and income in a short time.

Matt and Pat had been corresponding during the final months of Pat's master's program, with Matt trying to convince his twin brother to join him. But at the same time other offers came Pat's way. A large vet practice in Turlock, California showed interest in having him also join them. In retrospect, going west would have been totally out of character for a Sexton, since most had either stayed in the Midwest or gone east. Fortunately, Pat declined the offer in California and decided to join his brother.

Pat would be leaving school and immediately moving into his own practice, Matt's path there was more torturous. Way back to 1976, Matt, while dating Ginny, had finagled a job at her sorority Pi Phi. There is very little likelihood that such a job would interest him if there wasn't compensation beyond the puny wages, but then Matt was young and in hot pursuit.

Years later behind the door of the apartment they rented in Oelwein, the romance that had blossomed at Iowa State started to drop petals. By June of 1982 Ginny filed for divorce. The trauma experienced by the couple infected the entire family. Being much more vocal than Joe, Marilane engaged in vitriolic letter writing. She had never before been faced with divorce in the family, and the prospect was almost more than she could bear. Her brother Emmett had been divorced when he was relatively young, but no one ever talked about it; not even Emmett's children knew about it untilthey were much older.

Tranquility seemed to return when Ginny returned to Matt a month later. With Pat now joining him in Readlyn where in April 1982 their practice opened its door, their parents couldn't have been more proud; now four of their children had returned home. For over a decade family members who had ventured far from Sumner's orbit now were falling back toward the center. Oddly enough, Joe took this time to ponder leaving the continent.

Filtering through the vet school, word of an opportunity arose for a two year lecture assignment in Africa. The Botswana Agricultural College had offered a teaching position in its capital, Gaberone. Due north of South Africa, the nation did not share the remoteness of the Congo, but still it was truly other worldly when compared to Iowa. Marilane may have shared Joe's eagerness for the romantic thrill of foreign lands, but subtropical Africa may have been a stretch. She most likely didn't share his enthusiasm for setting up housekeeping in some third world country but she also didn't want to deny Joe the chance to experience a thrilling adventure in a distant land. We don't know if he willingly or begrudgingly abandoned the idea but in 1985 he was again caught up with the prospect of teaching in some less-than-typical setting. Joe had sent a letter to Ross University in Basseterre, St. Kitts in the West Indies, inquiring about a teaching position in large animal medicine. His dreams of alien lands were dashed again when the dean, Dr. T.H. Brasmer wrote to inform him that there were no openings at that time. Ever the dreamer, Joe just couldn't escape the mundane world he had been thrown into in 1942

The 'Golden' Years

Entering Readlyn from the north, in 1984, the main street curved east by the city park before turning south for three blocks. The downtown section of town was walled in by large grain bins which mark the southern end of town. The catalog of businesses was not a long list. In the heart of town sat the Center Inn, the prime watering hole and dance hall, it dominated the truncated business district, incongruously bordered by a garage and Readlyn Savings Bank. Directly across the street sat a butcher shop, grocery store, and a small post office, which was the only entity with a chance of survival. At the end of downtown an abandoned brick gas station rested at an angle across the corner of the block. Here Matt and Pat's practice, the Readlyn Vet Associates, would open its doors, with the service bays being cannibalized as the twins' office and supply room. As the boys went about getting their practice off the ground, Joe couldn't stay away. Clearly proud of his sons, he was also captivated by all the activity.

That year, Joe and Marilane thankfully were not going to Africa, but Joe did finally commit to hanging up the boxing gloves. That same year, at least for Marilane, the chronic threat of a divorce in the family came true, but Matt had closure of some degree when his divorce was officially finalized. The summer did not bring all bad news for Matt's mother, however, Pat was 'doing the right thing' by marrying the woman he had been living with. A vet he'd dated in Canada while in graduate school. When he returned across the border she followed and moved in with him. Stephanie Mitcham was a Nova Scotian, who earned a degree in vet pathology at exactly the same time Pat completed his degree, and they took up residence in a farm house a few miles from Readlyn. Surely Marilane viewed this arrangement in the same vein as Maureen's travels with Dan in Europe, but in Pat's case she held her tongue.

Free now of the responsibilities of teaching, Joe bought tickets for himself and Marilane for a two-week vacation to New Zealand. Why he chose that distant southern archipelago is now anyone's guess. Of all his family members Joe had seen more of the world than anyone. Jim had seen Western Europe but from the cockpit of a cargo plane, Donna had hardly wandered from the central US, and George and Inez beyond their trip to Chicago rarely ventured out of the county. There had to have been something in Joe's youth that instilled in him the quest for travel and a love of nonconformity.

Joe had fallen in love with idea of New Zealand; the land the people and the animals. By the first of February 1985, the gallivanting couple was packing to leave Naples, Florida. They had sold the home they had just built only years before and were now back to renting. Eastern Airlines took them from Atlanta to Los Angeles, where they barely made the connection but their luggage did not. Safely on the plane they flew overnight to Auckland on a mind numbing fourteen-hour flight. When they passed the international date-line they lost an entire day having left on Tuesday and arriving on Thursday. After waiting a day for their trailing luggage in a hotel room overlooking Auckland Harbor, they joined a tour on its way to Rotorua, a local attraction known for thermal hot springs. Not unlike Yellowstone here the smell of hydrogen sulfate permeated the air. Stuck with the tour group, they were ushered to see the "glow worm" caves. Totally unimpressed by illuminated annelids Joe wrote of the experience "unworthy of 10,000 miles travel." The next day proved more rewarding. He and Marilane played what is known as a Scottish course which had volcanic craters, and pot bunkers. It might be hard to picture incorporating volcanoes into a golf course.

Separating themselves from the tour group in Wellington, they rented a car for the drive to Palmerston North, the home of New Zealand's vet school. After languishing there two days, they returned to Wellington and caught the ferry to Christchurch. Driving south they entered a little hamlet called Riversdale and by accident befriended a local couple who insisted they play golf with them and have dinner later.

Departing from their newfound friends, they traveled further south towards Queenstown, which was framed by snowcapped mountains. Joe thought the place was absolutely beautiful. Driving up into the mountains the next morning, they turned in the direction of Mt. Cook, at the base of which they came across a small resort motel where they procured lodging for the night.

The next morning outside the entrance of the quaint hotel a man was sitting on a rock waiting for a bus. Experiencing one of those flash moments when a face looks so familiar that you swear you know the person, Joe asked the gentleman "You wouldn't happen to be Dr. Wallingo would you?" Just as astounded that in some remote corner of the earth someone would know his name, the man looked up and in astonishment said, "Joe Sexton!" Here on a rock in the middle of nowhere was a classmate from vet school; the two had not seen each other since graduation. The two men filled the short time till the bus arrived, hastily compressing forty years of living into a twenty-minute conversation.

Over a week later, rested and back in Florida, Joe painstakingly documented the daily happenings of their trip for the family newsletter. Either for his family's education or his own gratification, he loved to expound on travels, compiling at the end of the letter a detailed description of the country, the climate, the environmental differences between the two main islands, the exchange rate, the population, and the number of cattle and sheep. If you just read the last paragraphs, you might assume Joe was giving a geography lecture.

By summer, Joe was already antsy for something to do, so he applied for a part-time job with the Racing Commission (horse racing) in Iowa. If he got the job, it would at least supply employment, albeit rather mundane, for a couple days every month. That summer Tom became a frequent visitor in their home. In his law firm, Tom had narrowed his legal focus to only dealing with bank sales and acquisitions. Now versed in the composition of bank deals, he saw no reason why he could not acquire a bank himself. With their practice now considered a part of the community, the twins saw the value in the Readlyn area and its local bank, and their assessment did not escape Tom's notice.

On a whim, Tom walked into the Readlyn Bank one day and confronted the president Burton Stumme about possibly buying the bank. Burton, a staid older gentlemen, probably did not give much credence to this young upstart. As president of that small town country bank, he found the offer flattering, but Tom was an outsider. Besides, in Burton's community almost every soul could trace their linage back to a handful of family names, and the Sexton name wasn't among them. With a single-minded pursuit Tom started stopping at the bank every time he was in the area. He finally started to win Burton over or maybe wear him down, and in 1986, he closed a deal to purchase a majority share of the Readlyn Savings Bank, signing the impromptu agreement on Burton's kitchen table and spelling out the details on a scrap of paper.

Joe initially became a shareholder in the holding company Tom had put together. Joe had to have been impressed that one of his sons would become a banker. Since his childhood, the Casses and Heyers who ran the banks in Sumner were always men of stature in the community, and the thought probably never occurred to him that someday his family would share that status.

Following rapidly in succession, the banks in Tripoli and Britt, Iowa fell under Tom's control. Joe still remembered the Bowlings' theory of paying off one acquisition before starting another, and the pace of acquisition was more than Joe felt comfortable with, so he asked to exchange his equity stock for preferred stock. To his thinking, this was far less risky.

Twelve months after the closing on the Readlyn Savings Bank, everything was going according to plan. The banks in the Midwest, after passing through the agricultural crisis of the 80's which saw land prices plummet and defaulted loans destroying multiple banks, banks in the area were making a rebound. The rash of closed banking institutions slowed considerably, marking the farm economy's stabilization. Enthused about the future, Tom invited his brother-in-law, Steve Sampson, who was still working for the First National Bank of Iowa City to move to Readlyn and work for him. Now another sibling would be moving back. By all appearances life was good, and Joe and Marilane were gradually gathering their family around them.

In 1988 the news arrived that was not unexpected but still unwelcome; Thomas Devine had died. For five years he had battled colon cancer. The first of Doc and Lillian's children to die shed a sobering light over the family. The tidings came on the back of two prior deaths, Nan Devine, Emmett's wife who had passed away the previous year and Margaret Goodenow's eldest son John.

John, a cardiologist, had inherited a congenital heart defect. While pumping gas at a station in southern California, he suffered a massive heart attack and died. If there can be irony in tragedy, in this case John had momentarily stopped on his way to give a lecture on CPR (cardio pulmonary resuscitation), and no one at the gas station at the time of John's heart attack knew CPR.

Barring the news from New Jersey, Joe and Marilane were vitally engaged that year. They'd placed their Ames condo on the market and it quickly sold. While the sale was pending and already in the works, a Tripoli contractor, Pete Moeller, had footings poured for the house Joe was building. On an ideal acreage just south of Tripoli the house they were having built was intended to be their retirement home. Pete, a man who probably enjoyed talking more than construction, secured the job, more than likely because he was Matt's father-in-law.

Matt had remarried the previous summer. His small blonde German Lutheran bride, Gail Moeller, scheduled the wedding in a large church in Tripoli not two blocks from the bank, but the reception was held in Readlyn just up the street from the vet office at the Center Inn. Of all the Sexton weddings this reception surely had the greatest attendance.

On the south side of the Readlyn Savings Bank a narrow, poorly light staircase led to the second story, which held three aged apartments. When Tom purchased the bank he also became a landlord. The building was old and this was reflected in the apartments, which were adequate but hardly palatial. With the Ames house sold and Pete still pounding nails on the new house, Joe and Marilane moved into the northwest apartment. Considering their journey from the little rental of Main Street, this without a doubt was huge step backwards. Fortunately for them they would not be at the apartment the entire year.

With the onset of winter they escaped the cramped apartment, renting a home back in Rivera Golf Estates and there they would stay until March at which time Joe and Marilane would go "back down under," but this time to Australia.

Dan the previous fall had uprooted his family from Oklahoma and had settled them for the next twelve months in Australia. Logistically this had been quite a feat. Arranging to move his family to Melbourne for an entire year, Dan initiated the journey, taking Maureen and the three children half way around the world and stopping in three continents along the way. The first leg of the journey took them to Dublin where the family celebrated Christmas with the ghosts of Gaelic kings. Moving through London, their expedition swung south into Africa where they spent eight days in Kenya and then on to Asia. The stop over in Bangkok introduced Dan's young son, Zack, to the commercial side of human sexuality when his father pointed out some working women coming off duty in a hotel lobby at 6:00am. Zack may not have fully comprehended what his father was pointing out that morning, but he did realized that Dan did know about these things.

Dan and Maureen and their children were well settled in Melbourne, having been there for three months when Joe and Marilane's flight arrived. With only a couple days to decompress from the wrenching flight, the couple reorganized their luggage for another plane ride. Dan had scheduled a side trip to Tasmania, but on this excursion he would accompany them. An island just off the southern tip of Australia, Tasmania was once a penal colony, just like Australia itself, but now it was visited only for its stunning beauty.

Once they returned to Australia, Dan's tour guide duties ended, since Dan and Maureen were working and the children were in school. Joe and Marilane were on their own, so they traveled by themselves, first taking a sleeper car up through the majestic snowy mountains along the coast to Sidney. These days in Australia would be entered in the last chapter of Joe and Marilane's book on independent travel. With the exception of a trip to Ireland with their Canadian friends the Mosses, their days of great excursions were coming to an end. Like most things as we age the discontinuation of anything usually isn't an abrupt decision but rather a gradual acceptance and so it was with travel on their own. It had to have been a bitter sweet reflection on things that were and will never be again.

The decade of the 80's were drawing to a close, a period significant for its sense of being unsettled, and that sense transferred through much of what Joe and Marilane did. Joe's annual decision to teach could only be described as mercurial, and where the couple chose to live was just as capricious. They began by building a retirement home in Florida only to sell it within twenty-four months, then bought a condo in Ames after renting for years only to sell it and start construction on a permanent home in Tripoli. As stable as Joe and Marilane's living arrangements would be in the next decade, mutability was the key word for the 90's.

The ledger of life in the 50's and 60's contained some negative entries, but Joe and Marilane by and large finished strongly in the black. The balance between life's triumphs and tragedies would begin to reverse in the 90's. In May of 1991, Mardy was diagnosed with lung cancer and surgery was scheduled at the local hospital in Elmhurst.

The morning of the surgery Mardy, Donna, and Deb Sexton rode together to the hospital. Deb had become a frequent guest of the Mardorf's, since her business brought her to Chicago several times a month. If there was any anxiety it could not have been perceived in the events of the previous night. All three had spent the spring evening in the middle-class living room, with Mardy watching the Cubs on TV, seemingly unconcerned about the impending operation and Donna and Deb practicing their natural talent for conversation. After Deb parked the car in the lot in front of the hospital, Mardy led the three-some toward the entrance with his x-rays under one arm and a light jacket over the other, just in case the unpredictable spring weather might turn.

Inside, after the ubiquitous paperwork, Donna and Mardy sep-arated from Deb. While they ventured to his room, Deb left for the airport to collect their son Chris, who was returning from a job.

Donna was just walking out of the elevator when Deb and Chris en-tered the waiting room. Mardy was already being wheeled into surgery. It would be hours before any word of his condition arrived.

Possibly two hours had passed before a nurse appeared in the door-way of the crowded waiting room. Glancing side to side, she announced Donna's name. Finding her the nurse related that Mardy had come through the procedure and was now in recovery.

It wasn't moments after the nurse had disappeared down the hall-way that the words "code blue" could be heard coming from that hall-way. Deb remembers thinking to herself that the code had something to do with Mardy, and her fears were realized when the nurse returned and soberly asked the family to accompany her to a small room not far from the waiting room. There, because the doctor had left for his home, it became the nurse's unpleasant duty to inform them of Mardy's death. It seems that the void left when the diseased lobe of his lung was removed allowed the remaining lung tissue to shift, twisting a blood vessel, strangling the gentle man.

After respectfully allowing the family to digest the grim news the nurse asked if Donna and Chris wished to have a few moments with Mardy's body. Without hesitation Donna declined and Chris, hearing his mother's refusal, never offered any reply.

As sad as Mardy's passing was the succeeding years would bring more losses of friends and relative. There would be a sober manifest of people Joe and Marilane knew during their lifetime that would now be leaving them. Dori Ritter and Lucille Schutte were gone. Jim and Virginia Whitmire, Horace and Vera Karsten, Gilly and Ruby Wells and the entire social group from their first years in Sumner were gone. The Millers were gone and Christmas celebrations in their basement were now mere memories. Sumner had also changed.

The countryside now had more idle barns than functioning ones. Milking parlors and hog houses where Joe and Earl had spent a large portion of their working lives were either accumulating dust and cobwebs or were converted into storage buildings. Many of their clients had died or moved to town. Acres of land that were once lush green pastures dotted with black and white cows and alfalfa fields exuding the sweet smell of fresh cut hay were now rows of corn.

In town the three auto dealerships ceased to exist, their garages either repurposed or torn down. By the end of the decade there would be only farm implement dealer left and Adolph Miller's building now housed an antiques dealership. The bakery where Joe and Mike had worked as young men closed, depriving the citizens of the aroma of fresh baked bread and Bismarck donuts with grape jelly oozing from their centers when you took the first bite. Also gone were the daily trains that fueled Sumner's early growth. Closed too was Wayne Schutte's plant which sat next to their tracks. The business when sold was moved to Waterloo. The remaining Meadowbrook golf course had morphed into a shadow of its former self; once a summertime hub of social activity for the community, it now was frequented by only a small cadre of golfers who remained. Cub Park once echoing the cheers of nearly two thousand baseball fans was erased from the landscape. Main Street, which during the late 50's needed a cop to direct traffic on some Saturday nights, now looked deserted on similar evenings.

Golf, the passion of Joe's life, also had slipped into an altered phase. Marilane, true to her word, passionately took up the game. Beyond being casual player, she embraced golf. She was never proficient, but she still loved it. While wintering full seasons in Naples, both she and Joe had their own golf days. Besides playing together in the short Riveria course, she played one day a week with the ladies at the Hibiscus course nearby and Joe played one day over at Royal Palms with Wayne Schutte and Earl Ritter who had remarried and moved to Lehigh just south of Riveria.

This happy arrangement ended in 1992 when the Sextons rented for the winter in the Sebring area. Located in the central part of Florida ninety miles south of Orlando the land did not possess any natural beauty. Flat as a table top with shrub brush, low lying palmetto plants with their spiky leaves and tufts of wiry grass on which scrawny cattle grazed surrounded the enclaves of retirement homes. Why they chose to relocate there is open to debate. Had they grown bored with Naples? Had Naples, which was expanding rapidly, grown too large and congested? Or was it money? Sebring in the center of the state was less than picturesque, but with less traffic and a more moderate life style, Joe and Marilane may have found Sebring more appealing.

It was during the Sebring era that Joe, frustrated with his golf game, considered going to golf school. Not really wanting to go alone he called two of his sons to join him, Pat and Tim. The three of them signed up for a three day course held outside Tampa. It was well attended; all the enrollees were separated into groups of six under the tutelage of one instructor. Joe's teaching pro was a middle aged man who may have given an autobiographical answer to a question about scratch golfers one a day at lunch. Without a moment's hesitation the teacher replied, "one thing you can tell about a scratch golfer is that he has probably been divorced and fired from at least one job."

Joe had wanted to attend the school for one specific reason; he was approaching 80 years of age, and the powerful golf swing he'd once had was deteriorating. He wanted to rejuvenate his swing, which had served him well for over 70 years. The school's format was quite simple; for hours every morning and again every afternoon, the students would hit balls on the driving range with the instructor walking behind his six charges handing out advice or encouragement. The last afternoon each got individual time with the pro, hopefully to clear up any lingering issues they might have with their swing.

When Joe's allotted time arrived he was anxious to seek the answer to his problem. When he explained that all he wanted was more distance from his shots, his instructor took a second to compose his most tactful answer. Joe was not ever going to regain his youthful power; it was gone, and Joe would need to adjust his golf game accordingly. This wasn't what Joe wanted to hear. He had been like someone with an incurable disease who'd heard stories of a similarly affected person cured by eating a particular root or drinking some bizarre concoction. In his heart he knew the answer before he even asked it, but knowing and accepting do not always coexist.

All through the decades of the 80's and 90's Joe was an eager participant in the family golf trips. Starting in the early 80's, the six brothers, Joe and Peg's husband Ed (nicknamed the Jaguar for his ability to fully utilize his large handicap) gathered every fall for three days of golf. The eightsome maintained that yearly tradition till 1999 when the event expanded to incorporate more family members. That year the outing was held at Pinehurst, North Carolina. Two years later in 2001, the group descended on Horseshoe Bay near Austin, Texas. This was shortly after the 9/11 attack on the United States, and that weekend half-full airplanes and a nearly deserted golf resort spoke to the populations reluctance to travel again so soon. Those memorable three days would be Joe's last golf trip. He would relinquish his spot to younger players.

Part of Joe's decision to quit the group came from his health. During the previous thirteen years, gradual steps had brought him to that point. Everything seemed to have started back in 1988 when Joe drove to Norman, Oklahoma for full hip implant surgery. A recommendation from Dan had put Joe in contact with Dr. Howard Prior who had consented to perform the surgery. The timing of the surgery happened to coincide with the onset of the AID's scare. Rumors of transmission of the virus through blood held in blood banks had prospective surgical patients scrambling to protect themselves. Joe had been informed to expect at least one blood transfusion at the time of surgery so months prior Joe had 'banked' his own blood. On the day of the operation and far too late to alter plans, he was informed that of the two units of his own blood shipped to Oklahoma, only one had survived in a usable state.

The operation proceeded uneventfully and as planned the couple left for Iowa only days after Joe's release from the hospital. Back home after only a few days, Joe became lethargic and lost his appetite. He should have known something was wrong. Years of vet medicine had taught him any animal not eating had some underlying problem. The symptoms became more pronounced: chills, nausea, chest pain, and shortness of breath. Finally his daughter Mary, a nurse, insisted he be hospitalized. Reluctantly Joe agreed but by this time found he was too weak to get to the car. An ambulance was dispatched to transport him to the hospital. Initially his case was diagnosed as an emboli clot which might be lodged in his lungs. Monitored overnight his condition refused to improve. He would need to be transferred to a larger facility, Allen Hospital in Waterloo.

A second diagnosis confirmed his problem. He had pneumonia, also known as "the old man's friend" since a percentage of elderly succumb to pneumonia secondary to some other debilitating ailment. Joe, a life long asthmatic, was aware of the fragile nature of his lungs and the distinct possibility of not surviving. For the first time he faced his own mortality. Joe would be changed by the experience. The roles were reversed from the time of Marilane's auto accident; she now took the dominant role. In a note Joe even hinted the same sentiment "With quiet patience, resolve and love she bullied, jawed, suggested and forced me to do things I should do. She took over all the duties of paying bills, seeing people and checking everything out."

Joe would recuperate but the altered dynamics of their relationship would never return to their previous state.

Two years later Joe would have another scare. He had been playing golf with Mel Krumm, a friend from Tripoli. Mel, now retired from the presidency of American Savings Bank which Tom had purchased, had formed a friendship with Joe, and the two frequently played golf together. Partway through the round one afternoon, Joe started to feel ill. The symptoms were much like the prior episode. This time Joe didn't procrastinate. He called his good friend Tom Mangan. Tom, now divorced from Vera, had left Forest City and gone to the Mayo Clinic in Rochester. By that evening Joe was in St. Mary's and under Tom's care. The whole episode proved to be a false alarm, but Joe wasn't done with the medical profession. In the fall of 1966 he stepped out of the shower in the new house Pete Moeller had built for them. Joe slipped on the wet floor while he was in an awkward position, the fall caused his hip joint to pop out of its socket. Rushed to the hospital in excruciating pain, Joe would require anesthesia to reset the joint.

Two years later, for Joe's 80th birthday the family flocked to Wisconsin to celebrate at Tom and Bea's vacation house on Deer Lake. For three days the entire family enjoyed the mild July weather and for Joe, a man who for years had made his birthday an annual celebration, this was the ultimate birthday party, surrounded by his voluminous family. There was no reason to think otherwise and Joe never let on, but a close examination of his face in the group picture taken that week-end told a different story.

The picture was taken from the cabin's porch looking downward toward the lake shore with a grove of white birch trees framing a picture. Scanning the faces looking up and smiling there was only one sober visage. The man who should be beaming was looking down. Unknown to everyone that day was the fact that Joe was sick.

The reunion photo for Joe's 80th birthday.

Just days after the photo Joe found himself sitting in an examination room in the Mayo Clinic. A bevy of tests led to a diagnosis of cardiomyopathy. His heart was not pumping enough blood. There was evidence from the exam that Joe may have suffered a previous small heart attack which had left a portion of his heart damaged. There was no evidence to prove it but it, may have occurred that afternoon while he'd been playing golf with Mel Krumm.

Treatment of the condition required surgically implanting a pace maker and a regime of a daily anticoagulant. Back home, there had always been a ritual of cocktails after work with one or more of his local children, usually Matt, Pat, Mary or Tim, but now Joe, because of his heart condition, declined to drink. Once when he was sitting at the kitchen table watching everyone having a drink, Mary asked him, "Do you miss having a drink?" Joe, completely as ease with the situation, replied, "No during my lifetime I think I've had more than my share".

Joe would dutifully stick to the physician's recommendation until a couple years later when one evening, with possibly a fatalistic viewpoint, he decided to join the evening cocktails. Suffering no ill affects, Joe would thereafter question the merits of medical restrictions for a man in his eighties.

His health may have been stabilized the following year, but an even more traumatic happenstance would cause a near dissolution of the family. In 1990, the serving president of the Readlyn Saving Bank, Virgil Mathias retired and Steve Sampson, a loan officer at the time, was elevated to the position of president. Smart, gregarious, young, and energetic, Steve appeared to be prefect for the job and an ideal fit. Joe in particular would applaud Steve's advancement.

There was no secret in the family that Joe took different views of his daughters and sons when it came to their futures. Possibly chauvinistic, he worried more about daughters. Boys he figured should be able to take care of themselves, but girls would need to rely on their husbands over whom he had no control. A creature of the period when only the men went to work, he hadn't fully embraced the new era of the two income family.

The first two years the bank functioned smoothly, but small dark clouds began to appear on the horizon. In board meetings during discussions of problem loans Steve's analysis gave hints to his thinking. When a delinquent loan appeared on the bank's daily ledger, Steve felt that the debtor had personally affronted him. His explanation in the subsequent board meeting would carry a vindictive tone, and he would stray from a business like assessment toward the recovery of the loss. Tom was first to notice this change in Steve and expressed to Tim who was also on the board, his misgivings about Steve's attitude and his fears that his advancement to president may have been premature.

The issue came to a head in the fall of 1998 when behind the building where Tim had a satellite dental office Steve and Tim stood talking. Steve was enraged. Two of his staff members at the bank were quitting and a few clients had moved their accounts to other banks. He felt these changes were a personal insult. The hour long meeting left Tim with a conviction that indeed Steve, though gifted, did not have the temperament for the job. Tim called Tom that evening, and a few days later they confronted the situation and reached the conclusion that something had to change. Though they realized this would be an unpleasant affair, Tom and Tim had no idea of the firestorm that would be coming at them, nor did Joe, at the time unaware of the situation, see the potential fracturing of his family.

With the announcement of Steve's impending release, the other family members immediately aligned behind Theresa. It was a case of the strong against the weak, and it was viewed that by their actions Tom and Tim were turning their sister out into the cold. Becoming the head spokesman for everyone in the family who supported Theresa, Marilane vociferously took to defending her daughter. In fact, late one night in a phone conversation, she told Tom that he and Tim were no longer her children. The emotions boiled over, with some family members rigidifying their stance and turning their backs on their brothers.

Joe remained generally silent all through this tempest. Prodded by both factions to join their rank he refused. Internally he had his own storm. During this tempest, Joe one morning at 4:30 AM typed a letter to Tim. In it he expressed the torment he was going through writing, "Recently we are faced with a situation that has no real answers. Theresa...needs our love badly. I realize that what started out to an answer to a problem turned out to be a real donnybrook...My own role is that of 'damage control.' I see a situation that has gotten out of control, and I'm sure neither you nor Tom wanted anything like this to develop. But it did! Both mom and I worry about both of you and Tom, but our immediate concern now is to try and support Theresa…We are torn both ways, and most of time feel we aren't doing a very good job no matter how you look at it." The family which had given him so much pride and satisfaction was devouring itself before his eyes and he could not stop it.

The die was cast. Tim and Tom along with the twins, who because of ownership in the bank were reluctantly thrown into the 'bully' camp, forced a vote at a board meeting to finalize the situation. Both camps thought they had a shot of turning the board in their favor. Steve's stance that he had been treated unfairly and the boys should leave the board was the option he floated. Tim and Tom obviously took the opposite position. On that afternoon as a verbal vote was taken around the board table, Steve's hope sank as the board members one after another sided with Tim and Tom. With the last vote cast, Steve stood up from the table and without saying one word walked out of the bank never to return.

At this point the rift within the family seemed to be cast in stone, and Joe could only view the dim prospect of a divided family. Fate, however, had another outcome in mind. Unknown to everyone, marital issues had developed in the Sampson household. Shortly after his firing, Theresa filed for divorce, the basis of which had no correlation with the bank. Now all the venom pooled within family members flowed out onto alienated Steve. Wounds inflicted during the incident would take years to heal, but Joe had his family back.

The Final Years

Though the disastrous implosion of the family had been averted there was one adversity Joe would not see overthrown: time. Marilane was the first to recognize the need for change. Their home on the Tripoli blacktop was lovely, but it was several miles from any town, which caused a sense of insecurity in both Marilane and Joe, both now in their 80's. Forcing the issue, the Tripoli house was put up for sale and they located a recently built house which satisfied their needs in Sumner. Butting up against the northern edge of Allen Kroblin's old business headquarters, a modest housing development had cannibalized several acres of an adjacent corn field. Settling into their latest home, the couple had the piece of mind of being only a few blocks away from the hospital, and shopping downtown. Oddly enough their last home would be only four blocks from their first home, the little rental house. Somewhat telling, Joe convinced Mary and Rod to part with the cast iron kettle from their backyard and he eagerly put it in his new yard. Just steps off the back porch, the kettle's relocation was like having an old friend move in.

Winters in Florida saw their days numbered also. Joe was becoming forgetful and Marilane's macular degeneration continued its slow progression, leaving her with only limited eye sight. No longer able to drive the fourteen hundred miles to Florida, they flew. Their Buick Lassabre they had driven down to Orlando by a Readlyn man, Rick Thatcher. They wintered comfortably and everything was fine until the trip back to Orlando and the airport.

Cruising now on the Florida turnpike toward the Orlando airport Marilane strained to find the exit for the airport which was just past the interchange with the Anderson Beachline Expressway. Confused by all the traffic the Sextons missed their exit. Now they would need to go up to Interstate 4 and then cross over to the southbound lane. As Marilane navigated with her diminished eyesight and Joe struggled with his short term memory, panic soon ensued. For the next forty five minutes the twosome drove back and forth till seemingly by accident they exited to the airport. This was the last straw.

The next year Tom would fly down to Florida to escort his parents' home but their days in Florida were coming to an end. Joe and Marilane, the world travelers, now saw their world shrink to the streets of Sumner. Only accompanying their children were they still were able to leave town. Weddings were by now becoming one of the major family functions with all the grandchildren marrying, and Marilane and Joe, being escorted, were still able to attend.

In December 2003, the last family newsletter went into the mail. The Underwood typewriter Joe had purchased while still in practice finally quit working. The last letters needed to be hand written. The news and the letters themselves had shrunk in volume. Reduced to only a few short paragraphs, Joe would be strained to finish even in this abridged format. Writing earlier in July he lamented "It's taken me days to get this far in the note so I think it's time to call a halt."

As the couple grew increasing confined to their home behind Kroblin's, Joe's diary written during this time portrayed a man attempting to come to grips with his deteriorating condition. On retirement he would write, "Retirement has its down side – no goals, no projects. One grows wearing of talking almost of how things used to be." One day in March while looking out the window he scribbled, tongue in cheek," Snowy but most of it melts upon hitting the ground. A lazy day, dark and overcast. A day made for suicides."

The long hours of idleness also took a toll on Marilane. Joe would write," Today she snapped at me – yes snapped – at me and directed me to water the plants, etc. This was said in a demeaning voice – which I obeyed. Somehow I no longer felt Lord of the manor but I heeded her commands."

Summertime did present some relief. Every Sunday morning Joe, Matt, Pat and Tim played golf at Tripoli's Maple Hills Golf Course. Joe might not have been able to remember exactly how many shots he took on a hole, but he still demanded etiquette and punctuality on the golf course. Following a set pattern, the scenario on Sunday mornings was always the same. Arriving early for the tee off (usually 8am) Joe and Tim practiced putting on the green next to the first tee. Matt and Pat would always arrive late and after looking across to the parking lot anticipating the twins, arrival, Joe would ask Tim, "What time do you have on your watch?" If the answer came back 8:00 he would instruct Tim to go to the tee and hit away. Without fail, half way up the first fairway, Joe would see the twins jogging with their clubs on their backs in an effort to catch up. No matter his age, the Sunday morning lessons continued.

On one such Sunday morning the usual group arrived at the ninth hole at Maple Hills, a fairly long hole with an inconsequential stream bisecting the fairway at about two hundred yards, conditions that dictated a long drive. As was normally the case, the foursome had the entire course to themselves, which was the way they preferred it. Tim had already driven off and Joe now took his stance, prepared to hit his tee shot. The alignment of his feet and the tilt of his back were a carbon copy of the stance he'd had from childhood. He struck the ball, sending it arching weakly out from the tee, far short of the stream. The swing may have looked the same, but the youthful power was gone, robbed by the thief of time. Joe still plagued by a mind that knew thousands of shot that dominated the fairways couldn't come to grips with this old man who was a squatter in his body. When his shot fell far short of his expectations, Joe walked back toward the golf cart and stood there with a crestfallen look upon his face. Tim, seeing his father's disappointment, walked up next to him and put his arm over his shoulder quietly giving solace to the man. Now years after the late afternoon conversation with the teaching pro from Tampa, Joe was still stubbornly intolerant of ageing.

April in Iowa can be an unpredictable time. The days can be sunny and mild, and on these flawless spring mornings it surely feels like summer is just days away. Or it can be windy with clouds coming out of the north bringing a low grey ceiling with the ground only recently thawed and remaining cold supplying a chill to the air. This is an unforgiving time to plan an outdoor wedding but this is exactly what Theresa's son Joe and his bride Kelly Blegen had done. Their wedding was scheduled for the 30th of April, and though they hoped for the former, they would get the latter.

As the family gathered at Lake Panorama north of Des Moines the weather was in an ugly mood, but that surprisingly did not have everyone's attention. The rehearsal dinner on Friday night would be attended by Joe's father, Steve. Most of the family had not even seen him for years, and some family members had not talked with him since that afternoon at the bank. There was an obvious anxiety about the moment when they would all need to congregate in the same room. The air may have been trenchant at first as family and guests drifted into the hospitality room, but no one disgracefully broke the cordiality of the moment. Any deep-seated enmity never made it to the surface. To their credit, everyone maintained the exuberance of the occasion, probably much to the relief of the wedding party.

The next morning in between the resort's golf course and the condos was an open expanse specifically chosen for the wedding site. Intent on having an outdoor ceremony, Kelly and Joe bravely remained committed to their plan. Rows of white folding chairs were positioned on the grass lining both sides of the central aisle. The space was open to the elements, as the cold north wind had nothing to impede its assault on the wedding party. Everyone was cold, but no one more so than Kelly in her sleeveless bridal gown. The weather, though, seemed to dictate the pace of the ceremony. Intent up on conserving the decorum of the proceedings the minister did his best to appear to take his time, but he too felt the need to get in from the cold. The entire formality did not take much more than 15-20 minutes with the assembled guests doing their best to keep themselves warm.

Joe and Marilane courageously endured the frigid celebration, but this was enough for them even though there would be another wedding in a month. Graciously, they had declined to attend that celebration. Marrying in a month, Alison, Dan's daughter and Jamie Salvatori would reassemble the same crowd in North Carolina. The travel was just too much for the couple, now in their 80s, but Joe would send a letter to be read at the wedding. His words would be their only presence.

Seated at their kitchen table in their new home in Sumner, Joe and Marilane enjoyed an evening's cocktail no doubt thinking about their family a thousand miles away reveling in the Hope Valley Club House. Never before had they missed a family event. Dan had the honor of reading Joe's letter to his guests at the rehearsal dinner held in Duke Gardens. There among the sea of flowers, lilies, and water lotuses, many would be moved by Joe's words but no one realized the poignancy of the moment.

Early Sunday morning in their motel rooms, blurry-eyed partiers packed their bags and double checked their airline tickets. Most were leaving on early flights putting them back home by mid day. Mike would have the longest trip, having moved to Colorado.

Back in Sumner, Joe was also up early, but then he always got up early. By 5:00 AM, the sun on that morning of May 22nd, 2005, was already creeping over the horizon. The sky was still hazy but showed the promise of clearing. Because he was up at daybreak, Joe thought he would attend the early mass at 8:30 but Marilane, not feeling well, excused herself from attending. With Father Kleiner's retirement the

6:30 mass had been discontinued. After being retired for several years, the priest had died but the congregation was not entirely rid of him yet. In the basement of the church, which was named Kleiner Hall, hung a large picture of Immaculate Conception's long-time priest. Though Joe held Fr. Kleiner in utter contempt, he still had faithfully attended church, but you could count on one hand how many times Joe attended mass alone. The number truly paled in comparison to the thousands of times he attended mass accompanying his family. Those were stylish days, with Joe in a suit, and Marilane, required to cover her head, in a dress with large brimmed hat. Both of them book ended the children who always had their hair brushed and their shoes shined.

On that morning Joe, kneeling during communion with his arms folded and resting on the abutting pew, possibly never gave a thought to how far he had come from the little house two blocks away. In terms of distance, a mile circle would encapsulate a large portion of Joe's life. His influence, though, extended far beyond this little piece of land. It was odd to think of how far Joe had fantasized about traveling, but here he was one hundred yards from where he had started.

Leaving church that morning most likely none of those thoughts would have occurred to him. His focus now was narrowed to breakfast, his favorite meal of the day, a big breakfast of eggs, toast, and if possible some bacon and hash browns. Not long after breakfast, he just didn't feel right. Thinking it might help him feel better he reclined for a few minutes on the couch, but that didn't help. He actually felt worse, so much so that he thought probably he should go to the hospital. This was completely out of character. Joe would never voluntarily consider such a thing.

With eyes so bad that she couldn't drive, Marilane would need help. She called Rod Wells. Rod had not gone to the wedding because he had crops to put in. Marilane let the phone ring and ring and finally left a message for Rod. Obviously he was in the field and anxiously she tried to think of someone else who could help. Her next call was to Les Teeling. She explained the situation, and Les was there in minutes.

On call that morning when Joe arrived at the hospital was Dr. Mary Pat Rosman. She took one look at him and had him moved to an examination room. Only moments had passed since Joe had gone back when the heavy set doctor returned to the waiting room confronting Marilane and Les, who graciously waited with her. Dr. Rosman, with concern in her voice, told them Joe now unconscious, was being prepared to be transported to Allen Hospital in Waterloo. At that moment Rod arrived at the hospital. Hearing the phone message, he had grabbed his address book before heading out the door. Rod would be the first to admit he had no idea why he took the book with him, but it would prove to be a fateful act. Assessing the critical nature of the situation, Rod took it upon himself to start to alert family members now on their way home from North Carolina.

The emergency entrance to Allen Hospital was a relatively small area. The double doors of the entry way separated two distinct seating areas: one to the right was open to the hall with white chairs aligned in front of a TV and to the left was a small room closed off by a door. The whole area was contained by the long nurse's station. Marilane and Rod took up the vigil in the small room, which began to fill as more family members who were now alerted started to join them.

The diagnosis in Waterloo was that Joe had suffered an aneurysm, a tear in his renal artery. The bulge in the blood vessel wall had probably sat undetected for years but this morning it chose to rupture, releasing its red liquid into Joe's abdominal cavity. Dr. Otedessy, the surgeon on duty, had called in his staff who were preparing for a possible surgery but given Joe's age and condition he wanted to confer with the family first. A good friend of Theresa's, Julie Kline, happened to be one of the nurses called in, and she in turn called Theresa who was still en route from Minneapolis with her husband, Jeff Thompson, Mary, and Tom. Though there wasn't anything these family members could do, Julie felt compelled warn Theresa of her father's condition.

Theresa had not arrived at the hospital yet but other family members had found their way there. Matt, Pat, Tim, and their spouses were now all huddled in the small waiting room, nervously talking among themselves. Art Devine, also called, came to give comfort to his sister. Art, because of his years as a surgeon and his knowledge of the lethalness of the condition, awkwardly attempted to give everyone hope for Joe's survival.

A tense couple of hours passed with Joe in one of the emergency suites and the anxious family pooled in the waiting room. A decision needed to be made. In his blue surgical scrubs, Dr. Otedessy walked out past the nurse's desk to talk with Marilane. Uncomfortable with the conversation she turned toward Tim, "I need your advice," she said. Dr. Otedessy patiently reiterated his assessment of Joe's condition for Tim. Given their diagnosis, the ruptured artery would be fatal if surgery was not performed. However, Joe's heart and age gave him slim odds of surviving the surgery. Also, should he survive he would need to be on a respirator for an indefinite time and could be bed ridden for up to six months.

"What should we do, Tim?" Marilane asked. Always a strong woman, this was one decision she did not want to make. Looking into his mother's eyes, Tim knew he had to make the call.

"Dad would not want the surgery. I think we should not do it." Marilane only shook her head in agreement, not saying anything, almost as though she could not force the words out of her mouth.

"We will move your father to an IC unit on the third floor. Someone will come to escort you up to him," With that somber statement, Dr. Otedessy turned and disappeared behind the door to the emergency suites.

Marilane returned to the waiting room. The other family members needed to know what had happened. Tim, however, walked through the double doors and stood outside by himself. Seeing him standing alone, Deb went to join him. "I just told them to let my father die." Tim said hardly able to utter the words himself.

Arranged like a horseshoe, the Intensive Care Unit had an array of rooms all fronted by glass walls and positioned around a central nurse's station. Rather small, Joe's unit was just at the top of the horseshoe. A crowd gathered around Joe's bed with Marilane, Mary and Theresa at his head. Tom, Jeff, Matt and his son John, Gail, Matt Wells, Andy, Mark Sampson, Pat, Rod Tim, Deb, and their daughter Kathleen were all wedged into the small room aligned around the bed. The intubator which had sustained Joe the last few hours was gone and now Joe was only hooked up with an IV drip for morphine. Even today, no one present could tell you how long they stood in that room. Only Theresa and Mary spoke to their father saying,"It's ok, Dad." As his respiration gradually slowed, the girls continued their soothing utterance while the others were all locked in their own weighty thoughts.

When the moment came and the last breath left Joe's lungs, Marilane regained her strength. She leaned over and with almost reflexive motion kissed the handsome young man from the SAE house good bye.

Epilogue

I remember driving home that evening my father died. Kathleen was with me, Deb had taken by mother home thinking, she shouldn't be alone right now. It's odd what thoughts race through your mind during a time like that. Approaching the driveway to my farm that evening, I could see my father in that very field, helping me rip out an old row of fencing. It was hot and the work was monotonous. Ripping up barbed wire, rolling it up and stowing it on the wagon behind the tractor, we weren't talking much. Earlier in the day I had mentioned that Deb and I in a week would be picking up Kathleen from the adoption agency in Iowa City. Entirely detached from our task at hand he threw out, "The good thing about children is that they keep you from being selfish." This was classic Joe Sexton. He loved quotations. He kept a book in which he wrote down quotes he deemed worthy of remembering. That quote, however, I'm sure was his alone.

That next Monday morning brought a flurry of activity. Family members were making arrangements for the funeral. People flying in needed to be picked up at airport, and housing needed to be found for everyone. Father Purtell would set the date for the funeral mass, but most of the arrangements were already done except for little things like the gospels to be selected. This was rather embarrassing, since I doubt very much if my older brothers and surely myself had the slightest a clue about appropriate gospels.

A friend of mine, Bob Becker, was the funeral director in charge, and he related the story of my parents making their own funeral plans.

My parents had just moved from Tripoli to Sumner and had stopped by to talk to Bob. He said they could not have more different approaches as to what they desired. First, my mother wanted to be cremated but my father wanted a full funeral. While in the basement of the funeral home viewing possible caskets, Joe took one look around and walked immediately to the most plush and expensive casket and said "This one is for me."

I still saw patients that week, though several times I was interrupted by family members stopping by the office, I think not so much to see me but because they did not know what else to do with themselves. On one of these visits, Tom was in the office. Now replete in my personal office were things Deb preferred not to have me drag home. Leaning against the wall was a collection of persimmon headed Cleveland classic golf clubs, driver through five wood. Seeing them, Tom immediately walked over and grabbed the fivewood. Holding it up and after inspecting it closely, he announced, "Let's see if Bob will put this in the casket."

I loved that club. There was a moment's hesitation, but who to better have it than my father. In a very cavalier manner I replied, "Sure. Go ahead." I felt much better about it that evening at the visitation when I saw my club resting beside my father.

The visitation did not have the grimness that I remember from my brother Mark's wake. Seeing friends and neighbors and hearing fond memories made that evening fly by. Even Tom Mangan, then in his early 80s, drove down from Rochester.

Mike and Tom spoke at the funeral mass. Their poise and elegance could not have been matched by anyone else. Attending a funeral in Minnesota a few weeks prior, Tom had heard a gentleman sing at the service and he was so impressed that he solicited the singer to perform for our father. With the mass completed, the man in a clear and strong voice sang "O Danny Boy." The mournful tune left not a dry eye in the church, including those of Bob Becker, who you would think would be professionally immune.

As pall bearers my brothers and I had the limited responsibility of loading the casket into the hearse and then removing it by the gravesite. Just outside the church Bob told us, "Now get a good grip. I'm going to drop away my support." My thinking was how heavy can this be? My father barely weighed 150 pounds. However, when Bob released the casket into our hands, every one of us brothers was startled by its weight. It weighed a ton. Evidently the casket my father chose was made of solid bronze, the heaviest casket they make.

The white Cadillac hearse took the short drive to Mount Calvary Cemetery past the bridge over the Little Wapsi where Joe's casket was interred in the Sexton plot. Arrayed across the grass covered space five granite headstones gave notice of the Sexton's brief history in Sumner. On the far left, Karl Mardorf had his small stone with his grandparents, George and Inez, resting nearby. Donna and Mardy sharing a stone centered the row. On the far right, Joe and Mary Elaine's headstone was cradled next to Mark's lesser stone. All these seemingly unremitting granite tablets, like the mountains they came from, were destined to wash away in time, and with them the memory of their existence.

Normally after a funeral the ladies of Immaculate Conception would put out a lunch in the basement of the church, but to hold a luncheon in my father's honor in Kleiner Hall would have been sacrilegious. The two men despised each other. Instead we rented Meadowbrook County Club and opened the bar. Jim Sexton's daughters were there. Cathy, long since divorced, still lived in Minnesota and Debbie, remarried to Randy Schultz, now lived in Sumner. Chris Mardorf was there. His mother Donna, Joe's sister, had died a few years earlier. Years after Mardy died, she had sold her home and moved to Waverly, taking a room at the Bartels Home, a large nursing home for the elderly just past Wartburg College.

Jim Goodenow, my cousin, and his wife Susie had driven ten hours from Columbus Ohio to bring his mother Margaret to the funeral. Kenneth and Evelyn's daughters Renee and Katherine attended. Their father had passed away. He and Evelyn for years after retirement had lived on a boat cruising around Florida and up the eastern sea board. My parents had several times traveled to the Florida coast to meet them.

Art Devine came alone. His wife Marilyn had succumbed to alcoholism a few years prior, but he seemed quite adjusted to life as widower. Several of Joe's cousins like the O'Laughlins from Oelwein and Independence showed up en masse.

The next morning for those from out of town, the day brought hectic preparations as they headed for home and returned to work. For my mother, that first day when every one left and she was truly alone was a sobering moment. She surely felt periods of great sorrow, but she never showed this in front of the children.

Filling her days, she took to making me lunch on workdays, usually calling the office about 11:30 to make sure I was coming. I would have my 30-minute lunch with her, not long but enough to break up her day. Invariably every 7-10 days she would make creamed asparagus for lunch. This had been my father's favorite dish for lunch but it was not mine. I was not about to mention that fact, however. Completing her day, she still maintained a cocktail hour with the "locals."

Everyone settled into this comfortable pattern for the first few years. Mary, being the closest, oldest daughter, assumed the role of chauffeur, taking Mom to her appointments and shopping. This cozy routine was bound to end and it did one morning when my mother, while stepping out of the shower, fell. Though she suffered no threatening injuries, my mother on her own decided it was time to move to the nursing home. Deep down inside, the idea clearly repulsed her, but she wanted it to be her decision not a decision forced upon her. Behind this decision may have been an episode six years earlier that was traumatic enough to have left psychological scars.

It was October 15, 2001. Mary had just left our parents' home when the phone rang. "Mother has fallen and is lying in the hallway. I can't get her up." Joe said. Immediately returning to their house Mary when she walked through the front door heard her father say, "Let's get her up." Mary paused and took a second to assess the situation. Mother prone on the carpet and in pain appeared to have rotated her right foot beyond its normal position and Mary suspected something had broken.

Dubious of her condition Mary cautioned, "We better not Dad." Hip fractures in persons her mother's age were a constant danger, and Mary astutely made the right diagnosis.

When the ambulance crew arrived they gingerly transferred her to the gurney, then loaded her for transport to Waterloo. She had suffered a fracture. The Sumner hospital was not equipped to handle her condition, and she was going to need surgery. An x-ray at Allen Hospital located the fracture. The hip itself had not broken, but the femur had a horizontal break just below the socket. When Mary drove Dad to the hospital, she met Theresa there, having called her just before they had left Sumner. Luckily for Dad, now anxious about the situation, he had both girls, who were nurses, with him to take command.

Mary and Theresa were both familiar with hospital operations and they thought their mother was not being treated with the urgency she deserved. Mary was known well by the Chief of Medicine of Allen Hospital, and she left Theresa and her father to find him. Smiling at first when he saw Mary, the white smocked physician would not be smiling long.

Meeting both girls, the doctor quietly listened as they laid out their arguments for immediate surgery. Diplomatically, the doctor tried to find some common ground reassuring them that within 24 hours the surgery to reattach the bone would be performed, but he didn't realize the bobcats that had grabbed his tail. The doctor saw that these women were serious about having the surgery done immediately. Sympathetic giving in to their demands, the doctor agreed to their demands and called in a surgical team to perform the hip repair that evening.

Months later her healing complete but the incident still fresh in her mind, Mother fell again, in the kitchen in the middle of the night. The clamor awoke Dad. Finding her on the floor, conscious and claiming she was not hurt, he didn't have the strength to help her to her feet. Since the fracture Mom had worn a "first alert" pendant around her neck, and it had been triggered by the fall. To assess the nature of the alert, the first-alert call center had summoned Mary to investigate the situation. Within fifteen minutes Mary with a winter coat covering her pajamas, walked into the scene. On the floor lay her mother covered by a coat, and sitting next to her in a captain's chair was her father.

Turning around and seeing Mary, he said, "What are you doing here?"

She answered "Dad, I got a call from first alert".

All along Dad had planned on waiting until morning to call someone. "We didn't want to bother anyone," he explained

"We can't leave her lying on the floor, Dad" Mary replied, walking over to her mother. Sitting her up Mary realized nothing was broken. Her mother wasn't injured. Grabbing her under her arms she hoisted her to her feet.

Having regained her balance and certainly able to walk, Mom took one step, stopped, and commanded Mary, "Throw away that cake pan. Your father had me pee in it!" A few seconds later, having walked around the kitchen counter, Mother started to cry. The fear and anxiety still lingering from months before came back.

This brings us back to October 16th, the day after her third fall. This time she was all alone. Held in conjunction with the daily cocktail party, a family conference was called to discuss their mother's options. All their expounding did little good, Mom had made up her mind. The next day, alone with Mary and by now her confidence repaired, she rendered her decision "Mary, I am going to the nursing home. Now please go. I am going to have a cry."

Her first room was clear in the back of Hillcrest Home, just a few feet from the rear entrance. She had a single room, not because she was antisocial but she was a private, proud woman. Also it was dubious how a roommate would tolerate her small refrigerator stocked with beer and wine and the daily cocktail party which had merely moved to a new location. With her eye sight failing, to fill the hours she listened to books on tape and the radio. An ardent conservative while Dad was alive, she reveled in political conversation, often vehemently arguing her point. There were times when even Dad thought she'd crossed the line into being irrational. Certain politicians could instantly trigger that hyper response. The Clintons, for one, would bring forth her venom, but that was nothing compared to the hatred she had for Tom Harken. Ever since Mike lost the election to Ruth Harken, clear back in the 70's, the mere mention of the name Harken caused her eyes to grow tight and her voice to lose its warmth.

After a year in the back, she moved to the front of the nursing home. This was the original section of Hillcrest Home which at one time had been a room shared by three residents, but now Mom had it all to herself. It worked out quite well. The added room allowed her to bring more of her furniture from home. A sofa, two chairs, a dresser, and, of course, her refrigerator made a comfortable sitting area out of the west half of her room. Though her room was large, her world began to shrink. She listened less and less to books on tape. And the world outside grew less interesting. News about current events no longer engaged her conversation. Only the family seemed to arouse her curiosity. Along with her eye sight, her hearing was diminished, and this led to amusing exchanges concerning family gossip. Filtering family information through infrequently used hearing aids, the retelling by Mom of information she had gathered sometimes abused the true nature of the facts.

At first Mom still got out a lot. Able to walk unaided, she attended family gatherings around the area, but these episodes became fewer and fewer till the family needed to gather at the nursing home for celebrations. Congregating in the chapel, Mom still presided over family functions albeit in a wheel chair. After one of her birthday parties, when everyone was cleaning up and Mom was going back to her room, someone yelled out "We'll see you next year!"

Sardonically she replied, "I hope not!"

Her sight grew worse. Even eating became a chore. Unable to discern the food on her plate, she began to find eating embarrassing. She proudly requested that she be allowed to eat in her room, but the house staff thought it best she eat with the other residents and socialize. Not considered in their 'cook book' protocol was the fact that she didn't care anymore and no amount of psychological engineering would alter that fact. Again, Mary came to her defense, adamantly requesting what my mother wanted. Her evening meal from then on would be brought to her room. Her days grew more tedious. Sleeping most of the day out of boredom, Mom grew less and less ambulatory with each passing month. Her only passions were seeing her children and chocolate. Her ardent love of candy relentlessly destroyed her beautiful teeth.

My practice allowed me to finish my workday usually by 4:00 pm, well ahead of my other siblings, Matt, Pat and Mary. There was a running joke perpetuated around this scheduling. When after 5:00pm the other locals would arrive, Mother would relay that I had already been to see her and would add her impression of how hard I was working. This proved to be a consistent irritant for them since their efforts never seemed to count, and just as frustrating for them was that no matter their argument Mother could not be dissuaded from her conclusion.

Late one Thursday afternoon, I arrived to visit Mom, walking by the deserted front desk. Partway down the hallway toward my mothers room and just outside her door in a little sitting area, I passed without speaking a woman I didn't know watching TV. Entering her room I saw that Mom's evening meal had already arrived. She was in her blue chair, leaning over her tray picking at the food. Raising her head she said, "Is that you Tim?"

I replied," Yep, it's me Mom."

"You're done early," she shot back without looking up.

"No, not really. It's almost five." It was futilely answering a woman who really didn't care about time.

I pulled up a chair and switched on the lamp next to us. I knew she couldn't see much but there was no reason to sit in the gloom. "What are you eating?" I asked.

Still aimlessly running her fork around the plate she grumbled, "Same old stuff. I don't care for any of it." In this case she was right. Anyone would get tired of the bland food. I noticed however she had managed to eat the cake.

She needed to eat. She was just skin and bones. "At least eat the sandwich," I encouraged.

"No Pat always takes that for the cat," she answered slowly, but shot back without a moment's hesitation, "Get me some chocolate!"

That was the daily ritual. The woman was being kept alive by the Hershey Company. I opened the drawer of the little dresser. There were bags of bite sized chocolates. Riffling to the bottom I took out three foil wrapped pieces, unwrapping each and placing it on her tray. She grabbed the first one with almost childlike joy, I thought, here is a woman who can't see, can't hear, can't walk and finally has been relegated to only one pleasure in life.

She was barely finished with the last piece of chocolate when she asked me, "Tim get the nurse, I want to go back to bed." For the last few months Mom had preferred to stay in bed. I'm sure it was uncomfortable for her to sit up anymore. The nursing staff, however, wanted her out of bed at least part of the day. I know they thought it was best for her, but Mom had passed the point of caring about what was best. I pled the case that she should stay up at least till Mary and the boys stopped by, but even that argument did not hold.

"I want to go back to bed!" She was more adamant this time. As stubborn as she was, I was just as bull headed. I wasn't going to jump up and run down a nurse. The stalemate ended when I saw her face change and her voice soften. "Why won't God take me?"

There I sat without an answer. I reached over and grabbed her had. Her fingers were thin and soft. Standing up I leaned over and gave her a kiss and said "I love you. I'll see you tomorrow."

～◦〇

Friday morning, I had been at the office looking at records for the day. I heard Diane, my receptionist, and Kris my assistant talking as they came in the back door just then the phone rang. It's never a good sign when the phone rings early in the morning before office hours. Yelling from the back room I said "Diane can you get that?" I certainly did not want to answer, for fear it might just be a patient.

Diane picked up the phone and gave a cheery, "Hello, Dr. Sexton's office. This is Diane." She remained silent for several seconds and then said, '"OK I'll tell him." I could see from her face this wasn't going to be good.

"That was the nursing home. It's your mother," she said without any expression on her face. Evidently early that morning the nursing staff had found Mom unresponsive.

When I arrived at her room Mary was already there. We both realized Mom would not be coming back. Within the next few hours, Matt, Pat and Theresa had joined us, and the vigil had begun. The day wore on without change. Mother's breathing, though irregular, continued. Mary and Theresa volunteered to stay that night. By this time the entire family had been put on alert. It was just a matter of time now.

As odd as it may seem, the next day there wasn't anything sober about it. Gail, Deb, and Jeff joined the crew, bringing food and beer. Later in the afternoon, the new priest, Father Jim, stopped by to commiserate with the family. He had to have been surprised to walk in on loud talking and laughing. That night, all the siblings decided to stay. Graciously the staff at the nursing home supplied mattresses and sheets for everyone, and the occasion had the air of a childhood sleep-over, lying in the dark, telling stories, and falling asleep one by one.

The next day Tom and Bea drove down from St. Paul. Their arrival had an awkward feel to it. Here was someone truly grieving, while the locals, who after two days of lamentation had gone beyond the initial shock, were almost festive, lacking any morose atmosphere. Art also came to see his sister, loudly talking to her as if she would awaken and answer. Art, I felt, in his own way said his good by.

As the light of day faded, Mom's breathing became more limited. Before this time Mom had just been someone in the room with us; now she became the focus of our full attention. With the inevitable facing us, we decided to make a list of everyone who needed to be called and split up the list among us. It may seem cold and business-like, but I'm convinced our parents would have been impressed. With the space between Mom's breaths growing longer and longer, Matt, Pat, Theresa, Mary and I with our spouses stood beside her bed. It was several minutes of tender concentration. There was only one event in the universe: these last labored breathes. Finally, with the last breath on Sunday night October 22, 2012, both our parents had left us.

For several minutes everyone said their good by's, drifting out of the room one by one. I walked back out the front entrance of the nursing home alone to make my calls. I had remained composed those three days, but now, having to voice the words, "our mother is dead" when I had Dan on the line that injured little child living in my soul came rushing to the surface.

Saying good night, Deb and I headed home. The hour was late and the night was still. The whole experience had an eerie feel about it. As we passed through downtown, there wasn't a person or a car to be seen anywhere. The only activity was the time and temperature sign flashing on the First National Bank building, right where Franklin West had had his restaurant.

Deb and I didn't talk much heading home. In fact, once there we both went right to bed. When I switched off the light next to the bed, Deb rolled over on her side pulling the sheet up and snuggling up next to me. I just lay there on my back, exhausted but I couldn't go to sleep yet. Like an 8mm movie, a flickering recollection of my youth played in my head. Emotionally I didn't know how I should feel: relieved, sorrowful, alone. I lay awake for the longest time before sleep finally came.